Communications in Computer and Information Science 1718

Rationale

The CCIS series is devoted to the publication of proceedings of computer science conferences. Its aim is to efficiently disseminate original research results in informatics in printed and electronic form. While the focus is on publication of peer-reviewed full papers presenting mature work, inclusion of reviewed short papers reporting on work in progress is welcome, too. Besides globally relevant meetings with internationally representative program committees guaranteeing a strict peer-reviewing and paper selection process, conferences run by societies or of high regional or national relevance are also considered for publication.

Topics

The topical scope of CCIS spans the entire spectrum of informatics ranging from foundational topics in the theory of computing to information and communications science and technology and a broad variety of interdisciplinary application fields.

Information for Volume Editors and Authors

Publication in CCIS is free of charge. No royalties are paid, however, we offer registered conference participants temporary free access to the online version of the conference proceedings on SpringerLink (http://link.springer.com) by means of an http referrer from the conference website and/or a number of complimentary printed copies, as specified in the official acceptance email of the event.

CCIS proceedings can be published in time for distribution at conferences or as postproceedings, and delivered in the form of printed books and/or electronically as USBs and/or e-content licenses for accessing proceedings at SpringerLink. Furthermore, CCIS proceedings are included in the CCIS electronic book series hosted in the SpringerLink digital library at http://link.springer.com/bookseries/7899. Conferences publishing in CCIS are allowed to use Online Conference Service (OCS) for managing the whole proceedings lifecycle (from submission and reviewing to preparing for publication) free of charge.

Publication process

The language of publication is exclusively English. Authors publishing in CCIS have to sign the Springer CCIS copyright transfer form, however, they are free to use their material published in CCIS for substantially changed, more elaborate subsequent publications elsewhere. For the preparation of the camera-ready papers/files, authors have to strictly adhere to the Springer CCIS Authors' Instructions and are strongly encouraged to use the CCIS LaTeX style files or templates.

Abstracting/Indexing

CCIS is abstracted/indexed in DBLP, Google Scholar, EI-Compendex, Mathematical Reviews, SCImago, Scopus. CCIS volumes are also submitted for the inclusion in ISI Proceedings.

How to start

To start the evaluation of your proposal for inclusion in the CCIS series, please send an e-mail to ccis@springer.com.

Ana Fred · David Aveiro · Jan Dietz ·
Jorge Bernardino · Elio Masciari · Joaquim Filipe
Editors

Knowledge Discovery, Knowledge Engineering and Knowledge Management

13th International Joint Conference, IC3K 2021
Virtual Event, October 25–27, 2021
Revised Selected Papers

Springer

Editors
Ana Fred
Instituto de Telecomunicações
Lisbon, Portugal

University of Lisbon
Lisbon, Portugal

Jan Dietz
Delft University of Technology
Delft, The Netherlands

Elio Masciari (iD)
University of Naples Federico II
Naples, Italy

David Aveiro (iD)
Universidade da Madeira
Funchal, Portugal

Madeira-ITI
Funchal, Portugal

Jorge Bernardino
Polytechnic Institute of Coimbra - ISEC
Coimbra, Portugal

Joaquim Filipe
Polytechnic Institute of Setúbal
Setúbal, Portugal

INSTICC
Setúbal, Portugal

ISSN 1865-0929   ISSN 1865-0937 (electronic)
Communications in Computer and Information Science
ISBN 978-3-031-35923-1   ISBN 978-3-031-35924-8 (eBook)
https://doi.org/10.1007/978-3-031-35924-8

This Springer imprint is published by the registered company Springer Nature Switzerland AG
The registered company address is: Gewerbestrasse 11, 6330 Cham, Switzerland

Preface

The present book includes extended and revised versions of a set of selected papers from the 13th International Joint Conference on Knowledge Discovery, Knowledge Engineering and Knowledge Management (IC3K 2021), which was exceptionally held as an online event, due to COVID-19, from 25–27 October.

The purpose of IC3K is to bring together researchers, engineers and practitioners in the areas of Knowledge Discovery, Knowledge Engineering and Knowledge Management. IC3K is composed of three co-located conferences, each specialized in at least one of the aforementioned main knowledge areas.

IC3K 2021 received 103 paper submissions from 47 countries, of which 9% were included in this book.

The papers were selected by the event chairs and their selection is based on a number of criteria that include the classifications and comments provided by the program committee members, the session chairs' assessment and also the program chairs' global view of all papers included in the technical program. The authors of selected papers were then invited to submit a revised and extended version of their papers having at least 30% innovative material.

The papers selected to be included in this book contribute to the understanding of relevant trends of current research on Knowledge Discovery, Knowledge Engineering and Knowledge Management, including: Information Extraction, Knowledge Representation, Mining Text and Semi-Structured Data, Natural Language Understanding, Knowledge Acquisition, KM Strategies and Implementations, Explainable AI, Domain Ontologies, Domain Analysis and Modeling and Deep Learning.

We would like to thank all the authors for their contributions and also the reviewers who have helped to ensure the quality of this publication.

October 2021

Ana Fred
David Aveiro
Jan Dietz
Jorge Bernardino
Elio Masciari
Joaquim Filipe

Organization

Conference Chair

Joaquim Filipe — Polytechnic Institute of Setubal/INSTICC, Portugal

Program Co-chairs

KDIR

Ana Fred — Instituto de Telecomunicações and University of Lisbon, Portugal

KEOD

David Aveiro — University of Madeira, NOVA-LINCS and ARDITI, Portugal

Jan Dietz — Delft University of Technology, The Netherlands

KMIS

Jorge Bernardino — Polytechnic of Coimbra - ISEC, Portugal

Elio Masciari — University of Napoli Federico II, Italy

KDIR Program Committee

Amir Ahmad — United Arab Emirates University, UAE

Mayer Aladjem — Ben-Gurion University of the Negev, Israel

Maria Aramburu Cabo — University Jaume I, Spain

Eva Armengol — IIIA CSIC, Spain

Gloria Bordogna — CNR - National Research Council, Italy

Amel Borgi — Université de Tunis El Manar, Tunisia

Jesús Carrasco-Ochoa — INAOE, Mexico

Arnaud Castelltort — University of Montpellier, France

Zhiyuan Chen — University of Maryland Baltimore County, USA

Patrick Ciarelli	Universidade Federal do Espírito Santo, Brazil
Paulo Cortez	University of Minho, Portugal
Thanh-Nghi Do	Can Tho University, Vietnam
Antoine Doucet	University of La Rochelle, France
Markus Endres	University of Applied Sciences Munich, Germany
Iaakov Exman	Azrieli College of Engineering Jerusalem, Israel
Thiago Ferreira Cuvõcs	Universidade Federal do ABC, Brazil
Pedro G.	University of Porto, Portugal
Susan Gauch	University of Arkansas, USA
Jennifer Harding	Loughborough University, UK
Beatriz de la Iglesia	University of East Anglia, UK
Arti Jain	Jaypee Institute of Information Technology, India
Mouna Kamel	CNRS, France
Ron Kenett	KPA and the Samuel Neaman Institute, Technion, Israel
Ikuo Keshi	Fukui University of Technology, Japan
Margita Kon-Popovska	Ss Cyril and Methodius University, North Macedonia
Nuno Lau	Universidade de Aveiro, Portugal
Anne Laurent	University of Montpellier, France
Carson Leung	University of Manitoba, Canada
Jerry Chun-Wei Lin	Western Norway University of Applied Sciences, Norway
Jun Liu	University of Ulster, UK
Fadi Al Machot	University of Klagenfurt, Austria
J. Martínez-Trinidad	Instituto Nacional de Astrofísica, Óptica y Electrónica, Mexico
Sérgio Matos	University of Aveiro, Portugal
Edson Matsubara	UFMS, Brazil
Dulani Meedeniya	University of Moratuwa, Sri Lanka
Engelbert Mephu Nguifo	Université Clermont Auvergne, France
Manuel Montes y Gómez	INAOE, Mexico
Agnieszka Mykowiecka	Institute of Computer Science, Polish Academy of Sciences, Poland
Nayden Nenkov	Konstantin Preslavsky University of Shumen, Bulgaria
Mitsunori Ogihara	University of Miami, USA
Elias Oliveira	Universidade Federal do Espirito Santo, Brazil
Fabrício Olivetti de França	Universidade Federal do ABC, Brazil
Alberto Pinto	INESC TEC and University of Porto, Portugal
Colm Riordan	University of Galway, Ireland
Milos Savic	University of Novi Sad, Serbia

Christoph Scholz   Fraunhofer IEE, Germany
Filippo Sciarrone   Universitas Mercatorum, Italy
Atsuhiro Takasu   National Institute of Informatics, Japan
Marco Temperini   Sapienza University of Rome, Italy
Ulrich Thiel   Fraunhofer Gesellschaft, Germany
Kar Toh   Yonsei University, South Korea
Alicia Troncoso Lora   Pablo de Olavide University of Seville, Spain
Domenico Ursino   Università Politecnica delle Marche, Italy
Xing Wei   Pinterest Inc., USA
Nicola Zeni   University of Trento, Italy
Yan Zhang   California State University, San Bernardino, USA
Yi Zhang   University of Technology Sydney, Australia

KDIR Additional Reviewers

Zheng Fang   Pinterest, USA
Matheus Fernandes   UFABC, Brazil
Imran Sk Hossain   University of Clermont Auvergne, France
Kevin Labille   University of Arkansas, USA
Jerry Lonlac   IMT Nord Europe, France
José Martins   INESC-TEC, Portugal
Dickson Owuor   Strathmore University, Kenya
Omar Salman   University of Arkansas, USA
Fernando Sánchez-Vega   Centro de Investigación en Matemáticas, A.C.
                                    (CIMAT), Mexico

KEOD Program Committee

Mara Abel   Universidade Federal do Rio Grande do Sul,
                                    Brazil
José Abreu Salas   Universidad de Alicante, Spain
Mamoun Abu Helou   Al-Istiqlal University, Palestine (State of)
Raian Ali   Hamad Bin Khalifa University, Qatar
Vaibhav Anu   Montclair State University, USA
David Aveiro   University of Madeira, NOVA-LINCS and
                                    ARDITI, Portugal
Michael Bada   University of Colorado Anschutz Medical
                                    Campus, USA
Stephen Balakirsky   GTRI, USA
Claudio Baptista   Universidade Federal de Campina Grande, Brazil

Fevzi Belli   University of Paderborn, Germany
Christoph Benzmüller   Freie Universität Berlin, Germany
Rafael Berlanga   Universitat Jaume I, Spain
Pierrette Bouillon   University of Geneva, Switzerland
Vladimír Bureš   University of Hradec Králové, Czech Republic
Radek Burget   Brno University of Technology, Czech Republic
Guoray Cai   Penn State University, USA
Soon Chun   City University of New York, USA
João Costa   Institute of Computer and Systems Engineering of
                                    Coimbra, Portugal
John Edwards   Aston University, UK
Maria Ganzha   Warsaw University of Technology, Poland
Francisco García-Sánchez   University of Murcia, Spain
Martin Giese   University of Oslo, Norway
Josiane Hauagge   Mid-West State University (UNICENTRO),
                                    Brazil
Xudong He   Florida International University, USA
Martina Husáková   University of Hradec Králové, Czech Republic
Maizatul Akmar Ismail   University of Malaya, Malaysia
Hans Kamp   University of Stuttgart, Germany
Dimitris Kanellopoulos   University of Patras, Greece
Jakub Klímek   Charles University and Czech Technical
                                    University in Prague, Czech Republic
Dimitris Kontokostas   Diffbot, USA
Egor V. Kostylev   University of Oslo, Norway
Konstantinos I. Kotis   University of the Aegean, Greece
Dmitry Kudryavtsev   Saint-Petersburg University, Russian Federation
Tomislava Lauc   University of Zagreb, Croatia
Antoni Ligeza   AGH University of Science and Technology,
                                    Poland
Paulo Maio   Polytechnic Institute of Porto, Portugal
Riccardo Martoglia   University of Modena and Reggio Emilia, Italy
Andre Menolli   Universidade Estadual do Norte do Parana, Brazil
Nives Mikelic Preradovic   University of Zagreb, Croatia
Michele Missikoff   ISTC-CNR, Italy
Óscar Mortágua Pereira   University of Aveiro, Portugal
Regina Motz   Universidad de la República, Uruguay
Jørgen Nilsson   Technical University of Denmark, Denmark
Hervé Panetto   University of Lorraine, France
Carlos Periñán-Pascual   Universitat Politècnica de València, Spain
Dimitris Plexousakis   FORTH, Greece
Mihail Popescu   University of Missouri-Columbia, USA

Amar Ramdane-Cherif	University of Paris Saclay, France
Domenico Redavid	University of Bari "Aldo Moro", Italy
Thomas Risse	Goethe University Frankfurt, Germany
Renato Rocha Souza	Getulio Vargas Foundation, Brazil
Oscar Rodriguez Rocha	Teach on Mars, France
Colette Rolland	Université Paris 1 Panthèon-Sorbonne, France
Lloyd Rutledge	Open University of the Netherlands, The Netherlands
Fabio Sartori	University of Milano-Bicocca, Italy
Cogan Shimizu	Kansas State University, USA
Nuno Silva	Polytechnic Institute of Porto, Portugal
Petr Tucnik	University of Hradec Králové, Czech Republic
Jouni Tuominen	Aalto University, Finland
Manolis Tzagarakis	University of Patras, Greece
Bingyang Wei	Texas Christian University, USA
Gian Zarri	Sorbonne University, France
Nianjun Zhou	IBM, USA
Qiang Zhu	University of Michigan, Dearborn, USA

KEOD Additional Reviewers

| Mário Antunes | Instituto de Telecomunicações Aveiro, Portugal |
| Vasilis Efthymiou | Institute of Computer Science, FORTH, Greece |

KMIS Program Committee

Leon Abdillah	Bina Darma University, Indonesia
Michael Arias	Universidad de Costa Rica, Costa Rica
Al Bento	University of Baltimore Merrick School of Business, USA
Giuseppe Berio	University of South Brittany, France
Semih Bilgen	Istanbul Okan University, Turkey
Kelly Braghetto	University of São Paulo, Brazil
Abhijit Chaudhury	Bryant University, USA
Cindy Chen	University of Massachusetts Lowell, USA
Vincent Cheutet	Université de Lyon, INSA Lyon, France
Chin Wei Chong	Multimedia University, Malaysia
Ritesh Chugh	Central Queensland University, Australia
Malcolm Crowe	University of the West of Scotland, UK

Susan Cuddy	Commonwealth Scientific and Industrial Research Organisation (CSIRO), Australia
Stephen Flowerday	Rhodes University, South Africa
Joan-Francesc Fondevila-Gascón	CECABLE (Centre d'Estudis sobre el Cable), UPF, URL, UdG (EU Mediterrani) and UOC, Spain
Matteo Gaeta	University of Salerno, Italy
Francisco García-Sánchez	University of Murcia, Spain
Bogdan Ghilic-Micu	Academy of Economic Studies, Romania
Annamaria Goy	University of Torino, Italy
Severin Grabski	Michigan State University, USA
Michele Grimaldi	University of Cassino, Italy
Gabriel Guerrero-Contreras	University of Cádiz, Spain
Jennifer Harding	Loughborough University, UK
Keith Harman	Oklahoma Baptist University, USA
Mounira Harzallah	University of Nantes, France
Eli Hustad	University of Agder, Norway
Anca Ionita	University Politehnica of Bucharest, Romania
Omar Khalil	Kuwait University, Kuwait
Marite Kirikova	Riga Technical University, Latvia
Tri Kurniawan	Universitas Brawijaya, Indonesia
Dominique Laurent	Cergy-Pontoise University - ENSEA, France
Michael Leyer	University of Rostock, Germany
Kecheng Liu	University of Reading, UK
Carlos Malcher Bastos	Universidade Federal Fluminense, Brazil
Nada Matta	University of Technology of Troyes, France
Brahami Menaouer	National Polytechnic School of Oran (ENPOran), Algeria
Michele Missikoff	ISTC-CNR, Italy
Norshidah Mohamed	Prince Sultan University, Saudi Arabia
Luis Molina Fernández	University of Granada, Spain
Shahrokh Nikou	Åbo Akademi University, Finland
Iraklis Paraskakis	South East European Research Centre, Greece
Wilma Penzo	University of Bologna, Italy
Filipe Portela	University of Minho, Portugal
Nicolas Prat	Essec Business School Paris, France
Arkalgud Ramaprasad	Ramaiah Public Policy Center, India
Colette Rolland	Université Paris 1 Panthèon-Sorbonne, France
Xiao-Liang Shen	Wuhan University, China
Malgorzata Sterna	Poznan University of Technology, Poland
Goce Trajcevski	Northwestern University, USA
Shu-Mei Tseng	I-Shou University, Taiwan, Republic of China

Costas Vassilakis   University of the Peloponnese, Greece
Anthony Wensley   University of Toronto, Canada
Uffe Wiil   University of Southern Denmark, Denmark
Qiang Zhu   University of Michigan, Dearborn, USA

KMIS Additional Reviewers

Sara Balderas-Díaz   University of Cadiz, Spain
Edwin Frauenstein   Walter Sisulu University, South Africa
Olutoyin Olaitan   Walter Sisulu University, South Africa

Invited Speakers

Eric Yu   University of Toronto, Canada
Bhavani Thuraisingham   University of Texas at Dallas, USA
Jan Mendling   Humboldt-Universität zu Berlin, Germany
Deborah L. McGuinness   Rensselaer Polytechnic Institute, USA

Contents

Contents

Pathology Data Prioritisation: A Study of Using Multi-variate Time Series Without a Ground Truth

Jing Qi[1(✉)], Girvan Burnside[2], and Frans Coenen[1]

[1] Department of Computer Science, The University of Liverpool, Liverpool L69 3BX, UK
J.Qi7@liverpool.ac.uk
[2] Department of Biostatistics, Institute of Translational Medicine, The University of Liverpool, Liverpool L69 3BX, UK

Abstract. In any hospital, pathology results play an important role for decision making. However, it is not unusual for clinicians to have hundreds of pathology results to review on a single shift; this "information overload" presents a particular challenge. Some form of pathology result prioritisation is therefore a necessity. One idea to deal with this problem is to adopt the tools and techniques of machine learning to identify prioritisation patterns within pathology results and use these patterns to label new pathology data according to a prioritisation classification protocol. However, in most clinical situations there is an absence of any pathology prioritisation ground truth. The usage of supervised learning therefore becomes a challenge. Unsupervised learning methods are available, but are not considered to be as effective as supervised learning methods. This paper considers two mechanisms for pathology data prioritisation in the absence of a ground truth: (i) Proxy Ground Truth Pathology Data Prioritisation (PGR-PDP), and (ii) Future Result Forecast Pathology Data Prioritisation (FRF-PDP). The first uses the outcome event, what happened to a patient, as a proxy for a ground truth, and the second forecasted future pathology results compared with the known normal clinical reference range. Two variation of each are considered: kNN-based and LSTM-based PGR-PDP, and LSTM-based and Facebook Profit-based FRF-PDP. The reported evaluation indicated that the PGR-PDP mechanism produced the best results with little distinction between the two variations.

Keywords: kNN · LSTM-RNN · Facebook prophet · Time series · Pathology data

1 Introduction

The problem of information overload has become a global phenomena, fueled by the large quantities of data that are produced currently, on a continuous basis. One specific example is the increasing number of pathology results generated in hospitals. Clinicians usually use the results to provide support for decision making when treating patients, such as whether some urgent intervention is required, or some particular medication needs to be prescribed or further tests need to be carried out. However, even for experienced doctors, this procedure is complex and time consuming. One solution is to prioritise pathology results using the tools and techniques of machine learning so

A. Fred et al. (Eds.): IC3K 2021, CCIS 1718, pp. 1–20, 2023.
https://doi.org/10.1007/978-3-031-35924-8_1

as to provide a "look at these first" style of help to accelerate the process of analysing pathology results. Highlighting significant results to be considered first will prevent the condition of patients from worsening due to the delays in treatment.

However, the biggest challenge for the prioritisation of pathology data using machine learning is, in many cases, the absence of ground truth data. In practice, experienced clinicians can recognise a priority result when they see one, but do not have the resource to use their experience to generate bespoke training data sets. Thus traditional, well established, supervised learning techniques can not be used directly. One proposed solution, reported in [10], is to use an unsupervised anomaly detection approach whereby anomalous records are considered to be priority records. In [10] a set of clusters was generated using historical data and any new pathology result which could not be readily fitted into a cluster labeled as an outlier and therefore assumed to be a priority record. The flaw in this approach was that, just because a record was unusual, it did not necessarily mean it was a priority record (and vice-versa). In [9] the idea of using a proxy ground truth was proposed; an idea that addresses the criticism directed at the anomaly detection approach described in [10]. This paper builds on the ideas presented in [9] by reconsidering the proxy ground truth concept. This paper also presents an alternative to this previous work founded on the idea of forecasting future pathology results and comparing these with the expected normal clinical range.

In more detail, two mechanisms are presented in this paper: (i) Proxy Ground Truth Pathology Data Prioritisation (PGT-PDP) and (ii) Future Result Forecast Pathology Data Prioritisation (FRF-PDP). The PGT-PDP mechanism, founded on ideas first proposed in [9], uses a proxy training data set to build a pathology data classification model. The proxy ground truth in this case was obtained from meta-knowledge about patients concerning the "final destination" of patients, what is known as the *outcome event* for each patient. Three outcome events were considered: Emergency Patient (EP), an In-Patient (IP) or an Out Patient (OP). Then, given a new pathology result and the patient's pathology history, it would be possible to predict the outcome event and then use this to prioritise the new pathology result. For example if we predict the outcome event for a patient to be EP, then the new pathology result would be assigned a *high* priority; however, if we predict that the outcome event will be IP the new pathology result would be assigned *medium* priority, and otherwise *low* priority. The hypothesis that we seek to establish here is that there are patterns in patients' historical lab test results which are markers as to where the patient "ended up", and which can hence be used for prioritisation. To variations of the PGT-PDP mechanism are considered for classification model generation, Long Short-Term Memory (LSTM) and k Nearest Neighbour (kNN). The first is a well established deep learning approach, and kNN is a classic way of classifying time series data that has previously been used in the medical domain [19]. A value of $k = 1$ was adopted for the kNN, as suggested in [1], and Dynamic Time Warping (DTW) was used as the similarity measure.

The FRF-PDP mechanism uses the normal range for a test result. This will vary from test to test, and patient to patient, and may even change with time. A "quick and easy" solution would be to prioritise a new pathology results if it fell outside of the normal range. However, waiting till this happens may be too late. Instead it is argued here that a better approach would be to use the patient's history and, given a new pathology result, predict what the next pathology result value in the sequence will be. If this next value is out of range then we have a priority pathology result. In other words, the idea promoted by this mechanism is to use time series forecasting as a tool for prioritising pathology data. More specifically, the mechanism utilises the idea of time series regression. Two regression approaches are considered: (i) LSTM regression and (ii) Facebook Prophet (FP). LSTM regression is a well established regression approach. FP forecasting is founded on a novel Bayesian forecasting model whereby the influencing factors that affect the trend associated with a set of time series are decomposed so as to identify patterns. Unlike LSTM regression, FP can operate using irregular time intervals (pathology data is collected in an irregular manner). In the case of the LSTM regression a unit time interval needed to be assumed.

The main contribution of this paper are thus: (i) a more detailed consideration of the event-based pathology prioritisation than that presented in [9], (ii) a new mechanism to prioritise pathology data using future result forecasting, and (iii) an in depth comparison of the operation of the two mechanisms. To act as a focus for the comparison the domain of Urea and Electrolytes (U&E) pathology testing was considered; a domain that features five types of pathology result. More specifically U&E data provided by Arrowe Park hospital in Merseyside in the UK was used.

The remainder of this paper is organised as follows. A review of relevant previous work is presented in Sect. 2. This is followed, in Sect. 3, by a review of the Urea and Electrolytes pathology application domain used as a focus for the work presented in this paper. A formalism for the pathology prioritisation problem is also presented. The proposed mechanisms, PGT-PDP and FRF-PDP, are then presented in Sects. 4 and 5 respectively. The comparative evaluation of the mechanisms is presented and discussed in Sect. 6. The paper is concluded, in Sect. 7, with a summary of the main findings and some suggested avenues for future work.

2 Previous Work

This previous work section commences by considering the general concept of data prioritisation, followed by some discussion of existing work directed at pathology data prioritisation. The reminder of this previous work section considers the classification model generation and forecasting approaches utilised in this paper with respect to the two proposed mechanism, PCT-PDP and FRF-PDP.

Data prioritisation is concerned with the applications of techniques to a data source to determine which examples should be "ranked" higher than others. The techniques used range from the application of simple heuristics to the application of sophisticated models generated using the tools and techniques of machine learning. In the medical domain, the term "triage" is frequently used instead of prioritisation; especially in the context of hospital emergency departments. The Emergency Severity Index (ESI), a five-level emergency department triage algorithm, that arranges patients into five tiers from 1 (most urgent) to 5 (least urgent), is frequently used. In [11] several machine learning models, Random Forest and Lasso regression, were adopted to categorise patients using the five-level ESI stratification. Favourable comparisons were made with the ESI algorithm. In [4] a support vector machine, coupled with free text analysis, was used to build an emergency department prioritisation prediction model. However, the work in [4,11] was directed at supervised machine learning approaches that assumed a suitable training set was available, not the case with respect to the focus of the work presented in this paper. The work reported in [4,11] was also confined to emergency department triage only.

To the best knowledge of the authors there is little work directed at the use of machine learning to prioritise pathology data in the absence of a "ground truth". However, one notable approach, already referenced in the introduction to this paper, is the Anomaly Detection (AD) mechanism proposed in [10]. In [10] the assumption was that an anomalous record was a priority record. This was identified by generating a cluster configuration of pathology results and attempting to fit a new pathology result into this cluster configuration; if the new result could not be fitted to an existing cluster it was assumed to be anomalous and therefore the pathology result should be prioritised. Thus the pathology result prioritisation problem was defined as a two class problem, priority versus non-priority. Two variations were considered: (i) Point-based AD and (ii) Time Series-based AD. The distinction being that the second considered patient history while the first did not. However, given a large number of priority pathology results these would no longer be considered to be anomalous and therefore not be prioritised. It can also be argued that just because a record is unusual does not necessarily mean it is a priority record. The opposite can also be argued, just because a record is common it does not necessarily mean it is not a priority record. The results reported in [10] are referred to later in this paper for evaluation purposes to compare with the operation of the PGT-PDP and FRF-PDP mechanisms described. In response to the above criticism of the AD mechanism, in [9], an event-based proxy ground truth prioritisation mechanism was proposed [9], the PGT-PDP mechanism also considered in this paper and discussed further in Sect. 4.

The pathology data considered in this paper is in the form of multi-variate time series. There are two popular time series formats: (i) instance-based and (ii) feature-based. Using the instance-based format the original time series format is maintained. While using the feature-based representation, properties of the time series are used [17]. In this paper, the instance based format was adopted.

In the case of the PGT-PD mechanisms discussed in this paper, two approaches for generating the desired pathology data classification models were considered, kNN and LSTM. In the case of the proposed FRF-PDP mechanism, two approaches for forecasting pathology results were considered: LSTM regression and Facebook Profit (FP). Each of these approaches is considered in some further derail in the remainder of this literature review section.

The fundamental idea of kNN classification is to compare a previously unseen record, which we wish to label, with a "bank" of records whose labels are known. The class labels from the identified k most similar records are then used to label the previously unseen record. Usually $k = 1$ is adopted because it avoids the need for any conflict resolution. A significant issue when using kNN with respect to time series classification is the nature of the similarity (distance) measure to be used [18]. There are a number of similarity measure options, such as Euclidean, Manhattan and Minkowski distance measurement, but Dynamic Time Warping (DTW) is considered to be the most effective with respect to the instance-based format time series, and offers the additional advantage that the time series considered do not have to be of the same length [18]. DTW was therefore used for the work presented in this paper.

Among the various deep learning models that are available, the Long Short Term Memory (LSTM) Recurrent Neural Networks (RNN) model is one of most effective with respect to sequence (time series) data. LSTM can be applied in both the context of classification and forecasting. There are many examples in the literature where RNNs have been used with respect to time series analysis [13,14,20]. The ability to "memorise" and select which data in a sequence is important for predicting future values makes the LSTM model an obvious candidate for both the PGT-PDP and the FRF-PDP mechanism.

In recent years Facebook Prophet (FP) has attracted increasing attention due to its demonstrated better performance with respect to certain application domains [7,8]. FP models can deal with "regime shift" where the characteristics of a time series (mean and variance) changes over time, in some cases suddenly and in others gradually. Intuitively, pathology data time series features such regime shifts. FP was therefore experimented with in the context of the proposed FRF-PDP mechanism. An alternative might have been Autoregressive Integrated Moving Average (ARIMA) model [2,6].

3 Application Domain

This section presents the U&E application domain used as a focus for the work presented in this paper. The section is divided into two sub-sections. Subsect. 3.1 considers the practice of U&E testing, whist Subsect. 3.2 presents a formalism for the data.

3.1 U&E Testing

Urea and Electrolytes pathology testing (U&E testing) is commonly used to detect abnormalities of blood chemistry, primarily kidney (renal) function and dehydration. U&E testing is usually performed to confirm normal kidney function or to exclude a serious imbalance of biochemical salts in the bloodstream. The U&E test data considered in this paper comprised, for each pathology test, measurement of levels of: (i) Bicarbonate (bi), (ii) Creatinine (cr), (iii) Sodium (so) (iv) Potassium (po) and (v) Urea (ur). The measurement of each is referred to as a "task", thus we have five tasks per test. Therefore each U&E test result comprises five pathology values. Pathology results comprised of a number of tasks are not unusual. Normally, for each of the task results, there is a clinical reference range indicating whether the corresponding result value is abnormal or not. In the case of U&E data, abnormal levels in any of the tasks may indicate that the kidneys are not working properly. However, a one time abnormal result for a single task does not necessarily indicate priority. A new task result that is out of range for a patient who has a previous recent history of out of range task results, but the latest result indicates a trend back into the normal range, may not be a priority result either. Conversely, a new task result that is within the normal range for a patient who has a history of normal range task results, but the latest result indicates a trend heading out of the normal range, maybe a priority result. It is suggested that U&E pathology results can be prioritised more precisely if the trend of the historical records is taken into consideration. Thus for the mechanisms presented in this paper, historical results are considered.

3.2 Formalism

In the context of the U&E Testing domain, the data used for evaluation purposes with respect to the work presented in this paper comprised a set of clinical patient records, $\mathbf{D} = \{P_1, P_2, \dots\}$. Each patient record $P_j \in \mathbf{D}$ was of the form:

$$P_j = \langle Id, Date, Gender, T_{So}, T_{Po}, T_{Ur}, T_{Cr}, T_{Bi}, c \rangle \tag{1}$$

where T_{so} to T_{bi} are five multi-variate time series representing, in sequence, pathology results for the five tasks typically found in a U&E test: Sodium (So), Potassium (Po), Urea (Ur), Creatinine (Cr) and Bicarbonate (Bi) and c is the class label(proxy) taken from a set of classes C. Each time series T_i has three dimensions: (i) pathology result, (ii) normal low and (iii) normal high. The normal low and high dimensions indicate a "band" in which pathology results are expected to fall. These values are less volatile than the pathology result values themselves, but do change for each patient over time. Thus each times series T_i comprises a sequence of tuples, of the form $\langle v, nl, nh \rangle$ (pathology result, normal low and normal high respectively).

In the case of the PGT-PDP mechanism the class label for each record $P_j \in \mathbf{D}$ for the proxy ground truth was derived from the outcome event(s) associated with each patient. Three outcome events were considered: (i) Emergency Patient (EP), an In-Patient (IP) or an Out Patient (OP) which were correlated with the priority descriptors "high", "medium" and "low" respectively. Hence $C = \{high, medium, low\}$. The proxy data, formulated as described above was also used for the evaluation pf FRF-PDP mechanism.

4   Proxy Ground Truth Pathology Data Prioritisation

The fundamental idea underpinning the PGT-PDP mechanism, as already noted, was that although no ground truth training data was available, the final destinations of patients were known, and hence these could act as a proxy for a ground truth. In order to validate this idea, two classification model generation methods were considered, the kNN-DTW approach and the LSTM-RNN approach. Thus two variations of the PGT-PDP mechanism were considered: (i) kNN-Based and (ii) LSTM based. Each is discussed in further detail in the following two sub-sections.

4.1 kNN-Based Proxy Ground Truth Pathology Data Prioritisation

The kNN-based variation of the PGT-PDP mechanism used the well known kNN classification algorithm. As already noted, kNN used a parameter k, the number of best matches we are looking for. For the work presented here $k = 1$ was used because it is most frequently used in the context of time series analysis [1]. DTW was used for the similarity measure because of its ability to operate with time series of different length and because it has been shown to be more effective than alternatives such as Euclidean distance measurement [18]. The disadvantage of DTW, compared to the Euclidean distance measurement, is its high computational time complexity of $O(x \times y)$ where x and y are the lengths of the two time series under consideration. Two strategies for addressing this computational overhead were adopted with respect to the work presented here: (i) early-abandonment [12] and (ii) LB-Keogh lower bounding [16]. The first is a strategy whereby the accumulative distance between two time series is repeatedly checked as the calculation progresses and if the distance exceeds the best distance so far the calculation is "abandoned" [12]. The second involves pre-processing the time series to be considered by comparing the time series using an alternative "cheaper" technique and pruning those that are unlikely to be close matches and applying DTW to the remainder. One example of this, and that adopted with respect to the work presented in this paper, is the lower bounding technique proposed in [16], the so called LB-Keogh technique. This operates by superimposing a band, defined by a predefined offset value referred to as the lower bound, over each time series in the bank and calculating the complement of the overlap with the new time series. Where the calculated value exceeds a given threshold ϵ the associated time series is pruned.

The traditional manner in which kNN is applied in the context of time series analysis is to compare a query time series with the time series in the kNN bank. In the case of the U&E test data prioritisation scenario considered here the process involved five comparisons, once for each time series in the query record P_j, $T_{q_{so}}$, $T_{q_{po}}$, $T_{q_{ur}}$, $T_{q_{cr}}$ and $T_{q_{bi}}$. In addition, traditional kNN is applied to univariate time series, in the U&E pathology case each task time series was a three-dimensional multi-variate time series: (i) pathology value, (ii) normal low and (iii) normal high. Thus, from the foregoing, for each comparison five distance measures were obtained and combined to obtain a final prioritisation. These five distance measures therefore need to be combined to give a final prioritisation.

The final prioritisation was decided using a rule called the "High priority first and voting second" rule (Rule 1), which will be explained in more details in Subsect. 4.3 below. The application of kNN for prioritising pathology results P_j was as follows:

1. Calculate the average LB-keogh overlap for the five component time series separately and prune all records in D where the overlap for any one time series was greater than a threshold ϵ, to leave D'.
2. Apply DTW, with early-abandonment to each pair $\langle T_{q_i}, T_j \in D' \rangle$ where i indicates the U&E task.
3. Assign the class label c to the time series T_{q_i}, of a patient record P_j, associated with the most similar time series $T_i \in D'$.
4. Use the final prioritisation rule, Rule 1, to decide the final priority level for P_j (see Subsect. 4.3 below for further details).

With respect to the above the choice of the value for ϵ is of great importance as it affects the efficiency and the accuracy of the similarity search. According to [5], there is a threshold value for ϵ whereby the time complexity for the lower bounding is greater than simply using DTW distance without lower bounding. The experiments presented in [5] demonstrated that this threshold occurs when the value for ϵ prunes 90% of the time series in D. For the work presented in this paper $\epsilon = 0.159$ was used because, on average, this resulted in 10% of the time series in D being retained.

4.2 LSTM-Based Proxy Ground Truth Pathology Data Prioritisation

Using the LSTM classification approach, and given the U&E pathology prioritisation scenario, the PGT-PDP mechanism required the training of five LSTM models, one for each task: $LSTM_{so}$, $LSTM_{po}$, $LSTM_{ur}$, $LSTM_{cr}$ and $LSTM_{bi}$. Figure 1 illustrates the adopted LSTM architecture.

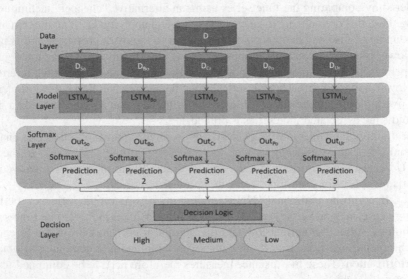

Fig. 1. LSTM architecture for the PGT-PDP mechanism [10].

From Fig. 1 it can be seen that the overall structure is expressed in four "layers" (i) the input layer, (ii) the model layer, (iii) the Softmax layer and (iv) the decision layer. The input is the five component task parts $T_{q_{so}}, T_{q_{po}}, T_{q_{ur}}, T_{q_{cr}}$ and $T_{q_{bi}}$ of data set D. Thus for each task, a multi-variate time series $T_i = \{V_1, V_2, ..., V_m\}$ was established, where $V - J$ is a tuple of the form presented earlier, and $m \in [l_{min}, l_{max}]$. Where necessary each time series T_i is padded to the maximum length, l_{max} using the mean values for the pathology test values, normal low and normal high values in T_i. Each time series T_i is then passed to the model layer and the LSTM constructed. And for each LSTM two hidden layers of cells were adopted. The output from the LSTM layer is then passed to a Softmax layer, where the first predictions will be made with respect to the task level. The Softmax function for normalising the output of each single task LSTM model was as follows:

$$y_i = \frac{e^{a_i}}{\Sigma_{k=1}^{|C|} e^{a_k}} \quad \forall i \in 1...C \qquad (2)$$

where: (i) $|C|$ is the number of classes (three in this case) and (ii) a_i is the output of the LSTM layer.

The last layer in Fig. 1 is the decision layer where the final label is derived. A logits component rule (Rule 2) in this layer is used to determine the final pathology result prioritisation label. Subsect. 4.3 presents further detail regrading Rule 2.

4.3   PGT-PDP Prioritisation Rules

Two rules were utilised in the foregoing to assign an overall pathology result prioritisation: (i) the final prioritisation rule, Rule 1, for kNN-based PGT-PDP, and (ii) the logits component rule, Rule 2, for LSTM-based PGT-PDP. Both are discussed in further detail in this sub-section. Rule 1 for prioritisation using kNN was as follows:

Rule 1. If one of the class labels is "high" the overall class label is high, otherwise voting will be adopted to derive the overall class label.

Rule 2 For prioritisation using $LSTM$ was a folows:

Rule 2. If there exists a prediction that equates to 'High' for one of the tasks then the overall prediction is high, otherwise average the five outputs produced by the Softmax function and choose the class with the maximum probability.

5   Future Result Forecast Pathology Data Prioritisation

The fundamental idea promoted using the FRF-PDP mechanism is that, given a current pathology result P_j, comprised of a number of task value sequences, the sequences can be appended to using forecasted next values, the $n + 1$ values. If a predicted $n + 1$ value is out of the normal clinical reference range the associated current task value should be labelled as a "priority" value. Thus given a new patient pathology result, P_j, the historical records for the patient were used to predict the $n + 1$ values which were then used to label P_j. The prioritisation problem thus becomes a "one-step" time series forecasting problem. The entire FRF-PDP process is illustrated in Fig. 2. The forecasting can be done using any appropriate forecasting algorithm, however two were considered with respect to the work described here, LSTM regression and FP. Two variation of the FRF-PDP mechanisms were thus considered: (i) LSTM-based and (ii) FP-based. Further detail concerning these two variations is presented in the following two sub-sections, Subsect. 5.1 and 5.2.

5.1   LSTM-Based Forecasting Future Results Pathology Data Prioritisation

LSTM classification was considered with respect to the PGT-PDP mechanisms described previously in Sect. 4. However, due to its versatility, LSTM can also be adopted for regression/prediction purposes. Hence it was adopted with respect to the FRF-PDP mechanism. LSTM prediction was applied to single tasks individually because earlier work, not shown here, had demonstrated that considering all tasks simultaneously produced a poor model. This was thought to be because of potential correlations between tasks that caused the model to become over-complex and lead to unstable solutions, consequently compromising the generalisability of the prioritisation model.

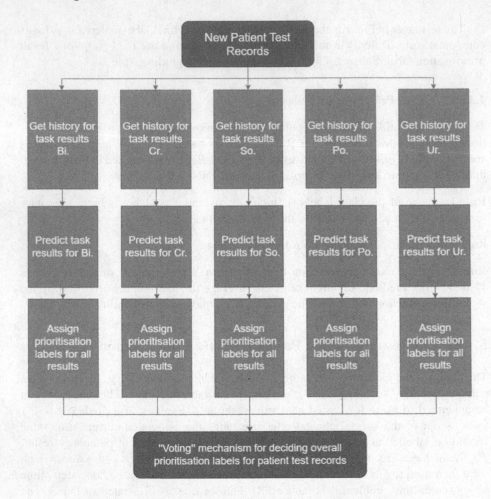

Fig. 2. Future Result Forecast Pathology Data Prioritisation process.

Thus individual LSTM models were generated for each task (as indicated in Fig. 2). For the evaluation data used in this paper this resulted in five LSTM models: $LSTM_{so}$, $LSTM_{po}$, $LSTM_{ur}$, $LSTM_{cr}$ and $LSTM_{bi}$. The overall prioritisation for each pathology result was then obtained by applying a predefined rule (discussed at the end of this sub-section). Further challenges, as in the case of LSTM-based PGT-PDP, were that:

1. Pathology (task) data features irregular time spacing, the time period between points was not uniform, both with respect to individual patients and between patients. LSTM prediction assumed regular spaced time series data. For the evaluation set used with respect to this paper the spacing varied from 3 to 52 days.
2. The overall length of the time series for each patient was not the same. LSTM requires all time series to be of the same length. Thus a padding techniques was applied to the time series so that they were all of the same length and therefore could be used to generate a LSTM model.

The overall architecture of the generated LSTM models was similar to the architecture of the LSTM used with respect to the PGT-PDP mechanism as shown in Fig. 1. The LSTM comprises three layers: (i) the input layer, (ii) the model layer and (iii) the decision layer. Each model took as input a task time series $T_i = [t_{i_1}, t_{i_2}, \ldots, t_{i_n}, t_{i_{n+1}}]$, where t_{i_n} is the current test result value, and $t_{i_{n+1}}]$ is the task value to be predicted. Where necessary, each time series T_i was padded to the maximum length, l_{max}, using the mean values for the pathology test values in T_i. For each LSTM model, 2 layers of LSTM blocks were used for the model layer, linked by the default Sigmoid activation function.

After obtaining all of the predicted future result values, one from each LSTM model, a "label computation function" was applied to predict the prioritisation labels for each task result. The equation for deriving a prioritisation label c taken from a set of labels $C = \{\text{priority}, \text{non-priority}\}$ is given by Eq. 3. Where: (i) $t_{i_{n+1}}$ is the predicted task next value, and (ii) x_l and x_h are the referenced clinical normal low and normal high values for the corresponding task and patient.

$$c = \begin{cases} \text{non-priority}, & \text{if } x_l < t_{i_{n+1}} \leq x_h \\ \text{priority}, & \text{otherwise} \end{cases} \tag{3}$$

Given the above, the process for generating a pathology result prioritisation label using a set of LSTM models (one per task) was as follows:

1. Given a new pathology test result for a patient j comprised of m tasks, thus m values, $\langle v_1, v_2, \ldots, v_m \rangle$, where v_k is a pathology value, add these values to the historical data for the patient j to generate m time series of the form $T_i = \{t_{i_1}, t_{i_2} \ldots t_{i_n}\}$ where $t_{i_n} = v_k$.
2. Input each time series into the corresponding LSTM model to produce predicted values $t_{i_{n+1}}$.
3. Use Eq. 3 to assign a label to each predicted values $t_{i_{n+1}}$.
4. Apply "Voting" to the task prioritisation labels to acquire the final prioritisation for the pathology result (see Subsect. 5.3 below for further detail).

5.2   FP-Based Future Result Forecast Pathology Data Prioritisation

For the FP-based FRF-PDP variation Facebook Profit (FP) was adopted. FP was created by Facebook's Core Data Science team for univariate time series forecasting. FP is an open source library for forecasting with time series that feature significant seasonal variation and that span a number of seasons. Unlike LSTMs, FP operates well with missing values. Models generated using FP operate in an "additive regressive" manner. The fundamental FP equation is as follows:

$$y(t) = g(t) + s(t) + h(t) + \epsilon_t \tag{4}$$

where: $g(t)$ is the trend factor, and $s(t)$ and $h(t)$ are the seasonal and holiday components respectively, and ϵ_t is an error term [3, 15].

Although specifically designed for use with time series that feature seasonality, the components $s(t)$ and $h(t)$ can be ignored. For the work presented in this paper the focus was on $g(t)$. There are two trend models for $g(t)$: (i) a non-linear saturating growth model and (ii) a piece-wise linear model. For the experiments reported on later in this paper the non-linear growth model was used, because of the non-linear nature of the task time series under consideration. Overall, the adopted procedure for pathology forecasting using FP was similar to that used with respect to LSTM-based FRF-PDP. Equation 3 was again used. The differences were: (i) the date of each point in each patient time series was added to the input training data, and (ii) no padding was required as FP was able to deal with time series data with different lengths.

5.3 Final FRF-PDP Classification

Once we have forecast the next value in a task time series and used Eq. 3 to label each task value in a new pathology result using a two class classification, priortity versus non-priority, the next stage was to determine the overall three-class (high, medium, low) prioritisation of the given pathology result. To this end a simple conditional rule was defined as follows:

$$c = \begin{cases} high, & \text{if } m \geq 4 \\ medium, & \text{if } 3 \leq m < 4 \\ low, & \text{otherwise} \end{cases} \quad (5)$$

where m is the number of tasks classified as "priority" tasks (see above). In the case of the evaluation presented in the following section, the U&E evaluation data used featured $m = 5$.

6 Evaluation

This section presents the evaluation of the two proposed mechanism and their two variation in each case: (i) kNN-based PCT-PDP, (ii) LSTM-based PCT-PDP, (iii) LSTM-based FRF-PDP and (iv) FP-based FRF-PDP. As established in the foregoing, the pathology prioritisation problem was conceptualised as a three class problem; hence solutions to the problems could be evaluated using the "standard" accuracy, precision, recall and F1 metrics. All the experiments were run using a windows 10 desktop machine with a 3.2 GHz Quad-Core IntelCore i5 processor and 24 GB of RAM. For the LSTM, a GPU was used fitted with a NVIDA GeForceRTX 2060 unit. The objectives of the evaluation were as follows:

1. To identify the optimum parameter settings for the proposed approaches.
2. To compare the operation of the kNN and LSTM-based PGT-PDP approaches.
3. To compare the operation of the FP and LSTM-based FRF-PDP approaches.
4. To compare the overall performance of the proposed mechanisms.

For the evaluation U&E pathology data provided by the Wirral Teaching Hospital in Merseyside in the UK was used. From this raw data an evaluation data D was created.

The remainder of this section is organised as follows. An overview of the U&E evaluation data sets is given in Subsect. 6.1. The LSTM parameter setting are considered in Subsect. 6.2. The results with respect to remainder of the above objectives are then discussed in Subsect. 6.3, 6.4 and 6.5 respectively.

6.1   Evaluation Dataset

The Wirral Teaching Hospital U&E pathology test data comprised four data tables: (i) Emergency Data (ED), (ii) In-Patient (IP), (iii) Out-Patient (OP) and Laboratory Results (LR). The data tables comprised of 180,865, 226,634, 955,318 and 532,801 records respectively. The primary table used for the evaluation of the proposed data prioritisation mechanisms considered in this paper was the LR data table. A single pathology task record in this table was of the form:

$$\langle ID, Task, Date, Value, Max, Min, Gender \rangle \tag{6}$$

This was used to generate a database **D** where, as noted in Sect. 3.2, each patent record $P_j \in \mathbf{D}$ was of the form:

$$P_j = \langle Id, Date, Gender, T_{So}, T_{Po}, T_{Ur}, T_{Cr}, T_{Bi}, c \rangle \tag{7}$$

Some data cleaning, such as removing patients with missing or non-numeric task values and feature scaling was undertaken with respect to **D**.

For the FRF-PDP mechanism, as noted in Sect. 5, an initial two class prioritisation, priority versus non-priority, was undertaken. The two-class distribution, per task, is given in Table 1. This two-class prioritisation was then converted into the desired three-class prioritisation, high, medium and low. In the case of the PGT-PDP mechanism the classification models were generated directly by using this three-class prioritisation. Table 2 shows the three-class distribution per patient.

Table 1. Two-class (priority, non-priority) distribution per task in the U&E LAB Dataset.

Task Name	Task Labels		Total
	Prior.	Non-prior.	
Bicarbonate (bi)	1,099	2,635	3734
Creatinine (cr)	1,639	2,095	3734
Sodium (so)	861	2873	3734
Potassium (po)	397	3,337	3734
Urea (ur)	1,373	2,361	3734
Total	5,369	13,301	18,670

Table 2. Three-class (high, medium, low) distribution per patient in the U&E LAB Dataset.

Event Proxy Truth	No. Patients Test Records
High	255
Medium	123
Low	3356
Total	3734

From the Table 2, it can be seen that there was a significant imbalance between the number of patients within each class. This is not an issue for the forecasting mechanism as the data was not required to train a classification model. But for the PGT-PDP mechanism, especially when using LSTMs, it was an issue, as highly imbalanced data may pose a bias towards the majority class. Thus we used an oversampling techniques to address this issue with respect to the LSTM-based PGT-PDP variation.

6.2 Parameter Settings

Two classification model generator approaches, kNN and LSTM; and two prediction mechanisms, LSTM and FP, were considered with respect to the two approaches presented in this paper, PGT-PDP and FRF-PDP. All these approaches require parameters. As already discussed above kNN required a value for k and a value for the associate $\epsilon = 0.159$ threshold. The values for these parameters are fairly easy to specify. As discussed above, $k = 1$ and $\epsilon = 0.159$ were used.

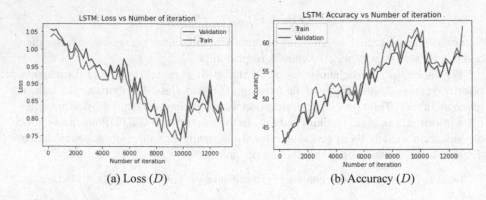

(a) Loss (D) (b) Accuracy (D)

Fig. 3. Loss and Accuracy curves for LSTM-based PGT-PDP as reported in [9].

Table 3. Parameter setting for LSTM-based PGT-PDP.

Parameter Name	Task				
	Bi	*Cr*	*So*	*Po*	*Ur*
Batch size	512	128	256	512	512
Learning Rate	0.01	0.01	0.01	0.01	0.01
Epochs	1,000	1,000	1,000	1,000	1,000

Table 4. Parameter setting for LSTM-based FRF-PDP.

Parameter Name	Task				
	Bi	*Cr*	*So*	*Po*	*Ur*
Batch size	128	64	128	128	128
Learning Rate	0.01	0.01	0.01	0.01	0.01
Epochs	45	45	45	45	45

LSTMs require three parameters: (i) the batch size, (ii) the learning rate and (iii) the number of epochs. The general way of finding the best LSTM parameters is to analyse the learning curves and accuracy plots of the training and validation data. The most popular learning curve used for this purpose is the "loss over time" curve. Loss measures the model error, which represents the performance of the model. As loss is usually a function indicating the difference between the derived values and the actual values, the lower the loss the better the model performance. A grid search was used to find the best combination of parameters according to the generated loss over time curves. Although the drawback of the grid search method is that it is computationally expensive, it is a simple and effective technique when there is a prior knowledge of the parameters range. Grid search, coupled with loss over time curves, were therefore used with respect to the work presented here. This was also the approach taken with respect to the work described in [9]. In this manner the most appropriate parameters with respect to each pathology task were identified. The average loss and accuracy plots obtained, as reported in [9], are presented in Fig. 3. In the figure the x-axis gives the number of times the weights in the network were updated, and the y-axis the loss value. From the figures, it can be seen that convergence is not obvious in all cases. Possible reasons could be: (i) the oversampling techniques used for addressing the class imbalanced problem was not suitable, and the information insufficient problem still exists, so there is not enough information for the LSTM to learn from; or (ii) that the proxy ground truth data set may not be entirely representative. Whatever the case, the derived LSTM parameters for the PGT-PDP mechanism are given in Table 3, and those for the FRF-PDP mechanism in Table 4. From the table it can be observed that: (i) the most appropriate batch size was different for each task, (ii) the learning rate was the same in all cases, and (iii) the number of epochs was required to be higher for PGT-PDP than for FRF-PDP.

The parameters for FP prediction approach were fairly straight forward to set. The original FP algorithm required three categories of parameters, which controlled the trend, seasonality and holiday effects. However, As noted above, in the case of the FP-based FRF-PDP mechanism only the trend part was utilised. Therefore the two parameters of concern were: (i) the number of trend changes within the data, and (ii) the change points scale which determines the flexibility of the trend, and in particular how much the trend changes at the trend change points. To identify the most appropriate FP parameter settings ranges of values wee considered. For the number of trend changes the selected range was from 3 to 52, incrementing in steps of 1. For the change points scale the selected range was from 0.01 to 0.5, incrementing in steps of 0.01. The identified parameters are given in Table 5.

Table 5. Parameter settings for FP-based FRF-PDP.

Parameter	Task				
Name	Bi	Cr	So	Po	Ur
N_changepoints	3	3	3	3	3
ChangePoints Scale	0.01	0.03	0.05	0.06	0.05

6.3 Comparison of Proxy Ground Truth Pathology Data Prioritisation Approaches

The comparison results for the kNN and LSTM-based PGT-PDP approaches, as reported in [9], are given in Tables 6 and 7 (best results for each fold highlighted in bold

Table 6. Average Precision and Recall of kNN-based PGT-PDP [9].

Fold Num.	Acc.	Pre. High	Pre. Medium	Pre. Low	Rec. High	Rec. Medium	Rec. Low
1	0.585	**0.414**	0.400	0.545	**0.637**	0.577	0.666
2	0.632	**0.534**	0.688	0.578	**0.678**	0.467	0.714
3	0.576	**0.412**	0.541	0.674	**0.588**	0.535	0.647
4	0.523	**0.598**	0.541	0.634	**0.712**	0.4688	0.505
5	0.566	**0.444**	0.384	0.598	**0.541**	0.487	0.785
Ave	0.576	**0.480**	0.510	0.605	**0.631**	0.507	0.663
SD	0.039	**0.082**	0.124	0.050	**0.068**	0.047	0.103

Table 7. Average Precision and Recall of LSTM-based PGT-PDP [9].

Fold Num.	Acc.	Pre. High	Pre. Medium	Pre. Low	Rec. High	Rec. Medium	Rec. Low
1	0.671	**0.578**	0.374	0.711	**0.811**	0.641	0.412
2	0.642	**0.475**	0.552	0.735	**0.758**	0.468	0.577
3	0.622	**0.553**	0.577	0.708	**0.669**	0.547	0.703
4	0.608	**0.615**	0.714	0.699	**0.712**	0.563	0.697
5	0.645	**0.466**	0.766	0.596	**0.699**	0.476	0.778
Ave	0.638	**0.538**	0.597	0.690	**0.730**	0.539	0.633
SD	0.024	**0.065**	0.120	0.054	**0.056**	0.071	0.143

font). Five fold cross validation was used to generate these results. The overall average (Ave) and standard deviation (SD) are also presented in the last two rows. Recall that a low SD values indicates that little variation existed across the folds. It can be observed from the table that LSTM-based PGT-PDP consistently out performed the kNN-based PGT-PDP. It might be argued that the recall and precision values are relatively low, this could be because the irregular distribution of the time stamps within the training data may have had an adverse effect.

6.4 Comparison of Future Results Forecast Pathology Data Prioritisation Approaches

Using the FRF-PDP mechanism forecast models were built for each task and then the results combined to produce a final priority classification. Hence, the evaluation was conducted on two levels, the Local Task level and the Global Test level. Accuracy, Recall, Precision, F1 score and Mean Square Error(MSE) were again used as the evaluation metrics, together with Five fold cross validation.

The results obtained at the local task level, using LSTM-based and FP-based FRF-PDP, are given in Tables 8 and 9 respectively. The tables are divided into two parts. The right hand side gives the average MSE values recorded with respect to the prediction for each task. The left had side gives the the average accuracy (Acc), Precision (Pre), Recall (Rec) and F1 values recorded with respect to the prioritisation classification.

From the Tables 8 and 9 it can be seen that the overall recall using FP-based FRF-PDP is much higher than when using LSTM-based FRF-PDP. In the context of pathology data prioritisation high recall is generally considered desirable over precision, given that it would be acceptable to classify a non-priority record to be a priority record mistakenly, rather than the contrary. But it can also be noticed that the average MSE using FP-based FRF-PDP, for the majority of the tasks is higher than when using LSTM-based

FRF-PDP, especially for the $MSE_{(so)}$, where the difference is considerable. Perhaps this is because FP takes account of the individual date stamps of values and because it does not require padding. Another possible reason for the better performance of FP is that the predicted values derived by FP for different tasks are further away from the true mean values ("outside" of the true values), than when LSTM is used. This would mean that the predicted values are likely to fall outside of the clinical reference range and hence be classified as "priority" values. This in turn would explain the relatively higher recall values when using FP compared to LSTM, as there is a higher chance of a priority record being labelled correctly; using FP the high priority classification is therefore favoured. However, this conjecture may also cause concerns about the stability and generalisability of the model. Whatever the case, in summary it can be seen that the overall performance of FP-based FRF-PDP, at least at the Local Task level, is better than LSTM-based FRF-PDP.

Table 8. Local Task Level Accuracy, Recall, Precision, F1-score and MSE using LSTM-based FRF-PDF.

Fold Num.	Acc.	Pre.	Rec.	F1	MSE(bi)	MSE(cr)	MSE(so)	MSE(po)	MSE(ur)
1	0.611	0.524	0.371	0.412	16.29	421.56	4.92	0.37	4.71
2	0.657	0.544	0.333	0.502	21.01	224.68	6.47	0.25	5.68
3	0.555	0.639	0.278	0.530	26.36	602.24	24.31	0.61	7.98
4	0.586	0.410	0.362	0.408	21.43	478.12	33.75	0.78	13.21
5	0.512	0.682	0.403	0.577	9.78	541.45	9.74	1.28	12.56
Ave	0.584	0.560	0.345	0.486	18.974	453.61	15.838	0.658	8.828
SD	0.049	0.095	0.042	0.066	5.594	129.494	11.285	0.362	3.485

Table 9. Local Task Level Accuracy, Recall, Precision, F1-score and MSE using FP-based FRF-PDF.

Fold Num.	Acc.	Pre.	Rec.	F1	MSE(bi)	MSE(cr)	MSE(so)	MSE(po)	MSE(ur)
1	0.674	0.523	0.701	0.511	15.31	602.31	81.32	3.41	9.45
2	0.712	0.612	0.682	0.576	17.45	487.56	77.45	1.74	8.73
3	0.667	0.662	0.674	0.611	21.68	512.37	98.56	2.01	6.55
4	0.721	0.549	0.660	0.554	19.21	345.87	74.31	0.93	10.32
5	0.732	0.522	0.736	0.568	23.85	324.63	88.63	1.21	3.96
Ave	0.701	0.574	0.691	0.564	19.500	454.548	84.054	1.86	7.802
SD	0.026	0.055	0.026	0.0324	3.017	104.839	8.688	0.863	2.291

Recall that at the global level three proxy ground truth class labels were used (high, medium and low). The evaluation results obtained are given in Tables 10 and 11; best results for each fold highlighted in bold font. From the Tables it can be seen that the average recall for LSTM and FP-based FRF-PDP is higher than the precision for almost all of the three prioritisation classes. The average recall for the classification of the high prioritisation class was 0.739 using LSTM-based FRF-PDP, and 0.712 using FP-based FRF-PDP; both higher than for the other classes; which, as noted earlier, is desirable as it entails a lower chance for missing any high priority pathology results. However, the average precision for the high prioritisation, using both approaches, is far lower than their recall, which may cause low prioritisation pathology results to be classified as higher level results. Thus the benefit of the prioritisation might not be significant if all

Table 10. Global Test Level Precision and Recall for the overall prioritisation using LSTM-based FRF-PDP.

Fold Num.	Acc.	Pre. High	Pre. Medium	Pre. Low	Rec. High	Rec. Medium	Rec. Low
1	0.512	**0.310**	0.325	0.338	**0.694**	0.546	0.516
2	0.572	**0.317**	0.412	0.454	**0.711**	0.597	0.537
3	0.582	**0.447**	0.334	0.497	**0.824**	0.611	0.498
4	0.611	**0.301**	0.378	0.523	**0.765**	0.547	0.564
5	0.504	**0.477**	0.364	0.437	**0.702**	0.511	0.536
Ave	0.556	0.370	0.363	0.450	0.739	0.562	0.530
SD	0.041	0.076	0.031	0.064	0.049	0.037	0.022

Table 11. Global Test Level Precision and Recall for the overall prioritisation using FP-based FRF-PDP.

Fold Num.	Acc.	Pre. High	Pre. Medium	Pre. Low	Rec. High	Rec. Medium	Rec. Low
1	0.587	**0.456**	0.441	0.663	**0.714**	0.402	0.537
2	0.572	**0.437**	0.467	0.538	**0.820**	0.331	0.584
3	0.513	**0.525**	0.493	0.507	**0.551**	0.227	0.623
4	0.538	**0.533**	0.541	0.463	**0.698**	0.380	0.609
5	0.607	**0.488**	0.552	0.497	**0.775**	0.534	0.497
Ave	0.563	0.488	0.499	0.534	0.712	0.375	0.570
SD	0.034	0.037	0.042	0.069	0.091	0.100	0.047

results were classified as high priority. In the extreme situation, the prioritisation might thus be meaningless!

6.5   Comparison of the Overall Performance of the Proposed Mechanisms

Table 12. Comparison of PGT-PDP, FRF-PDP and Anomaly Detection-based PDP.

Method	Acc.	Precision			Recall		
		High	Med.	Low	High	Med.	Low
LSTM-based FRF-PDP	0.56	**0.37**	0.36	0.45	**0.74**	0.56	0.53
FP-based FRF-PDP	0.56	0.49	0.50	**0.53**	**0.71**	0.38	0.57
LSTM-based PGT-PDP [9]	0.61	0.58	0.55	**0.69**	**0.79**	0.59	0.63
kNN-based PGT-PDP [9]	0.60	0.42	0.51	**0.85**	0.70	0.55	**0.75**
Point-based AD [10]	0.34	0.35			0.43		
Time Series AD [10]	0.45	0.45			0.43		

Table 12 shows a comparison of the performance between the four approaches proposed in this paper. The table includes the results, reported in [10], obtained when using the two Anomaly Detection (AD) pathology prioritisation approaches: (i) Point-based AD and (ii) Time Series-based AD. Note that in [10] only the overall precision and recall values were reported; and hence these have been reported in Table 12. From the table, it can be seen that the recall for the high prioritisation level using the both the PCT-PDP and FRF-PDP mechanisms is good, over 70%, although the overall precision is lower than when using the FRF-PDP mechanism. The AD mechanisms produced the worst performance. The reason behind the poor performance of the Point-based AD and Time Series AD is probably because, as noted earlier, anomalous pathology results do not necessarily equate to priority pathology results. From the table, the best performing mechanism was PGT-PDP, with little distinction between the LSTM abd the kNN variations. The results given in the Table 12 of course need to be tempered with the observation that the ground truth used was a proxy for the real ground truth.

7 Conclusions

This paper has discussed two mechanisms for prioritising pathology results in the context of the absence of a ground truth; pathology results made up of a number of task values. The first mechanism, the Proxy Ground Truth Pathology Data Prioritisation (PGR-PDP) mechanism was underpinned by the fundamental idea that new pathology test results could be classified (using a three level priority classification) according to the anticipated outcome event associated with the result. Two variations were considered, kNN-based and LSTM-based PGR-PDP. The second mechanism, the Future Result Forecast Pathology Data Prioritisation (FRF-PDP) mechanism was underpinned by the fundamental idea that new pathology results could be classified according to whether predicted future test values were inside or outside the expected normal range. Two variations were again considered, LSTM-based and FP-based FRF-PDP. The proposed approaches were comparatively evaluated using U&E pathology test data which comprised five tasks. The final comparative results demonstrated that the PGR-PDP mechanism produced the best recall and precision of 0.79 and 0.58 respectively for the high priority class. For future work the authors intend to: (i) investigate the generation of artificial evaluation data sets to provide for a more comprehensive evaluation, and (ii) undertake a comprehensive collaborate with clinicians to obtain feedback regarding the prioritisations produced and to test the utility of the best performing mechanism in a real setting. The authors are currently liaising with domain experts on the practical impact of the proposed pathology data prioritisation mechanisms presented in this paper.

References

1. Bagnall, A., Lines, J., Bostrom, A., Large, J., Keogh, E.: The great time series classification bake off: a review and experimental evaluation of recent algorithmic advances. Data Mining Knowl. Discov. **31**(3), 606–660 (2017)
2. Benvenuto, D., Giovanetti, M., Vassallo, L., Angeletti, S., Ciccozzi, M.: Application of the ARIMA model on the COVID-2019 epidemic dataset. Data in brief **29**, 105340 (2020)
3. Daraghmeh, M., Agarwal, A., Manzano, R., Zaman, M.: Time series forecasting using facebook prophet for cloud resource management. In: 2021 IEEE International Conference on Communications Workshops (ICC Workshops). pp. 1–6. IEEE (2021)
4. Horng, S., Sontag, D.A., Halpern, Y., Jernite, Y., Shapiro, N.I., Nathanson, L.A.: Creating an automated trigger for sepsis clinical decision support at emergency department triage using machine learning. PloS one **12**(4), e0174708 (2017)
5. Li, Z.X., Wu, S.H., Zhou, Y., Li, C.: A combined filtering search for DTW. In: 2017 2nd International Conference on Image, Vision and Computing (ICIVC). pp. 884–888. IEEE (2017)

6. Li, Z., Han, J., Song, Y.: On the forecasting of high-frequency financial time series based on ARIMA model improved by deep learning. J. Forecast. **39**(7), 1081–1097 (2020)
7. Mahmud, S.: Bangladesh COVID-19 daily cases time series analysis using facebook prophet model. Available at SSRN 3660368 (2020)
8. Park, J., Chang, B., Mok, N.: 144 time series analysis and forecasting daily emergency department visits utilizing facebook's prophet method. Annals Emerg. Med. **74**(4), S57 (2019)
9. Qi, J., Burnside, G., Charnley, P., Coenen, F.: Event-based pathology data prioritisation: A study using multi-variate time series classification. In: Proceedings of the 13th International Joint Conference on Knowledge Discovery, Knowledge Engineering and Knowledge Management - KDIR, pp. 121–128. INSTICC, SciTePress (2021)
10. Qi, J., Burnside, G., Coenen, F.: Ranking Pathology Data in the Absence of a Ground Truth. In: Bramer, M., Ellis, R. (eds.) SGAI-AI 2021. LNCS (LNAI), vol. 13101, pp. 209–223. Springer, Cham (2021). https://doi.org/10.1007/978-3-030-91100-3_18
11. Raita, Y., Goto, T., Faridi, M.K., Brown, D.F., Camargo, C.A., Hasegawa, K.: Emergency department triage prediction of clinical outcomes using machine learning models. Crit. Care **23**(1), 1–13 (2019)
12. Rakthanmanon, T., et al.: Searching and mining trillions of time series subsequences under dynamic time warping. In: Proceedings of the 18th ACM SIGKDD International Conference on Knowledge Discovery and Data Mining. pp. 262–270 (2012)
13. Reddy, B.K., Delen, D.: Predicting hospital readmission for lupus patients: an RNN-LSTM-based deep-learning methodology. Comput. Biol. Med. **101**, 199–209 (2018)
14. Roondiwala, M., Patel, H., Varma, S.: Predicting stock prices using LSTM. Int. J. Sci. Res. (IJSR) **6**(4), 1754–1756 (2017)
15. Toharudin, T., Pontoh, R.S., Caraka, R.E., Zahroh, S., Lee, Y., Chen, R.C.: Employing long short-term memory and facebook prophet model in air temperature forecasting. Commun. Statistics-Simul. Comput. 1–24 (2020)
16. Vikram, S., Li, L., Russell, S.: Handwriting and gestures in the air, recognizing on the fly. In: Proceedings of the CHI. vol. 13, pp. 1179–1184 (2013)
17. Wang, L., Wang, X., Leckie, C., Ramamohanarao, K.: Characteristic-Based Descriptors for Motion Sequence Recognition. In: Washio, T., Suzuki, E., Ting, K.M., Inokuchi, A. (eds.) PAKDD 2008. LNCS (LNAI), vol. 5012, pp. 369–380. Springer, Heidelberg (2008). https://doi.org/10.1007/978-3-540-68125-0_33
18. Wang, X., Mueen, A., Ding, H., Trajcevski, G., Scheuermann, P., Keogh, E.: Experimental comparison of representation methods and distance measures for time series data. Data Mining Knowl. Discov. **26**(2), 275–309 (2013)
19. Xing, W., Bei, Y.: Medical health big data classification based on KNN classification algorithm. IEEE Access **8**, 28808–28819 (2019)
20. Zheng, H., Shi, D.: Using a LSTM-RNN Based Deep Learning Framework for ICU Mortality Prediction. In: Meng, X., Li, R., Wang, K., Niu, B., Wang, X., Zhao, G. (eds.) WISA 2018. LNCS, vol. 11242, pp. 60–67. Springer, Cham (2018). https://doi.org/10.1007/978-3-030-02934-0_6

From Event Tracking to Event Modelling: Understanding as a Paradigm Shift

Nicholas Mamo[✉] [iD], Colin Layfield [iD], and Joel Azzopardi

University of Malta, Msida, MSD 2080, Malta
nicholas.mamo.14@um.edu.mt
https://www.um.edu.mt/ict/ai/

Abstract. In 1998, Topic Detection and Tracking (TDT), or event tracking, was only two years old. By then, however, event tracking's pioneers had already realized that for algorithms to accomplish their task, to detect and track events in the news media accurately, they had to understand events. Yet it has taken event tracking the decades since then to resolve what it means to understand events and how. Simple interpretations of understanding often failed; the rest never fulfilled the potential of event tracking. Without understanding, event tracking continues to struggle with the same, early problems, which social media aggravated and contemporary applications of events compounded. Therefore in this position paper, we argue that now, more than ever, event tracking needs event understanding. By comparing event tracking's interpretations of what it means to understand, we demonstrate how early understanding only failed event tracking because it remained too simple in its reliance on linguistics. We adopt a different definition of events, a structured and semantic description that revolves around Who did What, Where and When. Furthermore, we propose how event tracking can fill in the event structure automatically and ahead of time. In the end, we show that understanding remains a complex problem, but event tracking can find in event knowledge a new purpose and its much-awaited paradigm shift.

Keywords: Topic detection and tracking · Event tracking · Event modelling and mining · Twitter

1 Introduction

Understanding flowed from event tracking almost as naturally as the first results. Event tracking, formally Topic Detection and Tracking (TDT), launched in 1996 as a pilot study with a straightforward goal: to detect and track events in the news media [4]. The next year, as the research area reflected on its problems, it settled on a logical solution: event tracking had to understand events better [6]. Disappointingly, early forms of understanding often failed event tracking [32]; the rest brought few benefits. However, event tracking discovered it could progress without understanding events as long as it understood how they behaved. And so event tracking continued to detect and track, and not understand.

Event tracking never solved the early problems of accuracy. Now, event tracking has progressed from the news media to social media, and it faces the modern challenges of

A. Fred et al. (Eds.): IC3K 2021, CCIS 1718, pp. 21–36, 2023.
https://doi.org/10.1007/978-3-031-35924-8_2

Twitter and the complex demands of novel applications of events. Event tracking must make sense of Twitter streams [9], find a way to explain, not merely detect events [34], and model the structure of events to allow complex reasoning over how one interacts with the other [12]. Event tracking faces all these challenges without understanding.

This is our position in this paper: *understanding can be event tracking's paradigm shift*. Despite the past disillusions of understanding, many of event tracking's problems can be attributed to the research area's lack of knowledge about events. But more than just a solution to event tracking's problems, understanding can approach event tracking to event modelling. Therefore we argue on behalf of understanding as we make the following contributions:

– Today, understanding lingers as a failed experiment of event tracking. Nevertheless, the research area's past attempts to apply understanding to improve accuracy, denoise datasets and model events endure as pertinent lessons. In this paper, we review these lessons as we explore existing and prospective applications of understanding in event tracking.
– Many applications of understanding in event tracking often led to inadequate improvements. However, what misled techniques were the simplistic interpretations of event understanding, not knowledge itself. In this paper, we contrast event tracking's various interpretations of understanding and explain why simple approaches often failed.
– Proper understanding can transform the way we detect and track events. However, defining and generating knowledge automatically persist as an outstanding challenge. In this paper, we adopt a structured definition of events that describes Who did What, Where and When, and explain how event tracking can generate semantic understanding automatically.

This position paper extends our previous work [30]. The paper includes a broadened discussion throughout and many new examples. Most notably, however, this version makes the following novel contributions:

– An extended discussion of event tracking's history, now oriented towards the research area's challenges and applications for understanding. In this paper, we also establish understanding as the missing link between event tracking and the emerging area of event modelling and mining.
– A comparison of event tracking's interpretations of what it means to understand events. In this paper, we frame these interpretations in a conventional definition of knowledge to justify why past efforts to understand events failed.
– A new guideline on how understanding can assimilate event tracking with event modelling. In this paper, we portray event modelling as event tracking empowered with understanding, and illustrate how knowledge about events can facilitate answering Why and How they happened.

The ideas that we present here represent more than a theoretical exercise. This position paper forms the foundation of a doctorate on the role of machine understanding in event tracking. Initial results confirm the three principles in this paper: the importance of

developing the theory behind event understanding, the feasibility of generating semantic knowledge about events automatically, and the wide-ranging benefits that proper
understanding can have on event tracking algorithms. We will disclose our results in
more detail in future scholarly publications.

The rest of this paper is organized as follows. In Sect. 2, we explore the evolving
role of understanding in event tracking over the years, from the traditional applications of event knowledge in the news media to its modern relevance in social media.
In Sect. 3, we compare and contrast event tracking's interpretations of understanding.
In Sect. 4, we adopt a structured definition of events steeped in semantics and explain
how event tracking can understand events automatically and ahead of time. In Sect. 5,
we summarize our position.

2 Why Event Tracking Needs Event Understanding

The Topic Detection and Tracking (TDT) pilot study in 1998 ended on a hopeful note.
The pilot study launched with three goals: to segment streams of news articles into
stories, to detect new events, and to track them until they expired. Commenting on the
outcomes of the pilot study, Allan et al. (1998) deemed the first results positive and the
first techniques "adequate". However, the pilot study also left "substantial room-and
hope-for improvement" [4]. It was in this context that, shortly after, Allan et al. (1998)
first touted event understanding [6].

Allan et al. (1998) argued that understanding the identity of the event-what makes
the event itself-would trivialize event tracking. A system that understands events recognizes that one event shares its identity with another. Inversely, a system that understands events recognizes a new event because it does not share its identity with any
other. Thus, the authors conjectured, capturing the event identity-Who did What, Where
and When, and Why and How-could improve event tracking's accuracy, although they
feared understanding might not lead to large gains [6].

Early ventures into understanding vindicated Allan et al. (1998)'s fears. At its worst,
simple understanding failed event tracking completely. Makkonen et al. (2004)'s event
profiles split the Vector Space Model (VSM) into four dimensions-the Who, What,
Where and When-but performed worse than a traditional baseline [27]. And at its
best, simple understanding did not fulfil event tracking's hope for improvement [32].
Allan et al. (1998)'s prediction [6] had come true: limited understanding yielded limited improvements.

Instead of better understanding, event tracking sought alternatives. Event tracking,
originally a clustering task, inherited the same challenges, namely fragmentation and
complexity. In answer, Fung et al. (2005) proposed feature-pivot techniques [16], a class
of methods rooted in an earlier intuition about how events behave: that when an event
happens, news outlets publish more reports or use a different language [40]. Feature-
pivot techniques look for such changes. They understand how events behave generally
without understanding the idiosyncrasies of particular events.

Then, in 2006, Twitter launched.[1] Twitter gave event tracking a new role, a new
purpose. Social media made amateur reporters of regular social media users, and event

---

[1] https://twitter.com, accessed on May 21, 2022.

tracking capitalized on Twitter's API to track their reporting. Before Twitter launched, event tracking was an aggregator of news from the newswire. Now, after Twitter launched, event tracking itself became the newswire.

But Twitter also forced event tracking to reckon with modern challenges. Event tracking could no longer assume that every item was newsworthy [20]. Nor could it assume that tools developed for news media reports would work just as well on Twitter's distinctively-short tweets [18,36]. Event tracking had to revise its algorithms' most fundamental principles to adapt to Twitter.

Hampered by social media's challenges, event tracking stalled. Of course, artificial intelligence witnessed technological advances, which event tracking adopted. Event tracking applied machine learning [15], text embedding [14] and, more generally, increasingly convoluted solutions. However, if event tracking's performance improved, it did not improve substantially. We point to the same flaws in algorithms from 2011 [41] as we do in algorithms from 2021 [29]: algorithms still require large datasets to build timelines [18,36], and still struggle to eliminate noise and cover events comprehensively [29].

Nothing could quite overcome social media's challenges, and still, event tracking rarely studied understanding as a solution. But are event tracking's difficulties to accurately parse event streams not a failure to understand what is relevant, objective and important?

The occasional experiments with understanding brought success, if not a revolution. Hossny and Mitchell (2018) extracted words that describe protests to classify days with demonstrations [19]. Huang et al. (2018) built separate timelines for separate named entities [21]. And Löchtefeld et al. (2015) hand-crafted patterns to extract complex topics from football matches, such as which player scored a goal or received a yellow card [25].

But event tracking's solution was rarely to understand [9,13,26]. More often, event tracking turned to aggressive filtering for a solution. It became typical for algorithms to retain only the largest clusters [18] or to remove all retweets [10]. McMinn and Jose (2015)'s filtering curbed more than 90% of datasets [31].

However, event understanding did not disappear altogether. Understanding resurged in event modelling and mining, the task of representing events "in a semantically meaningful way"-Who did What, Where and When-and of identifying connections among them [12]. Event modelling in particular aspires to transform events into a resource, enabling new applications, such as to triangulate fake news [2] or identify journalistic angles [33]. Thus, event modelling reiterates Panagiotou et al. (2016)'s call that detecting events no longer meets modern needs, that "event detection requires the automatic answering of what, when, where, and by whom" [34].

Event tracking and event modelling and mining mainly differ in purpose. Event modelling feels like a downstream task to event tracking, whose output it models. Although Chen and Li (2020) make no reference to Allan et al. (1998)'s work [4,6], nor allude to event tracking in general, they describe events in the same way: Who did What, Where and When, and Why and How. Only understanding separates event tracking's output from event modelling's.

With understanding, event tracking and event modelling could have a symbiotic relationship. To event modelling, event tracking could be a guide that, driven by understanding, automatically describes Who did What, Where and When, as Panagiotou et al. (2016) envisioned [34]. After all, Löchtefeld et al. (2015)'s hand-crafted extraction patterns simultaneously track events and represent them semantically [25]. And to event tracking, event modelling and mining could be the modern equivalent of Twitter: a new role, a new purpose. Yet for event tracking to approach event modelling and undergo a paradigm shift, it first needs to resolve what it means to understand events. Therefore in the next section, we discuss event tracking's interpretations of understanding.

3   What It Means to Understand

Before event tracking could not understand events, it could not define them. Event tracking has always struggled to define events and remains to this day without a standard definition [36]. The most common definition today is also the earliest and no more expressive now than it was back in 1998, generally something that happens at a particular place and at a particular time [4]. Event tracking can hardly understand events without defining them, so in this section, we seek implicit definitions in the research area's interpretations of understanding.

Allan et al. (1998)'s event structure [6], for instance, expresses the composition of events like a definition. Every event "comprises at the very least what happened, where it happened, when it happened, and who was involved" [32]. Allan et al. (1998)'s event structure formalizes those components in one framework, the 'five Ws and one H': Who did What, Where and When, and Why and How [6].

The 'five Ws and one H', adapted from the news media [35], bound every event. Given the BBC's tweet in Fig. 1, we can effortlessly fill in the event structure [6]. We can infer When the event happened from the publication time and identify the rest of the components in the short text: "Indonesian Navy *[Who]* hunting for submarine *[What]* that has gone missing *[Why/How]* in waters north of island of Bali *[Where]*."

Nevertheless, Allan et al. (1998)'s structure on its own does not constitute event understanding. Framed in Plato's widely-accepted definition of knowledge [8], "justified true beliefs", the framework of the 'five Ws and one H' fails. The structure contains no propositions: no justifications, no truths and no beliefs. The structure constitutes only a template for research to fill in with event understanding.

Thus, structured understanding left researchers to interpret how to fill in the template, with difficulty. What does it mean to understand What happens in an event or with Whose involvement? Annotating the tweet above comes intuitively to a human, but the research community struggled to convey that intuition to an algorithm, to find the structure of events automatically. Event tracking commonly resorted to linguistics to fill in the template. Less commonly, it prioritised semantics. In the rest of this section, we explore three interpretations of what it means to understand and their fortunes when applied to track events.

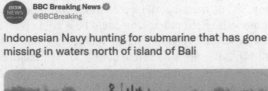

Fig. 1. Like in the above tweet [1], journalists use the Who, What, Where, When, Why and How to describe events. Figure reproduced from our previous work [30] with written permission from the publisher.

3.1 Linguistic Understanding

First, event tracking understood events with linguistics. There, in linguistics, event tracking found convenience and accessibility. The research area could experiment with understanding by exploiting progress in Natural Language Processing (NLP) to align the structure with articles and tweets: the When aligned comfortably with the publication time, the Who and the Where with named entities, and the What with most of what remained.

Early research recreated the event identity from articles in this manner. Makkonen et al. (2004)'s event profiles use Named Entity Recognition (NER) to capture Who was involved in an event and Where it happened, and Parts of Speech (POS) tagging to capture What happened [27]. More recent interpretations augment the old structure with modern metadata. Li et al. (2017)'s structure, otherwise identical to Makkonen et al. (2004)'s event profiles, views Twitter mentions like the Who and hashtags as the topics, the What [24].

Others focused narrowly on certain aspects of the event structure. Chen and Ku (2002) boost the weight of named entities, the Who and the Where [11], and McMinn and Jose (2015) cluster tweets separately for each named entity [31]. And others yet left behind the event structure altogether, although not the convenience and accessibility of linguistics. They interpreted understanding events as discovering the latent subjects in corpora through methods such as topic modelling [13] and text embedding [14].

Linguistic understanding failed frequently [32]. Makkonen et al. (2004)'s event profiles perform worse than the baseline [27]. De Boom et al. (2015)'s topic modelling [13] and Chen and Ku (2002)'s named entity boosting [11] only reduce errors when applied selectively. Even when linguistics succeeded, the progress appeared insignificant compared to the efforts and complexity of understanding.

The failures of linguistics should not surprise us. Applying conventional linguistics to the tweet in Fig. 1 would yield mixed fortunes. NER would correctly identify the *Indonesian Navy* as the Who and *Bali* as the Where, and POS tagging would correctly identify *hunting* and *submarine* as the verb and noun that describe What happened. Nevertheless, POS tagging would also erroneously identify *waters* and *island* as nouns that describe What happened despite having only a tangential relevance to the event. Many nouns and verbs describe What happens in events, but many others do not [11]. Linguistics failed because they understood language, not events.

Evidently, linguistics alone cannot replace true event understanding. The only justification that ties linguistics to events is the assumption that understanding language better can improve event tracking performance. Linguistics worked best when event tracking relied less on the assumption and adapted linguistic output: when Chen and Ku (2002) boosted only the discriminating named entities, rather than all entities [11], or when De Boom et al. (2015) applied topic modelling over hashtags, not entire tweets [13]. Event tracking may have found in linguistics convenience and accessibility, but not true event understanding.

3.2 Semantic Understanding

Second, event tracking understood events with semantics. Some research recognized that proper event understanding should be more meticulous than linguistic understanding. Event tracking did not need to understand the syntax or semantics of languages but the semantics of events. Like Chen and Ku (2002), event tracking needed to identify which named entities mattered to an event [11], or which nouns and verbs described its essence. We refer to such knowledge as semantic understanding.

Semantic understanding resembles linguistic understanding in form. Nouns like *goal*, *cross* and *foul* comprise the vast majority of Kubo et al. (2013)'s lexicon of 33 football terms for event summarization [22]. Differently from linguistics, however, you could study every term in Kubo et al. (2013)'s lexicon and identify a clear link with football. Alternatively-framed in Plato's definition of knowledge, the 33 terms represent true knowledge because their presence in the lexicon carries a strong justification.

Generating semantic understanding implies a more deliberate process than linguistics. Hua et al. (2016), for example, use a scoring metric to extract terms that distinguish one event from the other, and one event domain from the other [20]. Similarly, Hossny and Mitchell (2018) approach understanding as a feature selection problem, selecting the words that distinguish days with protests from peaceful days [19]. And Huang et al. (2018), who build separate timelines for each participant in an event, filter out infrequent named entities [21].

Semantic understanding appears less frequently than linguistics. Like Kubo et al. (2013)'s lexicon [22], semantic understanding can be defined manually to capture true event knowledge. When Buntain et al. (2016) mulled the possibility, however, they found the manual process infeasible, unreasonable and unscalable [10]. And ready-made knowledge bases seem like an inadequate option to the specific needs of particular domains [37]; WordNet contains 16 senses of the term *cross*, which appears in Kubo et al. (2013)'s lexicon [22], and not one relates to football.

Buntain et al. (2016) never considered the alternative, to generate semantic understanding automatically. The task poses a formidable challenge. We recognize that the word *waters* in Fig. 1 has little semantic bearing on the event-where else would a submarine be?-but struggle to explain *why* to an algorithm. The challenge is not only to generate semantic understanding automatically but to generate the type of reliable knowledge around which event tracking can design algorithms. So far, a common solution has eluded event tracking.

3.3 Event Models

Third, event tracking understood events with event models. Event models represent the most complete version of semantic understanding: the latter understands only What happens or only with Whose involvement; the former understands both, and maybe even how one relates with the other. For example, differently from Kubo et al. (2013)'s isolated terms [22] or Huang et al. (2018)'s detached named entities [21], the event model may link What happens with Who is involved. As a result, event models comprehensively fill Allan et al. (1998)'s structure of events with semantic understanding.

Löchtefeld et al. (2015) present what may be the best example of event models in event tracking literature [25]. The system hinges on a knowledge base of football teams and players from the German Bundesliga, the Who, and a set of hand-crafted extraction patterns that describe What may happen in a football match. When a pattern matches a participant from the knowledge base, the system deduces that a certain event must have happened, such as that a particular player scored a goal.

Event models like Löchtefeld et al. (2015)'s [25] seldom appear in event tracking literature. Constructing event models presents a complex challenge. To fill in the event structure with knowledge implies not only the same difficulties of generating semantic understanding but also a deeper knowledge about how events function. Semantics understand only What happens or only Who was involved in an event; event models understand how What happens relates to Who is involved, or Where and When the event happens.

Event models appear predominantly elsewhere, in event modelling and mining. Like Löchtefeld et al. (2015)'s extraction patterns [25], event modelling represents events "in a semantically meaningful way" [12]. ASRAEL, for example, automatically infers schemas for different types of events [35]. In turn, such machine-readable information enables event mining to infer more complex machine-readable information, such as which event caused the other.

Naturally, event modelling and mining has a different scope from event tracking. Event modelling understands events that happened in the past, whereas event tracking needs to understand, detect and track events in the future. Nevertheless, event models represent the type of understanding that event tracking should aspire to generate: complete, structured and semantic understanding. In the next section, we present our proposals for how event tracking can generate understanding automatically and early enough to drive event tracking.

Table 1. A selection of semantic definitions of the Who, What, Where and When in event tracking literature.

Who	"The entities that play a significant role in shaping the event progress" [21]; the persons, locations or organizations who affect or are affected by the event [30]
What	"An action, or a series of actions, or a change" [12]; "the subject, occasion, body or activity that [is] involved in the event" [32]
Where	The places or locations where the event takes place [32]
When	The date and time when the event takes place [32]

4   Understanding Events

Understanding events presents a complex challenge because it is a multi-faceted problem. It requires event tracking to answer various questions: what does it mean to understand events? How can we generate event understanding? And how can event tracking algorithms harness that understanding? The research we surveyed sought one common answer to all three questions. Generally, they failed. Therefore in this section, we answer, separately, what it means to understand events and how research can generate event understanding.

In this paper, we adopt Allan et al. (1998)'s structure [6] and propose how to fill it with semantic understanding automatically. Our interpretation represents only an elementary form of event models: we propose how to understand What may happen or with Whose involvement, but not how one relates to the other. We leave the study of more complete event models based on the semantic understanding we propose as future work.

We impose two conditions on the semantic understanding that must fill the event structure. First, event tracking must generate semantic understanding automatically. This first condition requires us to rationalize the information that fills the event structure: what it means to understand What may happen or Who may perform an action. To guide our rationale, we turn to Chen and Li (2020)'s definition of an event: "An action, or a series of actions, or a change *[What]* that happens at specific time *[When]* due to specific reasons *[How/Why]*, with associated entities such as objects, humans *[Who]*, and locations *[Where]*" [12]. Table 1 lists other complementary semantic definitions of the 'four Ws' in event tracking literature.

Second, event tracking must generate semantic understanding in time to drive event tracking. Understanding events retrospectively, like event modelling and mining does, limits the application of knowledge. It arrives too late to drive an event tracking algorithm or to improve performance. Therefore in the rest of this section, we propose how to understand events automatically and ahead of time. In particular, we focus on the entities associated with events, the Who and the Where, and the actions or changes in an event, the What.

4.1 Understanding Who Is Involved and Where

No form of event understanding appears as frequently as the participants who drive events. Some boosted the importance of participants [3, 11] or considered them separately from non-entity terms [27]. Others reasoned that events primarily concern named entities [31] and gave them a role to match; Huang et al. (2018)'s algorithm follows participants and builds individual timelines, one for each named entity and its coreferences [21]. Event tracking seems convinced it has understood an event's participants and their role.

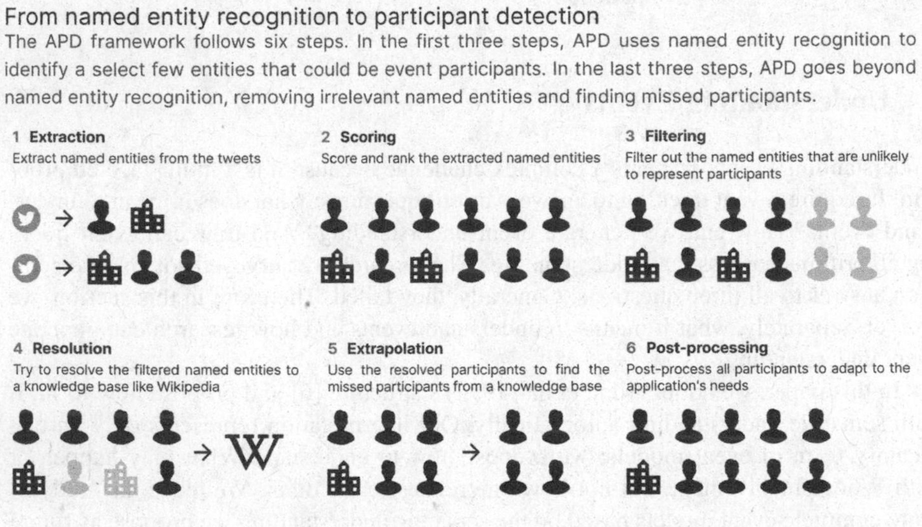

From named entity recognition to participant detection
The APD framework follows six steps. In the first three steps, APD uses named entity recognition to identify a select few entities that could be event participants. In the last three steps, APD goes beyond named entity recognition, removing irrelevant named entities and finding missed participants.

1 Extraction
Extract named entities from the tweets

2 Scoring
Score and rank the extracted named entities

3 Filtering
Filter out the named entities that are unlikely to represent participants

4 Resolution
Try to resolve the filtered named entities to a knowledge base like Wikipedia

5 Extrapolation
Use the resolved participants to find the missed participants from a knowledge base

6 Post-processing
Post-process all participants to adapt to the application's needs

Fig. 2. The six-step APD framework refines NER with semantics.

The prevalence of participants in event tracking literature leads to two reflections. First, it reflects the pivotal role that participants play in most events [31, 32]; exclude participants from the VSM and performance drops significantly [5]. Second, and perhaps most consequential to event tracking's view of understanding, it reflects the facility with which research could identify participants. Participants often represent persons, organizations and locations-named entities-so event tracking could rely on NER.

Regrettably, event tracking never progressed past NER. Despite Chen and Ku (2002) showing that only the discriminating named entities, the participants, contribute to event tracking [11], research continued to rely on NER. However, NER only provides linguistic understanding, named entities. It does not discern between a named entity with an active role in an event and one with a passive presence. Event tracking assumes, erroneously, that named entities could substitute for participants.

In our previous work, we revised this assumption [28]. We assumed that at least some of the named entities represent participants, and that they can lead us to the rest. Following this assumption, we proposed Automatic Participant Detection (APD), a six-step framework to understand Who participates in events or Where they occur. As shown in Fig. 2, in the first three steps, APD still relies on NER to identify, score and filter infrequent named entities. In the next steps, however, APD refines NER's output: it disambiguates named entities to retain only the relevant participants and extrapolates from them the missed participants.

The first iteration of our APD framework captured less noise and more participants than NER even before the event had started [28]. APD, however, represents more than a glorified NER filter. NER extracts named entities, mere strings, but APD extracts participants, semantic concepts. By disambiguating participants using a knowledge base, such as Wikipedia, APD allows event tracking to understand participants and their role in events better. And by extension, APD allows event tracking to understand events better. Therefore we propose that APD fills in the Who and the Where.

4.2 Understanding What May Happen

Like for the Who and the Where, event tracking looked for available solutions to understand the What. Event tracking routinely applied POS tagging to understand What mattered in events [27] and topic modelling to discover the latent events [13]. Differently from the Who and the Where, however, event tracking found the flaws of linguistic understanding of the What manifest. Kubo et al. (2013)'s manually-constructed lexicon [22] contrasts sharply with the crudity of linguistic understanding.

Nevertheless, event tracking had valid reasons to rely on linguistics to understand What happens in events. It is difficult to algorithmically distinguish a noun or a verb from a meaningful term. Even in other research areas, "the notion of term is mostly underspecified" [39]. We could find few exceptions to linguistics. Hua et al. (2018) identified event and domain terms with a term-weighting scheme [20], and Hossny and Mitchell (2018) applied feature selection [19] to the problem. Still, understanding What happens in events properly remains a fundamental aspect of event knowledge. No other component of the 'four Ws' describes events as expressively as the What [32].

To understand the What, we again revise the assumption of linguistic understanding. Events that share a domain may still involve different entities, and happen at different places and times. Hua et al. (2016) called these aspects the event terms because they distinguish one event from the other [20]. Fundamentally, however, events belong to the same domain because they share the possibilities of What may happen: a building collapses in an earthquake, a political party wins an election, a player scores in a football match. Therefore we assume that domain terms normally describe What happens in events.

Our assumption aligns the process of understanding What happens in events with Automatic Term Extraction (ATE). ATE is the task of identifying domain-specific terms from domain-specific corpora. Like event tracking itself, ATE techniques generally have a linguistic component and often rest on nouns. Unlike event tracking, however, ATE only rests on those nouns which describe domains. Apart from a linguistic component,

ATE techniques measure a noun's suitability as a domain term using a termhood statistic [7]. Thus, ATE can be a tool for event tracking to learn What happens generally in events from a domain.

Yet to understand What happens in events, event tracking must adapt, not adopt, ATE, for two reasons. First, ATE research into general domains abounds, but we could find little research into event domains. Event tracking needs domain terms to reflect, accurately, "an action, or a series of actions, or a change" [12]. Thus, it may discover that general domain terms do not suffice.

Second, neither could we find ATE research on Twitter. Despite tracking events on Twitter, Hua et al. (2016) resorted to the more reliable, authoritative news media to seek event domain terms [20]. But like event tracking detects events from Twitter, so must it also understand events in Twitter's language, which includes the social network's informal vernacular.

And then, when event tracking adapts ATE to its needs, the research area must accept Buntain et al. (2016)'s conundrum [10]. Buntain et al. (2016) reasoned that we could never enumerate every possibility in an event, so knowing What happens generally in certain events precludes the exceptional. How could a human foresee a parachutist landing in a stadium during a football match [38]? How could an algorithm? In service of the exceptional, Buntain et al. (2016) rejected manual and automatic understanding. Nonetheless, we argue that event tracking no longer affords to ignore understanding in service of the exceptional. Therefore we propose that ATE fills in the What.

4.3   Understanding Why and How an Event Happened

Even when event tracking thought it had understood Who does What, Where and When, it never ventured to understand Why an event happens or How. Their absence makes sense. The Why and the How, the task of mining events [23], represent relationships among events, like how a submarine gone missing prompts a hunt. Therefore understanding the Why and the How implies a deep knowledge of not only the event in question but other events too. In other words, the Why and the How imply reasoning, a complex task even for event mining [12].

Nevertheless, understanding Why and How events happen also poses difficulty because event modelling often falls at the same hurdles as event tracking. To mine the Why and the How, research understands and compares the events' 'four Ws' [23], which it often generates using linguistics. Therefore event modelling spends a lot of time understanding and, in the end, still does not understand events well. And how could an algorithm mine events without understanding them properly first?

We do not presume to solve event mining but merely to show that our vision of understanding can simplify the task. For event modelling, a precondition for mining, generating precise information about Who did What, Where and When remains an open research question [17]. However, our definition of events and interpretation of understanding align event tracking with event modelling and mining. Likewise, our interpretations apply to event modelling like they apply to event tracking. We have described, above, the framework of an event modeller that understands Who does What, Where and When with semantics.

More pertinently to this paper, our interpretation assigns event tracking a new role. An event tracking algorithm that understands events itself generates understanding. As Huang et al. (2018)'s model builds each named entity's timeline, it simultaneously understands Who performed an action or Where the change occurred [21]. Our vision of understanding of the Who and the Where, and the What-semantic, automatic and available before events start-can fulfil Panagiotou et al. (2016)'s own vision, of event tracking algorithms that do not only detect topics and events but model them too [34]. We summarize our position in the next section.

5   Conclusion

In 1998, understanding represented event tracking's hope to improve performance. Today, understanding represents the hope that event tracking could be more than a news aggregator or a tracker. Event modelling and mining shows us that event tracking could be what powers systems to reason about events [12], detect fake news [2] and find interesting angles in true news [33]. Event modelling and mining, however, also shows us that event tracking cannot become more than it is without understanding.

In this paper, we argued that understanding can be a paradigm shift for event tracking. History has shown us that proper understanding affects almost every aspect of event tracking. The failures of understanding do not reflect poorly on its value or potential but rather on event tracking's interpretations: the research area understood language, not events. Proper event understanding can become a solution for old problems and, by approaching event tracking to event modelling, a new purpose for modern applications: a paradigm shift.

Nevertheless, understanding events remains a long, arduous task. Event tracking must exchange the convenience and accessibility of linguistics for bespoke semantics. To that end, we showed how progress in adjacent areas, in particular APD and ATE, can spur event tracking to understand events, properly this time. Today's modern and complex applications for events make the question of whether event tracking requires understanding moot. The only relevant question now is not whether event tracking will understand but how.

Acknowledgements. The research work disclosed in this publication is funded by the Tertiary Education Scholarships Scheme.(https://education.gov.mt/en/education/myScholarship/Pages/TESS---Tertiary-Education-Scholarship-Scheme.aspx, accessed on May 21, 2022)

References

1. Indonesian navy hunting for submarine that has gone missing in waters north of island of Bali (2021). https://twitter.com/bbcbreaking/status/1384817851219988480. Accessed 5 Oct 2022
2. Abhishek, K., Pratihar, V., Shandilya, S.K., Tiwari, S., Ranjan, V.K., Tripathi, S.: An intelligent approach for mining knowledge graphs of online news. International Journal of Computers and Applications, pp. 1–9 (2021). https://www.tandfonline.com/doi/abs/10.1080/1206212X.2021.1957551

3. Aiello, L.M., et al.: Sensing trending topics in Twitter. IEEE Trans. Multimedia **15**(6), 1268–1282 (2013). https://ieeexplore.ieee.org/document/6525357

4. Allan, J., Carbonell, J.G., Doddington, G., Yamron, J., Yang, Y.: Topic detection and tracking pilot study final report. In: Proceedings of the DARPA Broadcast News Transcription and Understanding Workshop, pp. 194–218. Lansdowne, Virginia, USA (1998)

5. Allan, J., et al.: Topic-based novelty detection. In: Topic-Based Novelty Detection: 1999 Summer Workshop at CLSP, Final Report, pp. 1–51. August, Baltimore, MD, USA (1999)

6. Allan, J., Papka, R., Lavrenko, V.: On-line new event detection and tracking. In: SIGIR 1998: Proceedings of the 21st Annual International ACM SIGIR Conference on Research and Development in Information Retrieval, pp. 37–45. ACM, Melbourne, Australia (1998). https://dl.acm.org/citation.cfm?id=290954

7. Astrakhantsev, N.A., Fedorenko, D.G., Turdakov, D.Y.: Methods for automatic term recognition in domain-specific text collections: a survey. Programm. Comput. Softw. **41**(6), 336–349 (2015). https://link.springer.com/article/10.1134/S036176881506002X

8. Bolisani, E., Bratianu, C.: The elusive definition of knowledge. In: Emergent Knowledge Strategies. KMOL, vol. 4, pp. 1–22. Springer, Cham (2018). https://doi.org/10.1007/978-3-319-60657-6_1

9. Bontcheva, K., Rout, D.: Making sense of social media streams through semantics: a survey. Semantic Web **5**(5), 373–403 (2014). https://content.iospress.com/articles/semantic-web/sw110

10. Buntain, C., Lin, J., Golbeck, J.: Discovering key moments in social media streams. In: 2016 13th IEEE Annual Consumer Communications & Networking Conference (CCNC), pp. 366–374. IEEE, Las Vegas, NV, USA (2016). https://ieeexplore.ieee.org/document/7444808

11. Chen, H.H., Ku, L.W.: An NLP & IR approach to topic detection. In: Allan, J. (ed.) Topic Detection and Tracking. The Information Retrieval Series, vol. 12. Springer, MA (2002). https://doi.org/10.1007/978-1-4615-0933-2_12

12. Chen, X., Li, Q.: Event modeling and mining: a long journey toward explainable events. VLDB J. **29**(1), 459–482 (2020). https://link.springer.com/article/10.1007/s00778-019-00545-0

13. De Boom, C., Van Canneyt, S., Dhoedt, B.: Semantics-driven event clustering in twitter feeds. In: Proceedings of the 5th Workshop on Making Sense of Microposts, pp. 2–9. CEUR, Florence, Italy (2015). https://ceur-ws.org/Vol-1395/

14. Farnaghi, M., Ghaemi, Z., Mansourian, A.: Dynamic Spatio-temporal tweet mining for event detection: a case study of hurricane florence. Int. J. Disaster Risk Sci. **11**(3), 378–393 (2020). https://link.springer.com/article/10.1007/s13753-020-00280-z

15. Freitas, J., Ji, H.: Identifying news from tweets. In: Proceedings of the First Workshop on NLP and Computational Social Science., pp. 11–16. Association for Computational Linguistics, Austin, Texas, USA (2016). https://aclanthology.org/W16-5602/

16. Fung, G.P.C., Yu, J.X., Yu, P.S., Lu, H.: Parameter free Bursty events detection in text streams. In: VLDB 2005: 31st International Conference on Very Large Data Bases, pp. 181–192. VLDB Endowment, Trondheim, Norway (2005). https://dl.acm.org/doi/10.5555/1083592.1083616

17. Gallofré Ocaña, M., Opdahl, A.L.: Challenges and opportunities for journalistic knowledge platforms. In: CIKMW2020: Proceeding of the CIKM 2020 Workshops, pp. 1–9. CEUR-WS, Galway, Ireland (2020). https://ceur-ws.org/Vol-2699/

18. Hasan, M., Orgun, M.A., Schwitter, R.: Real-time event detection from the twitter data stream using the twitternews+ framework. Inf. Process. Manage. **56**(3), 1146–1165 (2019). https://www.sciencedirect.com/science/article/abs/pii/S0306457317305447

19. Hossny, A.H., Mitchell, L.: Event detection in twitter: a keyword volume approach. In: 2018 IEEE International Conference on Data Mining Workshops (ICDMW), pp. 1200–1208. IEEE, Singapore (2018). https://ieeexplore.ieee.org/document/8637560

20. Hua, T., Chen, F., Zhao, L., Lu, C.T., Ramakrishnan, N.: Automatic targeted-domain spatiotemporal event detection in twitter. GeoInformatica **20**(4), 765–795 (2016). https://link.springer.com/article/10.1007/s10707-016-0263-0

21. Huang, Y., Shen, C., Li, T.: Event summarization for sports games using twitter streams. World Wide Web **21**(3), 609–627 (2018). https://link.springer.com/article/10.1007/s11280-017-0477-6

22. Kubo, M., Sasano, R., Takamura, H., Okumura, M.: Generating live sports updates from twitter by finding good reporters. In: Proceedings of the 2013 IEEE/WIC/ACM International Joint Conferences on Web Intelligence (WI) and Intelligent Agent Technologies (IAT), vol. 1, pp. 527–534. IEEE Computer Society, Atlanta, Georgia, USA (2013). https://dl.acm.org/citation.cfm?id=2568811

23. Li, Q., Ma, Y., Yang, Z.: Event cube – a conceptual framework for event modeling and analysis. In: Bouguettaya, A., et al. (eds.) WISE 2017. LNCS, vol. 10569, pp. 499–515. Springer, Cham (2017). https://doi.org/10.1007/978-3-319-68783-4_34

24. Li, Q., Nourbakhsh, A., Shah, S., Liu, X.: Real-time novel event detection from social media. In: 2017 IEEE 33rd International Conference on Data Engineering (ICDE), pp. 1129–1139. IEEE, San Diego, CA, USA (2017). https://ieeexplore.ieee.org/document/7930053

25. Löchtefeld, M., Jäckel, C., Krüger, A.: TwitSoccer: knowledge-based crowd-sourcing of live soccer events. In: MUM 2015: Proceedings of the 14th International Conference on Mobile and Ubiquitous Multimedia, pp. 148–151. ACM, Linz, Austria (2015). https://dl.acm.org/doi/10.1145/2836041.2836055

26. Madani, A., Boussaid, O., Zegour, D.E.: What's happening: a survey of tweets event detection. In: INNOV 2014 : Proceedings of the Third International Conference on Communications, Computation, Networks and Technologies, pp. 16–22. IARIA, Nice, France (2014)

27. Makkonen, J., Ahonen-Myka, H., Salmenkivi, M.: Simple semantics in topic detection and tracking. Inf. Retrieval **7**(3), 347–368 (2004). https://doi.org/10.1023/B:INRT.0000011210.12953.86

28. Mamo, N., Azzopardi, J., Layfield, C.: An automatic participant detection framework for event tracking on Twitter. Algorithms **14**(3), 92 (2021). https://www.mdpi.com/1999-4893/14/3/92

29. Mamo, N., Azzopardi, J., Layfield, C.: Fine-grained topic detection and tracking on Twitter. In: Proceedings of the 13th International Joint Conference on Knowledge Discovery, Knowledge Engineering and Knowledge Management - (Volume 1), pp. 79–86. SciTePress, Remote (2021). https://www.scitepress.org/PublicationsDetail.aspx?ID=o+Iys1RHmPU=&t=1

30. Mamo, N., Azzopardi, J., Layfield, C.: Who? What? Event tracking needs event understanding. In: Proceedings of the 13th International Joint Conference on Knowledge Discovery, Knowledge Engineering and Knowledge Management - (Volume 1), pp. 139–146. SciTePress, Remote (2021). https://www.scitepress.org/PublicationsDetail.aspx?ID=o+Iys1RHmPU=&t=1

31. McMinn, A.J., Jose, J.M.: Real-time entity-based event detection for twitter. In: Mothe, J., et al. (eds.) CLEF 2015. LNCS, vol. 9283, pp. 65–77. Springer, Cham (2015). https://doi.org/10.1007/978-3-319-24027-5_6

32. Mohd, M.: Named entity patterns across news domains. In: Proceedings of the BCS IRSG Symposium: Future Directions in Information Access 2007, pp. 1–6. BCS, The Chartered Institute for IT, Glasgow, Scotland (2007). https://www.scienceopen.com/hosted-document?doi=10.14236/ewic/FDIA2007.5

33. Opdahl, A.L., Tessem, B.: Ontologies for finding journalistic angles. Softw. Syst. Model. **20**(1), 71–87 (2020). https://link.springer.com/article/10.1007/s10270-020-00801-w

34. Panagiotou, N., Katakis, I., Gunopulos, D.: Detecting events in online social networks: definitions, trends and challenges. In: Michaelis, S., Piatkowski, N., Stolpe, M. (eds.) Solving

Large Scale Learning Tasks. Challenges and Algorithms. LNCS (LNAI), vol. 9580, pp. 42–84. Springer, Cham (2016). https://doi.org/10.1007/978-3-319-41706-6_2

35. Rudnik, C., Ehrhart, T., Ferret, O., Teyssou, D., Troncy, R., Tannier, X.: Searching news articles using an event knowledge graph leveraged by Wikidata. In: WWW 2019: Companion Proceedings of The 2019 World Wide Web Conference, pp. 1232–1239. Association for Computing Machinery, San Francisco, CA, USA (2019). https://dl.acm.org/doi/10.1145/3308560.3316761

36. Saeed, Z., et al.: What's happening around the world? A survey and framework on event detection techniques on Twitter. J. Grid Comput. **17**(2), 279–312 (2019). https://link.springer.com/article/10.1007/s10723-019-09482-2

37. Syed, S., Spruit, M., Borit, M.: Bootstrapping a semantic lexicon on verb similarities. In: Proceedings of the 8th International Joint Conference on Knowledge Discovery, Knowledge Engineering and Knowledge Management (IC3K 2016) - Volume 1: KDIR, vol. 1, pp. 189–196. SciTePress, Porto, Portugal (2016). https://dspace.library.uu.nl/handle/1874/358283

38. Telegraph sport: parachutist landing on pitch disrupts inter's serie a win against sassuolo (2019). https://www.telegraph.co.uk/sport/2019/10/20/parachutist-landing-pitch-disrupts-inters-serie-win-againstsassuolo/. Accessed 21 May 2022

39. Velardi, P., Missikoff, M., Basili, R.: Identification of relevant terms to support the construction of domain ontologies. In: Proceedings of the ACL 2001 Workshop on Human Language Technology and Knowledge Management, pp. 1–8. Association for Computational Linguistics, Toulouse, France (2001). https://www.aclweb.org/anthology/W01-1005/

40. Yang, Y., Carbonell, J.G., Brown, R.D., Pierce, T., Archibald, B.T., Liu, X.: Learning approaches for detecting and tracking news events. IEEE Intell. Syst. Appl. **14**(4), 32–43 (1999). https://ieeexplore.ieee.org/document/784083

41. Zhao, S., Zhong, L., Wickramasuriya, J., Vasudevan, V.: Human as real-time sensors of social and physical events: a case study of Twitter and sports games (2011). https://arxiv.org/abs/1106.4300

Exploring Semantic Similarity Between German Legal Texts and Referred Laws

Harshil Darji⬚, Jelena Mitrović(✉)⬚, and Michael Granitzer⬚

Chair of Data Science, University of Passau, Innstraße 41, 94032 Passau, Germany
{harshil.darji,jelena.mitrovic,michael.granitzer}@uni-passau.de

Abstract. The calculation of semantic similarity is an important task in Natural Language Processing (NLP). There is a growing interest in this task in the research community, especially following the advent of new, ever-evolving neural architectures. However, this technique has not been explored in-depth in the realm of automatic processing of legal data, the area we often call Legal NLP or Legal Tech. In this paper, we aim to use semantic similarity to identify the relations between legal sentences that refer to a certain law and the law text itself. The semantic similarity score is calculated using cosine similarity between sentence embeddings. In our work, we use sentence transformers to get the sentence embeddings for our legal text. The results we achieve by using two separate sentence transformers, Cross English & German RoBERTa and all-MiniLM-L6-v2, provide a semantic similarity score of approximately 0.45 and 0.4, respectively.

Keywords: Legal language processing · NLP · Semantic similarity · Sentence transformers · Open legal data

1 Introduction

Investments in global legal technologies, supporting various stages of legal processes and proceedings, have grown from 17.32 billion U.S. dollars in 2019[1] to 18.4 billion U.S. dollars in 2021[2]. The legal research community has also taken note of this growing interest and is working toward applying the latest AI and Machine Learning technologies to build tools that can assist in efficient legal research. Research in legal tech differs based on the underlying legal system and countries. NLP-based systems adjust accordingly to investigate which studies can be translated and replicated across these different manifestations of the legal domain.

There exist different NLP tools and techniques, some are rule-based that focus more on pattern matching or fill-in-the-blanks tasks. Such methods, although proven to work well, do not work efficiently when generalized. Other tools are based on Machine Learning models, where some use probabilistic or linear classifiers while others use a state-of-the-art neural networks. However, the introduction of Transformers [20] in 2017 gave rise to improved and more efficient NLP tools such as BERT [4], RoBERTa [11], etc.

With an increasing amount of new cases, improved NLP tools are effective to gather important legal information, which is necessary to generate citation networks for legal

---

[1] https://www.statista.com/statistics/1155852/legal-tech-market-revenue-worldwide/.
[2] https://www.statista.com/topics/9197/legal-tech/.

A. Fred et al. (Eds.): IC3K 2021, CCIS 1718, pp. 37–50, 2023.
https://doi.org/10.1007/978-3-031-35924-8_3

purposes. Such citation networks can reveal critical information on precedents [3] based on the characteristics of the citations towards the precedent candidates. In previous work by Milz et al. [12], the authors demonstrated the scale-free behavior of the German case citation network. This citation network was built using a dataset similar to the one we use in our current work. They also make use of the PageRank algorithm to identify the most influential court decisions and laws. And finally, they claim the positive correlation between node- and text-based similarity scores. The citation network developed in their work is helpful for understanding court decisions, finding similar court cases based on similar court decisions, and finding background knowledge for a given case. However, for this to work, it requires manual reference to norms, which is not always feasible. For retrieval systems that do not rely on such manual annotations, it is necessary to utilize textual similarity techniques. In addition, we might also be able to conduct further analysis and downstream tasks such as developing a system that can differentiate between tenor and gründe using semantic similarities and also identifying clustering reasons in court decisions.

Our work is an extension of the original paper by Milz et al. [12] titled *"Analysis of a German Legal Citation Network"*. In this work, instead of using law references to identify node similarities, we try to identify similarities between the law text and legal text that refer to a given law. Additionally, legal sentences that refer to the same law should likely be semantically similar as well. To show this, we also work on finding semantic similarities between legal sentences that refer to the same law. The results from our experiment confirm that semantic similarity can be exploited to reference similar law texts. Semantic similarity between sentences or documents plays a significant role in Automated Short-Answer Grading, Machine Translation, and Image Captioning [17]. Techniques such as TF-IDF and Bag-of-Words (BoW) represent text as real-value vectors that can be used to find semantic similarity, but they do not account for the fact that similar words sometimes can have a different meaning or different words can sometimes be used to represent similar concepts [2].

Here, we use sentence transformers to generate sentence embeddings. A sentence transformer is a modification of the pre-trained BERT network that uses siamese and triplet network structures to derive semantically meaningful sentence embeddings [16]. These embeddings can then be compared using cosine-similarity to get a semantic similarity score. We use Cross English & German RoBERTa for Sentence Embeddings from T-Systems-onsite[3] and all-MiniLM-L6-v2[4] to generate embeddings and compare the performance of both.

Our paper is structured as follows: In Sect. 2, we summarise some of the related work in this field and indicate how our work can provide new insights into this area of research. In Sect. 3, we give details about the used dataset and how it differs from the original work. Next, in Sect. 4, we briefly summarise the work done by Milz et al. in the original work. In Sect. 5, we give details about the experiments done before presenting the results in Sect. 6.

[3] https://huggingface.co/T-Systems-onsite/cross-en-de-roberta-sentence-transformer.
[4] https://huggingface.co/sentence-transformers/all-MiniLM-L6-v2.

2   Related Work

In 2006, Li et al. [10] presented an algorithm that makes use of semantic and word order information. Because their algorithm derives semantic similarity from a lexical knowledge base and a corpus, it can adapt to different application areas using a corpus of that area. They evaluated their similarity algorithm on a set of sentence pairs from a variety of sources and achieved performance comparable to human participants.

In 2014, Kim et al. [7] published their work on legal Q&A using Ranking SVM and syntactic or semantic similarity. The dataset used by the authors for the evaluation is the first competition on legal information extraction/entailment (COLIEE) 2014, with two phases. The first phase was the identification of the relevance of Japanese civil law articles to a legal bar exam query. For this, they compared two baseline unsupervised models with Ranking SVM and concluded that the latter achieved performance far better than baseline models. In the second phase, they answer "yes" and "no" questions by comparing the query's meanings with the corresponding articles. For this purpose, they use semantic similarities with antonym relation identification. The authors claim that their method, combined with the rule-based model and the unsupervised model, outperforms the SVM-based supervised model.

In 2016, Mueller et al. [13] presented a siamese adaptation of the LSTM network to calculate semantic similarity between sentences. Their approach benefits from improved word-embeddings of sentences as pre-trained word-vectors are used as LSTM input. Furthermore, they form a highly structured space with complex semantic relationships by relying on a simple Manhattan metric [5]. Their results conclude that LSTMs are capable of effectively performing tasks that require complex understanding.

In 2020, Zhong et al. [21] published a paper explaining the use of NLP in legal tech. In addition, they also provide advantages and disadvantages of existing methods. Their work provides a comprehensive overview of different embedding-based and symbol-based methods. They conclude that although existing methods can provide good results for element extraction, they are not sufficient for corresponding applications.

In 2020, Paheli et al. [1] published their work on computing similarity between two legal documents. In this, they explored text-based and network embeddings-based methods for similarity computation on a set of 47 document pairs. Based on the Pearson correlation between the expert score and similarity implied by methods used, Node2Vec performed best for citation network-based measures while FullText Similarity achieved good performance for text-based measures.

Milz et al. published their work on German legal citation networks [12]. In this, they used the Jaccard similarity score between all pairs of nodes to identify similar court decisions. They compared the results of node similarity with simplified text-based similarity calculation. The results show that both similarity scores are in agreement more often. Furthermore, they performed a Pearson correlation test between the similarity measures of 1000 semi-randomly chosen court decisions and achieved a score of 0.64, implying a positive correlation.

In addition, another important research in terms of the use of NLP in German legal data was done by Leitner et al. [9] in 2019. Here, they created a dataset of Named Entity Recognition with 19 fine-grained classes, that can be generalized into seven coarse-grained classes. Then, they applied Conditional Random Fields (CRFs) and bidirectional Long-Short Term Memory Networks (BiLSTMs) to this NER dataset. Out of these two state-of-the-art models, BiLSTMs have better performance with an F1 score of 95.46 for the fine-grained and 95.95 for the coarse-grained classes.

To the best of our knowledge, there is no work on using sentence transformers to calculate semantic similarities between German legal texts. On the other hand, some research on using transformers for sentence similarity modeling does exist . For example, Laskar et al. [8] used contextualized word embeddings with the transformer encoder for the answer selection task. In this work, the authors presented feature-based and fine-tuning-based approaches for answer selection. In another work, Ormerod et al. [14] utilized independently fine-tuned transformers to calculate the average predicted similarity score.

3   Dataset

There is a noticeable discrepancy between the legal tech research output in North American and Europe.This is largely due to the lack of publicly available data in Europe. For example, there is a public dataset of 3.7 million U.S. precedential court decisions. Furthermore, Google search engine provides the option of searching through a vast data collection of the U.S. Case law. In European countries, Germany in particular, apart from the commercial datasets, there are only around 55000 publicly available court cases from the State Ministry of Justice (ger. Bundesministerium der Justiz). Many states in Germany also publish some records individually but do not allow users to scrape their content. This makes it difficult to have a centralized and openly available source for German legal data.

Ostendorff et al. [15] recognized this and published an openly available dataset called Open Legal Data. This dataset was used by Milz et al. in the original paper [12] to create a German citation network for legal data. The first step toward creating such a citation network is to extract citations from the decision text of cases. Due to the lack of distinctly identifiable references to previous court decisions or laws, extracting citations was not an easy task.

One of the reasons for this complication in extracting case-to-case citations is the lack of a properly structured unique identifier for court decisions. European Case Law Identifier can solve this problem, but this was only introduced in 2011, and not all the cases use it. In regards to law reference extraction, Milz et al. only considered citations that begin with the article sign ("§"). If there are multiple law references, they avoided such inconsistency by using the double article sign ("§§"). Overall they managed to extract 1,279,105 case-to-case citations and 2,234,934 case-to-law citations.

We tackle this problem of extracting the information from Open Legal Data in a different way. This dataset clearly mentioned information such as court, level of appeal, and ECLI. However, important text such as tenor, tatbestand, gründe, and entscheidungsgründe was available only in HTML format. One of the complications in extracting information from HTML was the inconsistency of HTML structure throughout the dataset. For example, not all the cases in the dataset use the same tags or identifiers to separate title from content.

Due to these inconsistencies in HTML structure in the dataset, we had to make some assumptions to extract the information from them. One of which was to assume that all the important titles, such as tenor and gründe are within the *h2* tag. In addition, to avoid false positives, we also made sure the content within *h2* tag is all alphabetic and is within a certain length. These assumptions lowered the number of cases to 43337.

The size of the resulting dataset is approximately 1.1 GBs, with 43337 rows and has the following 12 features:

Table 1. Features in the dataset with statistics and example content. Here, *slug* can be used to view the web-version of any case by appending it to *https://de.openlegaldata.io/ case/<slug>*.

Feature	Total	Example content
id	43337	127981
slug	43337	ag-volklingen-2002-07-10-5c-c-24102
ecli	10831	NaN
date	43337	2002-07-10
court	43337	Amtsgericht Völklingen
jurisdiction	43337	Ordentliche Gerichtsbarkeit
level_of_appeal	43337	Amtsgericht
type	43337	Urteil
tenor	36282	1. Die Beklagten werden als Gesamtschuldner
tatbestand	24243	Auf die Darstellung des Tatbestandes
gründe	27144	Die Klage ist zulässig und begründet. Die
entscheidungsgründe	24038	Die Klage ist zulässig und begründet. Di

One of the important features in this dataset is ECLI, an abbreviation for European Case Law Identifier. This identifier consists of five elements, separated by colons, **ECLI:[the country code]:[the code of the court]:[the year]:[an ordinal number]**[5].

The plot in Fig. 1 shows the number of cases per year, from 2002 to 2019. The reason for having very few cases in 2019 compared to previous years is because the data obtained from Open Legal Data only included cases up to the year 2019.

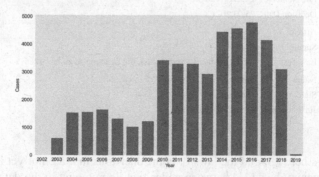

Fig. 1. Number of cases per year, 3 cases in 2002 and highest being in 2016.

This dataset is publicly available and can be downloaded from the provided link[6].

[5] https://e-justice.europa.eu/content_european_case_law_identifier_ecli-175-en.do.
[6] https://zenodo.org/record/6631931#.YqNkbxNBz0o.

4   German Law Citation Network

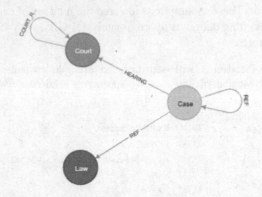

Fig. 2. Neo4j graph of the legal citation network [12].

Milz et al. [12] constructed a legal citation network for the German legal data. As stated in their work, they present a case-to-case citation network that also connects cases to the laws that are referenced within their decision text, as shown in Fig. 2. Table 2 shows the properties of nodes in the legal citation graph. Exactly one directed edge exists between two Case nodes (n) and (m) if (n) references (m) in the decision text at least once. For their analysis, it is of importance that a reference occurs, but not how often. Hence, multiple references from the same decision text to the same node are disregarded.

Table 2. Node properties of the legal citation graph [12].

Node	Property	Example
Case	DecisionText	Der Antrag des Antragstellers, §1 Abs. 5 Corona VV HE 4 im Wege der einstweiligen Anordnung
Case	File Number	IX ZR 70/20
Case	Decision Date	25.03.2021
Law	Article	§242
Law	Statute	BGB
Law	Law Text	Der Schuldner ist verpflichtet, die Leistung so zu bewirken
Court	Name	Finanzgericht Hamburg
Court	State	Hamburg
Court	Jurisdiction	Finanzgerichtsbarkeit

The authors here ignored the laws or court decisions that are not yet in the dataset since an edge cannot be added between nodes that do not exist in the dataset. Because of this, only 59.9% of law references can be added as edges, while only 16.3% of court decision references are represented in the graph.

4.1   Scale-Free Network

Similar to the case citation networks of the U.S. Supreme Court [18], the Austrian Supreme Court [6] and the European Court of Justice [19], German legal citation network also shows scale-free behavior. This behavior reveals that a very small cluster of court decisions holds a substantial amount of legal influence. This conclusion has been made considering the fact that the citation network shows that more than 70% of court decisions are not cited at all, and 92.6% of cases are cited less than five times.

This scale-free behavior is confirmed based on the case-to-case in-degree and case-to-law in-degree diagram (Fig. 3). As stated by the authors, "case and law references are not equally distributed, but there are in fact hub-like decisions and laws that are more likely to be cited".

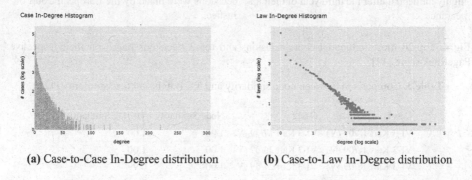

(a) Case-to-Case In-Degree distribution   (b) Case-to-Law In-Degree distribution

Fig. 3. Case and Law In-Degree distribution with log scale. This type of distribution suggests a scale-free network behaviour [12].

4.2   Centrality

One of the major aspects of legal research is to identify the most influential and important court decisions and precedents. One of the common practices to measure excellence is to count citations. In Milz et al. work, In-degree and PageRank scores have shown to be strong indicators for identifying precedents and influential cases. Figure 4a shows the twenty most important court decisions based on their overall PageRank rating. Figure 4b shows the top three decisions based on PageRank, but with respect to the year of the case.

4.3   Node Similarity

An important task of legal research is the identification or discovery of similar cases based on court decisions, topics, or law references. Previous work in this area has shown that despite being perspective to sparsity, network-based similarity does work. Milz et al. [12] used the Jaccard algorithm to find similarities between court decisions by calculating node similarity scores between all pairs of nodes in the Neo4j graph. The Jaccard algorithm considers a pair of nodes as similar if they share the majority of

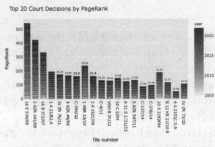
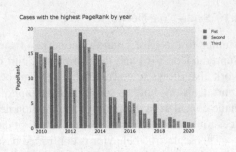
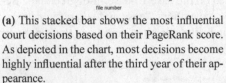

(a) This stacked bar shows the most influential court decisions based on their PageRank score. As depicted in the chart, most decisions become highly influential after the third year of their appearance.

(b) This plot shows the top three court decisions based on PageRank by year. This visualization shows that in some years the most important decisions were made by the European Court of Justice.

Fig. 4. Top-20 most influential court decisions and top-3 decisions based on their respective PageRank score [12].

Table 3. Comparison between node similarity and TF-IDF based text-similarity [12].

Case1	Case2	Node Similarity	TF-IDF Similarity
VI-3 Kart 18/09 (V)	VI-3 Kart 17/09 (V)	1.00	1.00
VI-3 Kart 18/09 (V)	VI-3 Kart 26/09 (V)	1.00	1.00
VI-3 Kart 18/09 (V)	VI-3 Kart 27/09 (V)	1.00	0.99
VI-3 Kart 18/09 (V)	VI-3 Kart 28/09 (V)	1.00	0.99
VI-3 Kart 18/09 (V)	VI-3 Kart 29/09 (V)	1.00	0.99
W 7 M 19.30082	W 7 M 19.30083	1.00	0.96
W 7 M 19.30082	5 L 1635/14.TR	0.88	0.69
W 7 M 19.30082	17 L 1610/14.A	0.81	0.71
W 7 M 19.30082	7 L 1224/14.A	0.58	0.55
W 7 M 19.30082	3 E 187/17	0.50	0.53
L 8 R 208/05	L 8 R 361/06	1.00	0.98
L 8 R 208/05	L 8 R 44/06	0.86	0.97
L 8 R 208/05	L 8 R 47/06	0.86	0.13
L 8 R 208/05	L 8 R 62/07	0.80	0.97
L 8 R 208/05	L 3 R 98/05	0.35	0.97

neighbors. Then as mentioned in Sect. 2, they compared this score with a text-based similarity measure to find a correlation.

Some examples of this comparison are shown in Table 3. As indicated by the scores in this table, node-based and text-based similarity scores agree more often. This agreement is quantified by calculating the Pearson correlation between the similarity measures of 1000 semi-randomly chosen court decisions and five corresponding counterparts. The positive correlation score of 0.64 indicates that case-similarity search methods can be further improved by adding network-based similarity measures.

5   Experiments

Our experiments in this publication focus on extending the similarity measures from node-similarity to textual or semantic similarities. Here, we focus on sentence-level text information instead of comparing entire cases. We use law references to not only compare their text with legal sentences that refer to them but also to compare legal sentences that refer to the same sentence.

5.1   Similarity Between Law Text and Legal Sentences

In the first experiment, we aim to find semantic similarities between the sentences from a legal case that refer to a law and the actual text from that law. To do so, one of the tasks here is to extract the law reference from the case. We extracted the law references directly from the HTML file. Most of the law references in the original Open Legal Data are within *verweis.norm* tag. We simply extracted the content within this tag and replaced the "Art." or "§§" sign with "§". Next, we gather the legal text from cases that surrounds these law references.

Since no API for getting a specific law and Absatz text exists, we relied on extracting this information from *Gesetze im Internet, Bundesministerium der Justiz*[7]. Because of a consistent HTML structure, we we were able to extract both the entire law text and the Absatz text.

After having the legal sentence and law text, the next step is to gather embeddings for both. This is done by feeding both the sentences to two separate sentence trans-formers, namely Cross English & German RoBERTa for Sentence Embeddings and all-MiniLML6-v2. One of the reasons for choosing sentence transformers above tra-ditional techniques such as TF-IDF is their ability to account for the fact that similar words can have different meanings based on context and vice versa.

Finally, we calculate the cosine similarity between these two embeddings to get the semantic similarity between the legal sentence and the corresponding law text.

The process of finding this semantic similarity is explained below with an example. Consider the following legal sentence:

> ... *Leben oder Freiheit besteht. Eine erhebliche konkrete Gefahr aus gesund-heitlichen Gründen liegt nur vor bei lebensbedrohlichen oder schwerwiegenden Erkrankungen, die sich durch die Abschiebung wesentlich verschlechtern würden (§60 Abs. 7 Satz 2 AufenthG). Es ist ...*

In this text, we can see one of the law's references is *§60 Abs. 7 Satz 2 AufenthG*. We extract the law text of this law from *Gesetze im Internet*[8], which says:

> ... *Es ist nicht erforderlich, dass die medizinische Versorgung im Zielstaat mit der Versorgung in der Bundesrepublik Deutschland gleichwertig ist. ...*

---

[7] https://www.gesetze-im-internet.de/.
[8] https://www.gesetze-im-internet.de/aufenthg_2004/__60.html.

We then simply get the embeddings of both texts using sentence transformers and find the cosine similarity between both embeddings. The following chart shows the simplified process of this experiment:

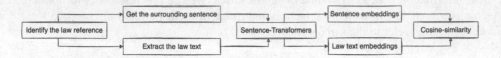

Fig. 5. Diagram depicting the simplified process of our experiment.

5.2 Semantic Similarity Between Legal Sentences

Next, we use the same embedding of legal sentences and plot a t-SNE visualization in 2-dimension. However, instead of checking for legal sentences that refer to the exact Absatz in a law reference, we only look for the semantic similarity based on the base law referred. For example, if two legal sentences refer to *§60 Abs. 7* and *§60 Abs. 9* respectively, we only look for the semantic similarity based on the base law referred, which is *§60*. Considering the higher number of law references in our dataset, we only plot the embeddings of legal sentences that refer to the same law more often (Fig. 6).

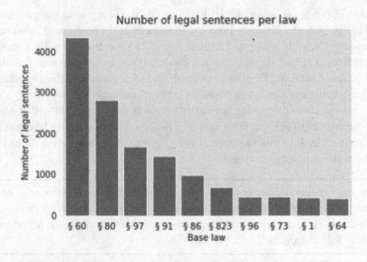

Fig. 6. The number of legal sentences that refer to the same law.

6 Results

Finding semantic similarities between law text and the sentences or paragraphs that refer to them is an important step towards generating or improving language models that can predict law references given legal text. In our work, we used two separate sentence transformers. In this section, we briefly compare the performance of both and the outcome of our experiment.

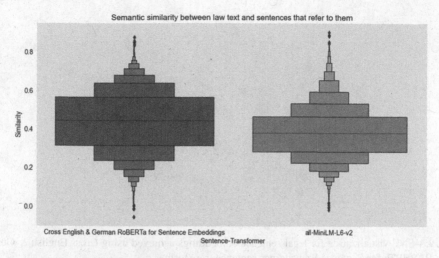

Fig. 7. Box plot comparing the performance of Cross English & German RoBERTa and all-MiniLM-L6-v2 sentence transformers. As can be seen here, the prior has higher performance than the later.

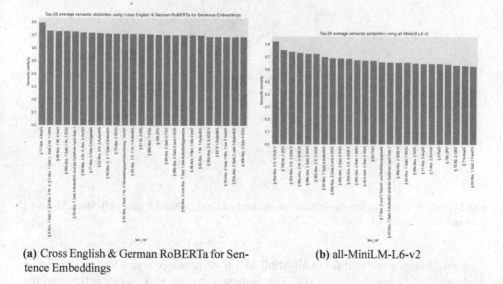

(a) Cross English & German RoBERTa for Sentence Embeddings

(b) all-MiniLM-L6-v2

Fig. 8. Bar chart depicting top-25 law references from our dataset that has highest semantic similarity with their surrounding text.

Embeddings generated using Cross English & German RoBERTa for Sentence Embeddings sentence transformers achieved a median value of approximately 0.45. The highest score for this model is 0.87, and the lowest score is −0.05. A higher number of law-text and legal sentence pairs resides between a semantic similarity score of 0.35 to 0.55.

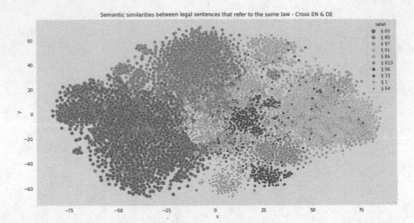

Fig. 9. t-SNE visualization for legal sentence embeddings achieved using Cross English & German RoBERTa for Sentence Embeddings sentence transformer.

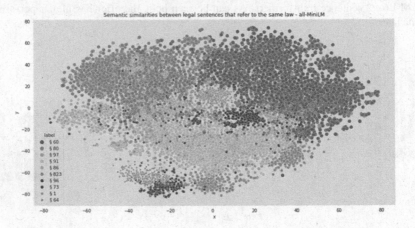

Fig. 10. t-SNE visualization for legal sentence embeddings achieved using all-MiniLM-L6-v2 sentence transformer.

Embeddings generated using all-MiniLM-L6-v2 sentence transformers achieved a median value of approximately 0.4. The highest score for this model is 0.9, and the lowest score is -0.01. A higher number of law-text and legal sentence pairs resides between a semantic similarity score of 0.3 to 0.45.

For the same pair where Cross English & German RoBERTa achieved the highest score, all-MiniLM-L6-v2 returns 0.84. And for the pair that later archives a high score, the former achieves 0.81. Figure 8 shows the top-25 law references with the highest average semantic similarities.

We also identified the semantic similarities between legal sentences that refer to the same law. However, as mentioned in Sect. 2, we only plot the t-SNE visualizations of embeddings of laws that have higher references in our dataset. As shown in Figs. 9 and

10, it can safely be said that sentences that refer to the same law are more semantically similar and grouped together.

From these visualizations, it is also clear that sentence embeddings retrieved from Cross English & German RoBERTa for Sentence Embeddings are better than all-MiniLM-L6-v2 as embeddings from prior have shown better grouping and thus higher similarity compared to the embeddings from the later.

7   Conclusion and Future Work

In this publication, we extended the work of Milz et al. [12] from finding similarities between court decisions to finding semantic similarities between law text and legal sentences that refer to them. We used two separate sentence transformers for our purpose. Using the embeddings from these sentence transformers, we calculate the cosine similarity between those.

In our experiment, Cross English & German RoBERTa for Sentence Embeddings achieved slightly better performance than all-MiniLM-L6-v2. Both sentence transformers achieve a 0.45 and 0.4 similarity scores. These results show that there do exist semantic similarities between the legal text and the law text. With improved embedding techniques, this can be exploited in certain downstream tasks such as predicting law references, identifying similar court cases and court decisions, and legal text entailment.

Finally, we show that legal sentences that have the same base law reference also have a higher semantic similarity. Their embeddings in embedding space are closely grouped. We can also use this technique to distinguish between text from tenor or gründe. This will be useful when extracting text from an improperly structured dataset.

The data from the published dataset can also be used to fine-tune existing language models for various legal tasks, such as assigning NERs or predicting the case outcome.

Acknowledgements. The project on which this report is based was funded by the German Federal Ministry of Education and Research (BMBF) under the funding code 01IS20049. The author is responsible for the content of this publication.

SPONSORED BY THE

Federal Ministry
of Education
and Research

References

1. Bhattacharya, P., Ghosh, K., Pal, A., Ghosh, S.: Methods for computing legal document similarity: a comparative study. arXiv preprint arXiv:2004.12307 (2020)
2. Chandrasekaran, D., Mago, V.: Evolution of semantic similarity-a survey. ACM Comput. Surv. (CSUR) **54**(2), 1–37 (2021)

3. Cross, F., Spriggs, J., Johnson, T., Wahlbeck, P.: Citations in the u.s. supreme court: an empirical study of their use and significance. University of Illinois Law Review, pp. 489–575 (2010)
4. Devlin, J., Chang, M.W., Lee, K., Toutanova, K.: BERT: pre-training of deep bidirectional transformers for language understanding. arXiv preprint arXiv:1810.04805 (2018)
5. Garner, H.L., Squire, J.: Iterative circuit computers. In: Proceedings of a Workshop on Computer Organization, pp. 156–181 (1963)
6. Geist, A.: Using citation analysis techniques for computer-assisted legal research in continental jurisdictions. SSRN Electronic Journal (2009). https://doi.org/10.2139/ssrn.1397674
7. Kim, M.-Y., Xu, Y., Goebel, R.: Legal question answering using ranking SVM and syntactic/semantic similarity. In: Murata, T., Mineshima, K., Bekki, D. (eds.) JSAI-isAI 2014. LNCS (LNAI), vol. 9067, pp. 244–258. Springer, Heidelberg (2015). https://doi.org/10.1007/978-3-662-48119-6_18
8. Laskar, M.T.R., Huang, X., Hoque, E.: Contextualized embeddings based transformer encoder for sentence similarity modeling in answer selection task. In: Proceedings of The 12th Language Resources and Evaluation Conference, pp. 5505–5514 (2020)
9. Leitner, E., Rehm, G., Moreno-Schneider, J.: Fine-grained named entity recognition in legal documents. In: Acosta, M., Cudré-Mauroux, P., Maleshkova, M., Pellegrini, T., Sack, H., Sure-Vetter, Y. (eds.) SEMANTiCS 2019. LNCS, vol. 11702, pp. 272–287. Springer, Cham (2019). https://doi.org/10.1007/978-3-030-33220-4_20
10. Li, Y., McLean, D., Bandar, Z.A., O'shea, J.D., Crockett, K.: Sentence similarity based on semantic nets and corpus statistics. IEEE Trans. Knowl. Data Eng. 18(8), 1138–1150 (2006)
11. Liu, Y., et al.: RoBERTa: a robustly optimized BERT pretraining approach. arXiv preprint arXiv:1907.11692 (2019)
12. Milz, T., Granitzer, M., Mitrovic, J.: Analysis of a German legal citation network. In: KDIR, pp. 147–154 (2021)
13. Mueller, J., Thyagarajan, A.: Siamese recurrent architectures for learning sentence similarity. Proceed. AAAI Conf. Artif. Intell. 30(1), 10350 (2016). https://doi.org/10.1609/aaai.v30i1.10350. http://ojs.aaai.org/index.php/AAAI/article/view/10350
14. Ormerod, M., Del Rincón, J.M., Devereux, B., et al.: Predicting semantic similarity between clinical sentence pairs using transformer models: evaluation and representational analysis. JMIR Med. Inform. 9(5), e23099 (2021)
15. Ostendorff, M., Blume, T., Ostendorff, S.: Towards an open platform for legal information. In: Proceedings of the ACM/IEEE Joint Conference on Digital Libraries in 2020, pp. 385–388 (2020)
16. Reimers, N., Gurevych, I.: Sentence-BERT: sentence embeddings using Siamese BERT-networks. arXiv preprint arXiv:1908.10084 (2019)
17. Sanborn, A., Skryzalin, J.: Deep learning for semantic similarity. CS224d: Deep Learning for Natural Language Processing Stanford, CA, USA: Stanford University (2015)
18. Smith, T.A.: The web of law. SSRN Electron. J. (2005). https://doi.org/10.2139/ssrn.642863
19. Malmgren, S.: Towards a theory of jurisprudential relevance ranking Using link analysis on EU case law. Stockholm University, Master Thesis (2011)
20. Vaswani, A., et al.: Attention is all you need. In: Advances in Neural Information Processing Systems 30 (2017)
21. Zhong, H., Xiao, C., Tu, C., Zhang, T., Liu, Z., Sun, M.: How does NLP benefit legal system: a summary of legal artificial intelligence. arXiv preprint arXiv:2004.12158 (2020)

Multidimensional Fairness in Paper Recommendation

Reem Alsaffar[1]([⊠]), Susan Gauch[1], and Hiba Al-Kawaz[2]

[1] University of Arkansas, Fayetteville, AR, USA
{rbalsaff,sgauch}@uark.edu
[2] Baghdad University, Baghdad, Iraq
hiba.m@csw.uobaghdad.edu.iq

Abstract. To prevent potential bias in the paper review and selection process for conferences and journals, most include double blind review. Despite this, studies show that bias still exists. This implicit bias may persist when recommendation algorithms for paper selection are employed instead. To address this, we describe three fair algorithms that specifically take into account author diversity in paper recommendation. In contrast to fair algorithms that only take into account one protected variable, our methods provide fair outcomes across multiple protected variables concurrently. Five demographic characteristics—gender, ethnicity, career stage, university rank, and geolocation—are included in our multidimensional author profiles. The Overall Diversity approach uses a score for overall diversity to rank publications. The Round Robin Diversity technique chooses papers from authors who are members of each protected group in turn, whereas the Multifaceted Diversity method chooses papers that initially fill the demographic feature with the highest importance. By selecting papers from a pool of SIGCHI 2017, DIS 2017, and IUI 2017 papers, we recommend papers for SIGCHI 2017 and evaluate these algorithms using user profiles with Boolean and Continuous-valued attributes. We contrast the papers that were suggested with those that were approved by the conference. We find that utilizing profiles with either Boolean or Continuous feature values, all three techniques boost diversity while experiencing just a slight decrease in paper quality or no decrease at all. Our best-performing algorithm, Multifaceted Diversity, recommends a set of papers that achieve demographic parity with the demographics of pool of authors of all submitted papers. Compared to the actual authors of the papers actually selected for the conference, the recommended paper authors are 42.50% more diverse and actually achieve a 2.45% *boost* in paper quality as measured by the h-index. Our approach could be applied to reduce bias in the selection of grant proposals, conference papers, journal articles, and other academic duties.

Keywords: User profiling · Paper recommendation · Diversity and fairness

1 Introduction

Our modern world is very diverse and individuals and institutions strive for inclusion. Despite gain in legislation and attitudes, there is still discrimination against people because of their race, color, gender, religion, national origin, disability or and age [1].

© The Author(s), under exclusive license to Springer Nature Switzerland AG 2023
A. Fred et al. (Eds.): IC3K 2021, CCIS 1718, pp. 51–72, 2023.
https://doi.org/10.1007/978-3-031-35924-8_4

These groups have legal protection within the United States, but discrimination, conscious or unconscious, still exists throughout society [13, 38]. Unfortunately, academia is no exception as evidenced by the fact that only 38% of tenure-track positions were awarded to women despite women receiving more than 50% of the Ph.D.'s awarded [15]. Computer Science is a long way from achieving diversity. [45] and [10] document the fact that only 18% of graduates in Computer Science are women and also only 18% are minorities. These statistics are reflected in the lack of diverse speakers at Computer Science conferences and in the demographics of conference attendees where minorities are underrepresented [28]. Racial, gender, and other types of discrimination among reviewers, editors and program committee might lead to bias in choosing papers for publishing [33] which has led to SIGCHI, one of the highest impact ACM conferences, announcing in 2020 an explicit goal of increasing the diversity of its Program Committee [40]. Merely using a double-blind review process fails to solve the problem of discrimination [9, 30]. Reviewers can often infer the authors of papers from previous publications or readily available electronic preprints even when using double-blind review, so the review process is not actually double-blind [1, 36]. Our approach is based on building a profile for each paper that reflects the paper's overall quality and also models the diversity of the paper authors. The demographic features most frequently identified as a source of bias are Gender, Ethnicity [7], Career Stage [31], University Rank [16] and geolocation [26], thus these are the features we use in our demographic user profiles. Our fair recommender system then uses this multi-dimensional profile to recommend papers for inclusion in the conference balancing the goals of increasing the diversity of the authors whose work is selected for presentation while minimizing any decrease in the quality of papers presented.

In our previous paper, we proposed two methods that use multiple attributes when picking a subset of authors from the pool to achieve demographic parity. We incorporated the diversity and the quality of the authors during the selection process to minimize the utility loss and maximize the diversity. We applied two different feature weighting schemes, Boolean and continuous, in demographic profiles used to increase fairness in paper recommendation. In this paper, we present three fair recommendation algorithms that balance two aspects of a paper, its quality and the authors' demographic features, when recommending papers to be selected by the conference. Because information about the review process is generally confidential, we simulate the results of the review process by creating pools of papers from related conferences within a specific field that have different impact factors. The highest impact factor conference papers will play the role of the papers that are rated most highly by the reviewers, the middle impact factor conference papers those with the second best reviews, and papers published at the conference with the lowest of the three impact factors will be treated as papers with lower reviews. Our main contributions in this work are:

- Modelling author demographics using profiles that contain multiple demographic features.
- Developing and evaluating fair recommendation algorithms for paper selections that balance quality and diversity.
- Achieving demographic parity between the accepted authors with the pool of all authors.

2 Related Work

We begin by discussing aspects of bias in academia, then we review previous work on the construction of demographic profiles for users. Finally, we summarize recent approaches to incorporate fairness in algorithmic processes.

2.1 Bias

Bias in Academia. Bias in academic research can be seen when one outcome or result is preferred over others during the testing or sampling phase, and also during any research stage, i.e., design, data collection, analysis, testing and publication [37]. Bornmann and Daniel discuss the evidence that gender, major field of study, and institutional affiliation caused bias in the committee decisions when awarding doctoral and post-doctoral research fellowships [5]. Flaherty investigates discrimination in the US college faculty focusing on ethnicity. The results showed that only 6% of professors are black versus 76% of white professors [17]. More recently, an article published by researchers from Stanford Graduate School of Education in 2021 showed that, in the United States, more doctoral degrees have been earned by women than men. Despite this, women are still less likely than men to receive tenured positions, have their research published, or obtain leadership roles in academia. After analyzing one million doctoral dissertations from US universities, they found that the authors whose topics are related to women or who used methodologies that refer to women have decreased career prospects versus those related to men [51].

Bias in Peer Review. Several studies have that the lack of fairness in the peer review process has a major impact on which papers are accepted to conferences and journals [41]. Reviewers tend to accept the papers whose authors have the same gender and are from the same region [33]. Double-blind reviews do not entirely solve this issue and some researchers demonstrate that bias still exists in the reviewing process. For example, Cox et al. concludes that the double-blind review did not increase the proportion of females significantly compared with the single-blind review [10].

2.2 Fairness

Demographic Profiling. User profiling can be used to understand the users' intentions and develop personalized services to better assist users [18]. Recently, researchers are incorporating demographic user profiles in recommender systems hoping to limit unfairness and discrimination within the recommendation process [14, 29]. Within academia, the demographic attributes of age, gender, race, and education are widely used and researchers often infer these features from the user's name [8, 39].

Demographic Parity. To achieve fairness, many approaches aim for *demographic parity*, which is when members of the protected groups and non-protected groups are equally likely to receive positive outcomes. However, this requirement generally causes a decrease in utility. Yang and Stoyanovich focus on developing new metrics to measure the lack of demographic parity in ranked outputs [46, 47, 48] address the problem of improving fairness in the ranking problem over a single binary type attribute when selecting a subset of candidates from a large pool while we work with multiple features at the same time. It maximizes utility subject to a group fairness criteria and ensuring demographic parity at the same time. We extended these works by using multiple attributes when picking a subset of authors from the pool to achieve demographic parity. We also incorporated the diversity and the quality of the authors during the selection process to minimize the utility loss and maximize the diversity. A study by [52] extended these works by using multiple attributes when picking a subset of authors from the pool to achieve demographic parity. Using Boolean profiles, they also incorporated the diversity and the quality of the authors during the selection process to minimize the utility loss and maximize the diversity. Further extensions [53] compared two different feature weighting schemes, Boolean and continuous, in demographic profiles used to increase fairness in paper recommendation [52]. Recently, some authors have been working on Generalized Demographic Parity (GDP) which is a group fairness metric for continuous and discrete features, to make fairness metrics more accurate. [54] proposed their method by displaying the relationship between joint and product margin distributions distance. They demonstrate two methods named histogram and kernel with linear computation complexity. Their experiment showed that GDP regularizer can reduce bias more accurately.

Fairness in Machine Learning. As more and more algorithms make financial, scholastic, and career decisions, it is very important that the algorithms to not perpetuate bias towards demographic subgroups. Many investigations show that machine learning approaches can lead to biased decisions [12]. Thus, researchers are working to improve classifiers so they can achieve good utility in classification for some purpose while decreasing discrimination that can happen against the protected groups by designing a predictor with providing suitable data representation [22, 49]. Other researchers attempt to improve fairness by training machine learning models without knowing the protected group memberships. In particular, [55] proposed an Adversarially Reweighted Learning (ARL) approach to improve the utility for the least represented protected groups when they train the model. During the training stage, they relied more on the non-protected features and task labels to identify unfair biases and train their model to improve fairness. Their solution outperformed state-of-the-art alternatives across a variety of datasets.

Paper Assignment Fairness. Some researchers have explored and measured fairness when choosing a suitable reviewer to review a paper. [32] and [42] focus on fairness and statistical accuracy in assigning papers to reviewers in conferences during the peer review process. Most of these studies propose methods to improve the quality of the reviewer assignment process. We contribute to this area by creating author profiles with multiple demographic features and using them in new fair recommendation algorithms to achieve demographic parity when selecting papers for inclusion in a conference.

3   Demographic Profile Construction

We first build a demographic profile for each paper by modeling the demographic features for the paper's authors so that this information is available during paper selection. Some demographic features are protected attributes, e.g., gender, race, that qualify for special protection from discrimination by law [25]. In this section, we will describe how we collect the demographic features for each author in our papers pool and then how we build the paper profile.

3.1 Data Extraction

For a given paper, our goal is to extract five demographic features that are Gender, Race, University Rank, Career Stage, and Geolocation for its author(s) then combine them to create a profile for the paper. Each feature is mapped to a Boolean value, either 1 (true) or 0 (false) based on that paper's author(s) membership in the protected group. We then extend our approach beyond current approaches by modeling demographics with continuous-valued features (each feature is mapped to a value between 0 and 1) to represent the complement of the proportion of each feature among computer science professionals. Table 1 outlines the protected and non-protected categories for each of our demographic features.

Table 1. Demographic Features and Categories.

Feature	Protected/Non-Protected Category
Gender	Female / Male
Ethnicity	Non-White / White
Geo-Location	Developing /Developed (by country)
	EPSCoR / Non-EPSCoR (by state in USA)
Career Stage	Junior / Senior
UniversityRank	Less than or equal mean/ more than mean

Gender. To gather information about an author's gender, we use the NamSor API v2, a data mining tool that uses a person's first and last names from different languages, alphabets, countries, and regions to infer their gender. The software processed more than 4 billion names with high precision and recall which are 98.41% and 99.28% respectively. The tool returns a value between -1 and $+1$ indicates that the name is male if it is close to $+1$ and female if it is close to -1. The accuracy of gender prediction using this tool is close to 99% [3]. After collecting each author's gender, we map females to 1 since they are the protected group and males to 0. To calculate the continuous value for gender, we map females and males to the complement of their participation in computer science. Women are considered a protected group since they make up only 27% of professionals in the computer science field [4]. **Ethnicity**: To predict ethnicity, we again use the NamSor tool, a web API that is used to predict ethnicity from the first and last names with the limitation of 500 names/month. It returns ethnicity as one of five values: {White, Black, Hispanic, Asian, other} [3]. Non-whites are considered a protected group since they make up less than 40% of professionals in the computer science field [4]. The continuous values for Ethnicity were calculated by mapping each category to the

complement of its proportion in the population of Computer Science professionals from [51] (Computer, engineering, & science occupations, 2020). Whites comprise 70.46% of computer science professionals, so they are mapped to 0.2954. Similarly, Black, Asian, Hispanic and others are assigned to 0.9295, 0.8237, 0.9281, and 0.7400 respectively.
Career Stage: In order to extract the academic position for each author, we utilize the researcher's Google Scholar pages [19] or their homepages. Researchers whose primary appointment is within industry are omitted from our data set. The results are then mapped to Boolean values, 0 if they are a senior researcher (Distinguished Professor, Professor, Associate Professor) and 1 if they are a junior researcher (Assistant Professor, Postdoc, Student). To calculate the continuous values for this feature, we map to six values equally distributed between [0,.., 1.0] in increasing order by rank, i.e., Distinguished Professor: 0/5 = 0.0; Professor: 1/5 = 0.2;…; Student: 5/5 = 1.0. Table 2 shows the values for each category.

Table 2. Career Stage Weight Allocation.

Position	Weight
Distinguished Professor	0.17
Professor	0.33
Associated Professor	0.50
Assistant Professor or Lecturer	0.67
Post-Doctoral or Research Fellow	0.83
Graduate Student	1.0

University Rank. Collecting this feature is done by extracting the institution's name from the Google Scholar page for the author [19] or their home pages and mapping it to the World University Rankings obtained from [44]. We partition the authors into low-rank (1) or high-rank institutions (0) using the median value. Then, we normalize the raw value to a continuous value by dividing the university rank (U_r) by the lowest university rank (L_r):

$$R_C = \frac{U_r}{L_r} \tag{1}$$

Geolocation. We set the researcher's geolocation (country and state if inside the US) based on information extracted from their institution's home page using the university name that was extracted. If the author is working inside the United States, we extract the state name as well. We find the category of the country (developed or developing) by mapping the country to the tables of the developed and developing economies that offered by the UN [35]. Thus, the Geolocation Boolean value is assigned to 0 if the researcher is working in a developed country (non-protected group) and 1 if a developing country (protected group). For those who live in the US, we use the EPSCOR (Established Program to Simulate Competitive Research) [34] to map the Geolocation to Boolean values. EPSCoR states which obtain less federal grant funding are the protected group with the value 1 and non-EPSCoR states values are 0. To calculate the continuous value for the Geolocation, we use the complement values of Human Development Index (HDI) ranking [24]. The values are ranging from 0.957 to 0.394 and Table 3 shows a sample of these values.

Table 3. Countries HDI sample.

Country	HDI
Norway	0.957
Ireland	0.955
Iceland	0.949
Germany	0.947
Sweden	0.945
Australia	0.944

H-index. We extract the h-index for each author from their Google Scholar page so we can measure the conference utility in our evaluation. If the author doesn't have a scholar page, we obtain their h-index using Harzing's Publish or Perish tool. This software calculates the h-index for the scholar using some impact metrics [23].

To conclude, each researcher has a demographic profile consists of five features (gender, ethnicity, career stage, university rank, and geolocation). Each feature has a Boolean weight that represents whether or not the candidate is a member of the protected group for that feature and a continuous value to represent the complement of the proportion of each feature among computer science professionals. In addition, we collect the h-index for each researcher using either their Google Scholar profile or is calculated and we use it to evaluate the utility of each accepted papers list in our evaluation.

3.2 Paper Profile Formation

We construct the demographic profile for each paper by combining the demographic profiles for all of the paper authors. Recall that each author has a Boolean value profile and a continuous value profile.

Boolean. The paper profile is created by doing a bit-wise OR on the paper's author profiles. Thus, the paper profile is 1 for a given demographic feature when any author is a member of that feature's protected group. We considered summing the author profiles, but this would give preferential treatment to papers with more authors and normalizing the summed profile would penalize papers with many authors.

Continuous. The paper's demographic profile is created by selecting the maximum value for each feature among the paper authors' profiles.

3.3 Paper Quality Profiler

There are several ways to measure a paper's quality such as the number of citations of the paper, the reputation of the editorial committee for the publication venue, or the publication venue's quality itself, often measured by Impact Factor (IF) [6]. Although the IF is not accurate for new venues that contain high quality papers with few citations, we use it as the basis of the quality profile for the papers in our research since the conferences in our dataset are all well-established [50]. We extract the Impact Factor (IF) for each paper's conference from Guide2Research website published in 2019 [21]. The IF was calculated by using Google Scholar Metrics to find the highest h-index for the published papers in the last 5 years [20].

3.4 Pool Distribution

When applying our proposed methods as described below, we rely on reaching demographic parity during accomplishing our goal. This means that we select the papers such that the demographics of the accepted authors match those of the pool of candidates. To achieve this, we measure the proportion of participants for each feature in the pool and store them in a vector (PoolParity).

PoolParity = < GenderWt, EthnicityWt, CareerWt, UniversityWt, GeoWt >

where each weight is the number of authors from that protected group normalized by the number of authors in the pool.

4 Approaches

The next goal is maximizing the diversity of the conference by applying three different methods to select papers with respect to each features' distribution in the pool and achieving demographic parity. The reason is to get a list of papers that have more diverse people in the high rank conferences while keeping the level of quality the same or with a little drop.

4.1 Overall Diversity Method

After creating paper demographic profiles as described in Sect. 3, paper diversity scores (PDScore) are calculated using formula (2) on the feature values:

$$PDScore = \sum_{i=1}^{5} f_i \qquad (2)$$

where f_i is the value for each paper's demographic feature (i.e., five features for each paper). Our first method to choose a diverse list of papers considers two different queues. The quality queue ($Qquality$) which contains the papers ranked by the Impact Factor (IF) as described in Sect. 3. This gives preference to the papers ranked highest by the reviewers, in our case represented by papers that appeared in the most selective conference. The demographic queue ($Qdemog$) which contains the ranked papers by

PDScore. Next, we pick papers from the top of (Qdemog) until satisfying the pool demographic parity for each feature then the remaining papers are added from the quality queue in order to meet the number of papers desired by the conference. Thus, as long as there are sufficient candidates in the pool, we are guaranteed to meet or exceed demographic parity for each protected group.

Algorithm 1. Overall Diversity.

---

1 Qquality, Qdemog ← Initialize two empty priority queues
　2 PoolParity ← Initialize an empty vector
3 Qq ← insert the papers and sort them based on Quality-Scores
　4 for each feature:
　5　　　PoolParity [feature] ← compute Demographic Parity
　6 for each paper:
　7 PDScore ← compute paper diversity score
　8 add paper to Qdemog and order them using PDScore
　9 If 2 or more papers have same PDScore:
　10　　Sort papers using Quality-Score
　11 while PoolParity Not satisfied:
　12Papers ← select a paper from top of Qdemog
　13delete selected paper from Qquality
　14 while # of conference papers not satisfied:
　15Papers ← select a paper from top of Qquality

4.2 Multi-faceted Diversity Method

The previous method selects papers based on the total diversity score for each paper. However, it does not guarantee that the selected authors from the protected groups are actually diverse. It might end up selecting papers that have high diversity scores but are all females from developing countries, for example, with no minority authors at all. To correct for this possibility, we extend the previous approach by creating five ranked queues (one per feature) and sorting the papers using one demographic feature at a time. Including the quality-ranked queue, we now have six queues total. Based on the pool demographics, we give the highest priority to the rarest features in the pool first, so we create the accepted papers list by selecting papers from the queues whose features have the fewest candidates in the pool until the demographic parity goal for those features is achieved. After satisfying demographic parity for all protected groups, the remaining papers are added in order from the quality queue.

Algorithm 2. Multi-Faceted Diversity.

---

1   FeatureName ← List of five queue names, one per feature
2   for each feature in FeatureName:
3   DivQueue[feature] ← Initialize empty priority queue
4   *Quality*Queue ← Initialize an empty priority queue
5   PoolParity ← Initialize an empty vector
6   *Quality*Queue ← insert papers and sort by Quality-Score
7   for each feature in FeatureName:
8   PoolParity [feature] ← compute Demographic Parity
9   for each paper:
10 PDScore ← compute paper diversity score
11 for each feature in FeatureName:
12 DivQueue[feature] ← add paper if this feature is 1
13 Sort papers based on Quality-Score
14 If 2 or more papers has the same Quality-Score:
15   Sort papers using PDScore
16 while PoolParity NOT empty:
17 LowFeature ← min (PoolParity)
18 while LowFeature Not reached demographic parity
19   Papers ← select top DivQueue[LowFeature]
20   delete selected paper from *Quality*Queue
21 delete LowFeature from DParity
22 while # of conference papers not satisfied:
23 Papers ← select a paper from top of *Quality*Queue

4.3   Round Robin Method

Our third method employs the same demographic queues as the Multi-Faceted Diversity method, but visits the queues using a round robin algorithm. It specifically creates one priority queue per demographic feature and selects from each in a round-robin fashion until the list of papers is formed. Since the proposed demographic profiles model five features, we create five priority queues, each of which orders all the papers by one specific feature based on PDScore. For example, one queue orders the papers based on gender, whereas another would order the papers based on academic position. Once all queues have been sorted, we apply round-robin selection by picking the highest sorted profile from each queue. Accordingly, the selected profile is then eliminated from all queues to endure that the same profile will not be selected again. This process continues iteratively until the list of papers reaches the desired size. We use this approach with both Boolean and continuous weight diversity profiles.

Algorithm 3. Round Robin.

---

1 FeatureName ← List of five queue names, one per feature
2 for each feature in FeatureName:
3   DivQueue[feature] ← Initialize empty priority queue
4 QualityQueue ← Initialize an empty priority queue
5 QualityQueue ← insert papers and sort by Quality-Score
6 for each paper:
7 PDScore ← compute paper diversity score
8 for each feature in FeatureName:
9 add profile to [feature] using PDScore[feature] as priority order
10 Papers ← empty list
11 While number of Papers < N:
12   feature ← FeatureName[0]
13   repeat:
14   paper ← get and remove profile from DivQueue[feature]
15   until paper is not in Papers
16   add paper to Papers
17   delete feature from FeatureName.
18 we now have N papers selected.

---

5   Experiment and Result

We now introduce our dataset and describe the process of evaluating our algorithms.

5.1   Datasets

For our driving problem, we focus on selecting papers for a high impact computer science conference from a pool of papers that vary in quality and demographics. To create pools of candidate papers that simulate the papers submitted to a conference, we select a trio of conferences based on several criteria: 1) the conferences should publish papers on related topics; 2) the conferences should have varying levels of impact {very high, high and medium} mimicking submitted papers reviewed as *high accept, accept, borderline accept*; 3) the conferences should have a reasonably large number of accepted papers and authors. Based on these criteria, we selected SIGCHI (The ACM Conference on Human Factors in Computing Systems), DIS (The ACM conference on Designing Interactive Systems), and IUI (The ACM Conference where the Human-Computer Interaction (HCI) community meets the Artificial Intelligence community). The papers published in SIGCHI represent papers rated highly acceptable by SIGCHI reviewers, DIS papers represent papers rated acceptable by SIGCHI reviewers, and IUI papers represent papers rated borderline acceptable. Excluding authors from industry, we create a dataset for each conference that contains the accepted papers and their authors (see Table 4). This dataset contains 592 papers with 813 authors for which we demographic profiles. We will expand this work to other conferences in the future.

Table 4. Composition of Our Dataset [56].

Dataset	Accepted Papers	Authors	Impact Factor
SIGCHI17	351	435	87
DIS17	114	231	33
IUI17	64	147	27

The demographic distribution of the authors in each conference is summarized in Fig. 1. These clearly illustrate each of the conferences had few authors from most of the protected groups with the lowest participation in the highest impact conference, SIGCHI, with gender being an exception. As an example, SIGCHI 2017 had only 8.28% non-white authors, DIS 2017's authors were only 16.45% non-white, and IUI 2017 had 27.21% non-white.

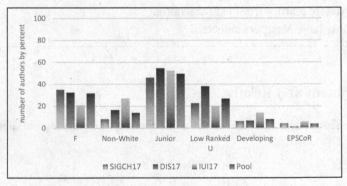

Fig. 1. Protected Group Membership of Authors for Three Current Conferences [56].

We define demographic parity as the participation rate for each of our demographic features in the pool created by combining the authors of all three conferences. Based on the 813 authors in our dataset, Table 5 presents the average participation in the pool for each feature and thus the demographic parity that is our goal.

5.2 Baseline and Metrics

Baseline. Our baseline is the original list of papers that were chosen by the program committee for SIGCHI 2017 and were represented in the venue. As shown in Table 2,

Table 5. Demographic Participation from protected groups in Three Current Conferences [56].

	Gender	Ethnicity	CStage	URank	Geoloc
SIGCHI	45.01%	7.69%	52.14%	25.64%	8.26%
DIS	57.89%	31.58%	72.81%	55.26%	11.40%
IUI	39.06%	56.25%	76.56%	28.13%	26.56%
Average	47.07%	18.71%	59.55%	32.33%	11.15%

the distribution of the protected groups in our baseline is: 45.01% female, 7.69% non-white, 52.14% junior professors, 25.64% authors from low ranked universities and 8.26 authors from developing countries.

Metrics. We evaluate our algorithms' effectiveness by calculating Diversity Gain (D_G) of our proposed set of papers versus the baseline:

$$D_G = \frac{\sum_{i=1}^{n} MIN(100, \rho G_i)}{n} \qquad (3)$$

where ρG_i is the relative percentage gain for each feature versus the baseline, divided by the total number of features n. Each feature's diversity gain is capped at a maximum value of 100 to prevent a large gain in a single feature dominating the value.

By choosing to maximize diversity, it is likely that the quality of the resulting papers will be slightly lower. To measure this drop in quality, we use the average h-index of the paper authors and compute the utility loss (UL_i) for each proposed list of papers using the following formula:

$$UL_i = \frac{U_b - U_{P_j}}{U_b} * 100 \qquad (4)$$

where U_{P_i} is the utility of the proposed papers for conference i and U_b is the utility of the baseline. We then compute the utility savings (Y_i) of papers for conference i relative to the baseline as follows:

$$Y_i = 100 - UL_i \qquad (5)$$

We compute the F measure [27] to examine the ability of our algorithms to balance diversity gain and utility savings:

$$F = 2 * \frac{D_G * Y_i}{D_G + Y_i} \qquad (6)$$

In order to measure how far away from demographic parity our results are, we calculate the Euclidean Distance [11] between our selected papers and the pool:

$$DemographicDistance = \sqrt{\sum_{i=1}^{5} (F1_i - F2_i)^2} \qquad (7)$$

where F1 is the participation of each feature in the proposed list of papers to select and F2 is the feature's participation in the pool. Finally, we normalized the distance values to obtain the similarity percentages between our results and the pool as shown in the formula below:

$$\text{DemographicSimilarity} = 1 - \frac{\text{DemographicDistance}}{\text{MaxD}} \qquad (8)$$

where MaxD is the largest possible distance between two vectors in our feature space.

To summarize the ability of the methods to balance the competing demands of increasing demographic parity and saving utility, we again apply the F measure using formula 6 calculated using DemographicSimilarity and Y_i.

5.3 Results

Our recommender system produces ranked list(s) from which we select to form the accepted papers list with the overarching goal of increasing the diversity in the papers. Both methods reported here select papers from a quality sorted queue and one or more demographic queue(s). Whenever there are ties in a demographic queue, those papers are sorted by their quality score.

5.4 Comparison with the Baseline

We report the differences between the accepted papers in SIGCHI 2017 and the accepted papers produced by the recommender system described in Sect. 4 using Boolean and Continuous profiles. Looking at Fig. 2., we can see that all algorithms succeeded in increasing the diversity in the recommended papers for acceptance across all demographic groups when using the Boolean profiles. However, it is obvious that Round Robin method produced the highest diversity in all the protected groups except gender.

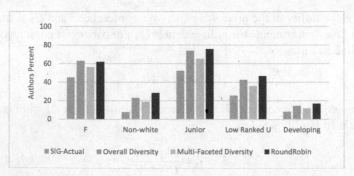

Fig. 2. Improvement in Protected Group Participation between the SIGCHI2017 and our Paper Recommendation Algorithms when using Boolean Profiles.

Figure 3 represents the protected groups participation with the Continuous profiles when applying our proposed recommendation algorithms. We can see that all methods

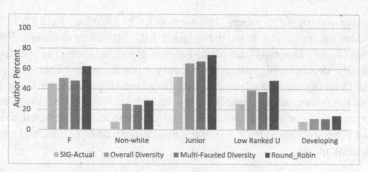

Fig. 3. Improvement in Protected Group Participation between the SIGCHI2017 and our Paper Recommendation Algorithms when using Continuous Profiles.

succeeded in increasing the diversity in the recommended papers for acceptance across all demographic groups.

Table 6 compares the participation of the protected groups between the actual accepted papers for SIGCHI with the accepted papers proposed by our three methods, and demographic parity based on the participation of the protected groups in the pool of authors in our dataset. We can see that all algorithms increase the diversity of authors across all protected groups. With the exception of female researchers for the Boolean profile, the Round Robin algorithm increases participation among the protected groups more than the Multifaceted Diversity algorithm across all demographics. As expected, these diversity-based recommendation methods overcorrected by including more authors from the protected groups proportionally than in the pool as a whole.

Table 6. Protected Group Participation for the recommender algorithms using Boolean and Continuous profiles.

Feature	SIGCHI	Overall Diversity (B)	Overall Diversity (C)	Multi-Faceted (B)	Multi-Faceted (C)	Round Robin (B)	Round Robin (C)	Pool
Female	45.01%	62.96%	50.71%	56.13%	48.15%	61.82%	62.39%	47.07%
Non-White	7.69%	23.08%	25.36%	18.80%	24.50%	28.21%	28.77%	18.71%
Junior	52.14%	73.79%	65.24%	64.96%	67.24%	75.50%	73.50%	59.55%
Low Ranked University	25.64%	42.45%	39.03%	35.90%	37.32%	46.44%	48.43%	32.33%
Develop Country	8.26%	14.53%	11.11%	11.68%	10.83%	16.81%	13.68%	11.15%

The recommended papers are a mix of papers from the three conferences in our datasets in different proportions as described in Table 7. The Multi-Faceted Diversity method selects the highest proportion of the recommended papers, 85.8% (Bool) and 78.06% (Cont.), from the actual SIGCHI papers, but Overall Diversity and Round Robin also selects the majority of its papers, 75.5% (Bool), 62.11% (Cont.) and 61.53% (Bool), 60.11% (Cont.) respectively, from the original SIGCHI selected papers. We further observe that Overall Diversity and Multi-Faceted algorithms selected the majority of papers from the demographic queue(s) with only a few from the quality-sorted queue. The Overall Diversity method selected 67.24% (Bool) and 66.67% (Cont.) of its accepted papers from the demographic queue and only 32.76% (Bool) and 33.33% (Cont.) from the quality queue. In contrast, the Multi-Faceted Diversity method selected nearly all of its accepted papers, 92.88%, from one of the five demographic queues, and only 7.12% from the quality queue.

Table 7. Proportion of Recommended Papers from each Conference.

	Overall Diversity (B)	Overall Diversity (C)	Multi-Faceted (B)	Multi-Faceted (C)	Round Robin (B)	Round Robin (C)
SIGCHI	265 (75.5%)	218 (62.11%)	301 (85.8%)	274 (78.06%)	216 (61.53%)	211 (60.11%)
DIS	59 (16.8%)	87 (24.79%)	47 (13.4%)	61 (17.38%)	84 (23.93%)	90 (25.64%)
IUI	27 (7.7%)	46 (13.11%)	3 (0.9%)	16 (4.56%)	51 (14.52%)	50 (14.25%)
Papers #	351	351	351	351	351	351

We also compare the performance of our algorithms with respect to the quality of the resulting accepted papers. Table 8 summarizes the diversity gain (D_G), Utility Savings (Y_i), and F scores for the accepted papers proposed by each algorithm when using the Boolean and Continuous profiles. All methods obtained Diversity Gains of over 40% for the proposed set of accepted papers, with the biggest gain occurring with the Round Robin algorithm. The gains in diversity occur with Utility Savings of 95.14% (B) and 94.06 (C) for the Round Robin algorithm versus 93.47% (B), 97.52%(B) and 97.52% (C), 102.45% (C) for the Overall Diversity and Multi-Faceted Diversity algorithms respectively. Based on these results, we conclude that the Round Robbin algorithm outperforms the other two algorithms and when considering author demographics and aiming for demographic parity, the quality of the selected papers actually increased.

Table 8. Diversity gain and utility savings for our algorithms versus the Baseline for Boolean and Continuous profiles.

	Overall Diversity	Multi-Faceted Diversity	Round Robin
D_G(Bool)	64.58%	46.00%	72.65%
Y_i(Bool)	93.47%	97.52%	95.14%
F-score (Bool)	76.39	62.51	82.39
D_G(Cont.)	44.90%	42.50%	66.80%
Y_i(Cont.)	102.49%	102.45%	94.06%
F-score (Cont)	62.44	60.08	78.12

Diversity-based algorithms may overcorrect and result in reverse discrimination, or the diversity gains may all be in one subgroup while other underrepresented populations are ignored. Tables 9 and 10 show the results when evaluating our algorithms' ability to achieve demographic parity with Boolean and Continuous features, respectively. We observe that, based on this criteria, the Multi-faceted Diversity algorithm produces results closest to Demographic Parity, with 95.01% similarity to the pool and a utility loss of just 2.48% when using Boolean profiles.

We further observe that the Multi-faceted method produces even better Demographic Parity of 95.12% when using continuous-valued features and actually results in a 2.45% increase in utility. This means that, by considering author diversity and aiming for demographic parity when selecting papers, the quality of the papers accepted to the conference could actually be improved.

Table 9. Demographic parity similarity and utility savings for our algorithms versus the baseline (Boolean).

Method	Demographic Similarity	Y_i	F-score
Overall Diversity	89.15%	93.47%	91.26
Multi-Faceted	95.01%	97.52%	96.24
Round Robin	87.40%	95.14%	91.11

Table 10. Demographic parity similarity and utility savings for our algorithms versus the baseline (Continuous).

Method	Demographic Similarity	Y_i	F-score
Overall Diversity	94.80%	102.49%	98.27
Multi-Faceted	95.12%	102.45%	98.44
Round Robin	87.38%	94.06%	90.60

5.5 Discussion

In the previous sections, we discuss the evaluation for our approaches by comparing them to the baseline using Diversity Gain (D_G), Utility Saving (Y_i), F-score metrics, and DemographicSimilarity. We compared three algorithms for our recommender system using Boolean and continuous weight features in the demographic profiles.

Diversity Gain Comparison. Table 11 summarizes the results for all experiment with each algorithm on both profile weights, evaluated using Diversity Gain, Utility loss, and the F-measure. From this we can see that the Overall Diversity method with Boolean profiles maximized diversity gain and the Overall Diversity method with continuous

Table 11. Diversity Gain and Utility Saving with Boolean and Continuous weights profiles.

	Profile	D_G	Y_i	F-score
Overall Diversity	Boolean	**64.58**	93.47	**76.39**
	Continuous	44.90	**102.49**	62.44
	Average	54.74	97.98	69.41
Multi-Faceted Diversity	Boolean	**46.00**	97.52	**62.51**
	Continuous	42.50	**102.45**	60.08
	Average	44.25	99.98	61.29
Round Robin	Boolean	**72.65**	**95.14**	**82.39**
	Continuous	66.80	94.06	78.12
	Average	69.73	94.60	80.26
Average	Boolean	61.08	95.38	73.76
	Continuous	51.40	99.67	66.88

weights minimizes the utility loss. However, the Overall Diversity method with Boolean weights produces the highest F-score that balances these.

All the Methods Comparison
Averaged over both feature weights, the Round Robin measure produces higher diversity gain, 69.73% versus 44.25% and 54.74%. The Multi-Faceted Diversity method produces a smaller drop in utility on average, 0.02% versus 2.02%. However, when balancing diversity gain with utility drop, the Round Robin method still produces better results with an average F-score of 80.26 versus 69.41 and 61.29 for the Overall and Multi-Faceted approach.

Boolean Versus Continuous Feature Weights
Averaged over the three methods, the Boolean profiles produces higher diversity gain, 61.08% versus 51.40% for Continuous. The Continuous profiles produces a little drop in utility on average, 0.33% versus 4.62% drop in utility for Boolean profiles. However, when balancing diversity gain with utility drop, the Boolean profiles still produces better results with an average F-score of 73.76 versus 66.88 for Continuous profiles.

Demographic Parity Comparison. Table 12 summarizes the results for all experiment with each algorithm on both profile weights, evaluated using Demographic Similarity, Utility loss, and the F-measure. From this we can see that the Multi-Faceted method with Continuous profiles maximized Demographic Similarity and the Overall Diversity method with continuous weights minimized the loss in utility. In fact, it actually produced a gain in utility! The Multi-Faceted method with Continuous weights also produces the highest F-score that balances these.

All the Methods Comparison
Averaged over both feature weights, the Multi-Faceted Diversity measure produces higher Demographic Similarity, 95.06% versus 91.97% and 87.39% for the other two

Table 12. Demographic Similarity with Boolean and Continuous weights profiles.

	Profile	Demographic Similarity	Y_i	F-score
Overall Diversity	Boolean	89.15	93.47	91.26
	Continuous	**94.80**	**102.49**	**98.27**
	Average	91.97	97.98	94.76
Multi-Faceted Diversity	Boolean	95.01	97.52	96.24
	Continuous	**95.12**	**102.45**	**98.44**
	Average	95.06	99.98	97.34
Round Robin	Boolean	**87.40**	**95.14**	**91.11**
	Continuous	87.38	94.06	90.60
	Average	87.39	94.60	90.86
Average	Boolean	90.53	95.38	92.87
	Continuous	92.43	99.67	95.77

methods. The Multi-Faceted Diversity method produces a smaller drop in utility on average, 0.02% versus 2.02% and 5.4%. Also, when balancing diversity gain with utility drop, the Multi-Faceted Diversity method still produces better results with an average F-score of 97.34% versus 94.76% and 90.86% for the Overall Diversity approach and Round Robin.

Boolean Versus Continuous Feature Weights
Averaged over both methods, the Continuous profiles produces higher Demographic Similarity, 92.43% versus 90.53% for Boolean profiles. The Continuous profiles produces a little drop in utility on average, 0.33% versus 4.62% drop in utility for Boolean profiles. However, when balancing diversity gain with utility drop, the Continuous profiles still produces better results with an average F-score of 95.77 versus 92.87 for Boolean profiles.

6 Conclusion

Our goal is maximizing diversity while reducing quality loss when recommending papers for inclusion in conferences. Thus, we provide new recommendation algorithms to select papers for publication in a conference. Our methods promote diversity by taking into account multiple demographic characteristics of authors in addition to paper quality. The majority of earlier research has concentrated on algorithms that ensure fairness based on a single Boolean attribute such as ethnicity, gender, or disability. In contrast, we profile the authors based on five attributes, i.e., gender, ethnicity, career stage, university rank, and geographic region. Furthermore, we extend previous work by comparing Boolean with Continuous-valued feature weights. To compare our algorithms for a real-world task, we created a dataset of authors whose papers were chosen for publishing at computer science conferences with varying impact factors to simulate papers judged by reviewers at various levels of acceptability in order to show our methodology.

We evaluated three algorithms: Overall Diversity, Multi-faceted Diversity, and Round Robin. The Overall Diversity method rates the papers based on an overall diversity score; the Multi-Faceted Diversity method chooses papers that satisfy the highest-priority demographic attribute participation goal first; and the Round Robin approach selects a single paper for each demographic attribute at a time. The resultant recommended papers were compared to the actual papers accepted in SIGCHI 2017 in terms of diversity gain and utility savings, where utility savings was measured based on how much, if at all, the h-index of the selected papers' authors declined. Our results showed that, based on the F-measure, the Round Robin approach with Boolean feature weights was the most effective strategy for maximizing diversity. It increased diversity by 72.6 % with only a 4.8 % reduction in utility. Also based on the F-measure, the Multifaceted Diversity algorithm with continuous features weights in the demographic profile was the most effective strategy for reaching demographic parity. With a 42.50% gain in diversity and a 2.45% boost in utility, it managed to achieve 95.12 % similarity to the demographics of the pool of authors of all submitted papers. *This finding indicates that, contrary to expectations, improving diversity actually raises the quality of publications that are accepted.*

In the future, we will investigate dynamic hill-climbing algorithms that modify the recommendation goals following each paper selection. Additionally, we will research the efficacy of fair deep learning approaches for paper recommendation.

References

1. Barak, B.: On double blind reviews in theory conferences. Windows on Theory (2018)
2. Blog, NamSor: Understanding NamSor API precision for Gender inference. Inferring The World's Gender and Ethnic Diversity using Personal Names (2018)
3. Blog, NamSor: NamSor US 'Race'/Ethnicity model helps estimate diversity in Chicago Police. Inferring The World's Gender and Ethnic Diversity using Personal Names (2019)
4. Khan, B., Robbins, C., Okrent, A.: Science and engineering indicator. NSF (2020). https://ncses.nsf.gov/pubs/nsb20198/demographic-trends-of-the-s-e-workforce
5. Bornmann, L., Daniel, H.D.: Selection of research fellowship recipients by committee peer review. Reliability, fairness and predictive validity of Board of Trustees' decisions. Scientometrics, **63**(2), 297–320 (2005)
6. Bornmann, L., Daniel, H.D.: The state of h index research: is the h index the ideal way to measure research performance? EMBO Rep. **10**(1), 2–6 (2009)
7. Cannon, S., et al.: Race and gender still an issue at academic conferences. The Conversation (2018)
8. Chandrasekaran, K., Gauch, S., Lakkaraju, P., Luong, H.P.: Concept-based document recommendations for citeseer authors. In: International Conference on Adaptive Hypermedia and Adaptive Web-based Systems, pp. 83–92. Springer, Berlin, Heidelberg (2008)
9. Code.org.: Women computer science graduates finally surpass record set 17 years ago, but percentages lag behind. Medium (2020)
10. Cox, A. R., Montgomerie, R.: The cases for and against double-blind reviews. PeerJ, 7, e6702 (2019). Data USA, Computer, Engineering, & Science Occupations (2020)
11. Draisma, J., Horobeţ, E., Ottaviani, G., Sturmfels, B., Thomas, R.: The Euclidean distance degree. In proceedings of the 2014 Symposium of Symbolic-Numeric Computation (SNC'14), pp. 9–16 (2014)

12. Dwork, C., Hardt, M., Pitassi, T., Reingold, O., Zemel, R.: Fairness through awareness. In: Proceedings of the 3rd Innovations in Theoretical Computer Science Conference, pp. 214–226 (2012)
13. eeoc.gov. (n.d.). US Equal Employment Opportunity Commission
14. Farnadi, G., Kouki, P., Thompson, S. K., Srinivasan, S., Getoor, L.: A fairness-aware hybrid recommender system (2018). arXiv preprint arXiv:1809.09030
15. Flaherty, C.: More faculty diversity, not on tenure track. Inside Higher Ed (2016)
16. Flaherty, C.: When Journals Play Favorites. Inside Higher Ed (2018)
17. Flaherty, C.: Professors still more likely than students to be white. Inside Higher Ed (2019)
18. Gauch, S., Speretta, M., Chandramouli, A., Micarelli, A.: User profiles for personalized information access. The Adaptive Web, 54–89 (2007)
19. Google Scholar (2020). Google. https://scholar.google.com/
20. Google Scholar (n.d.). https://scholar.google.com/citations?view_op=top_venues&hl=en&vq=eng
21. Guide2Research. Top Computer Science Conferences (2020). Guide2Research. http://www.guide2research.com/topconf/
22. Hardt, M., Price, E., Srebro, N.: Equality of opportunity in supervised learning (2016). arXiv preprint arXiv:1610.02413
23. Harzing, A.: Publish or Perish (2016). https://harzing.com/resources/publish-or-perish
24. Human Development Reports. (n.d.). Human development data center. human development reports
25. Inc. US Legal. (n.d.). Protected group member law and legal definition. https://definitions.uslegal.com/p/protected-group-member/
26. Jacob, B.A., Lefgren, L.: The impact of research grant funding on scientific productivity. J. Public Econ. **95**(9–10), 1168–1177 (2011)
27. Jardine, N.: The use of hierarchic clustering in information retrieval. Inf. Storage Retrieval **7**(5), 217–240 (1971)
28. Jones, T.M., Fanson, K.V., Lanfear, R., Symonds, M.R., Higgie, M.: Gender differences in conference presentations: a consequence of self-selection? Peer J. **2**, e627 (2014)
29. Labille, K., Gauch, S., Joseph, A. S., Bogers, T., Koolen, M.: Conceptual impact-based recommender system for CiteSeerx. In: CBRecSys@ RecSys, pp. 50–53 (2015)
30. Lemire, A.D.: Double-blind peer review is a bad idea. Daniel Lemire's blog (2020)
31. Lerback, J., Hanson, B.: Journals invite too few women to referee. Nat. News **541**(7638), 455 (2017)
32. Long, C., Wong, R.C.W., Peng, Y., Ye, L.: On good and fair paper-reviewer assignment. In: 2013 IEEE 13th International Conference on Data Mining, pp. 1145–1150. IEEE (2013)
33. Murray, D., et al.: Gender and international diversity improves equity in peer review. BioRxiv, 400515 (2019)
34. Naional Sciencef Foundation: Established Program to Stimulate Competitive Research (EPSCoR). NSF website (2019)
35. Nations, U.: The world economic situation and prospects 2020. Acessado em, 20 (2020)
36. Palus, S.: Is double-blind review better? American Physical Society (2015)
37. Pannucci, C.J., Wilkins, E.G.: Identifying and avoiding bias in research. Plast. Reconstr. Surg. **126**(2), 619 (2010)
38. Protected group. Wikipedia (2020). https://en.wikipedia.org/wiki/Protected_group
39. Santamaría, L., Mihaljević, H.: Comparison and benchmark of name-to-gender inference services. Peer J. Comput. Sci. **4**, e156 (2018)
40. SIGCHI: Diversity of the Program Committee for CHI 2020 (2019)
41. Sikdar, S., Marsili, M., Ganguly, N., Mukherjee, A.: Anomalies in the peer-review system: a case study of the journal of high energy physics. In: Proceedings of the 25th ACM International on Conference on Information and Knowledge Management, pp. 2245–2250 (2016)

42. Stelmakh, I., Shah, N. B., Singh, A.: PeerReview4All: fair and accurate reviewer assignment in peer review. In: Algorithmic Learning Theory, pp. 828–856. PMLR (2019)
43. Sugarman, D.B., et al.: Hate and violence: addressing discrimination based on race, ethnicity, religion, sexual orientation, and gender identity. Psychol. Violence **8**(6), 649 (2018)
44. Times Higher Education (THE). World University Rankings (2020)
45. ComputerScience. Women in computer science: getting involved in STEM. ComputerScience.org. (2021)
46. Yang, K., Stoyanovich, J.: Measuring fairness in ranked outputs. In: Proceedings of the 29th International Conference on Scientific and Statistical Database Management, pp. 1–6 (2017)
47. Zehlike, M., Bonchi, F., Castillo, C., Hajian, S., Megahed, M., Baeza-Yates, R.: Fa* ir: a fair top-k ranking algorithm. In: Proceedings of the 2017 ACM on Conference on Information and Knowledge Management, pp. 1569–1578 (2017)
48. Zehlike, M., Castillo, C.: Reducing disparate exposure in ranking: a learning to rank approach. In: Proceedings of the Web Conference 2020, pp. 2849–2855 (2020)
49. Zhong, Z.: A tutorial on fairness in machine learning. Towards Data Science (2018)
50. Zhuang, Z., Elmacioglu, E., Lee, D., Giles, C.L.: Measuring conference quality by mining program committee characteristics. In: Proceedings of the 7th ACM/IEEE-CS Joint Conference on Digital libraries, pp. 225–234 (2007
51. Andrews, L.E.: Stanford research reveals a hidden obstacle for women in Academia. Stanford News Service (2021). https://news.stanford.edu/press-releases/2021/12/16/hidden-obstacle-women-academia/
52. Zweben, S., Bizot, B.: 2018 CRA Taulbee survey. Comput. Res. News **30**(5), 1–47 (2018)
53. Alsaffar, R., Gauch, S., Alqahtani, M., Salman, O.: Incorporating fairness in paper recommendation. In: 2021 ACM/IEEE Joint Conference on Digital Libraries (JCDL), pp. 318–319. IEEE (2021)
54. Al-Saffar, R., Gauch, S.: Multidimensional demographic profiles for fair paper recommendation. In: KDIR, pp. 199–208 (2021)
55. Jiang, Z., Han, X., Fan, C., Yang, F., Mostafavi, A., Hu, X.: Generalized demographic parity for group fairness. In: International Conference on Learning Representations (2022)
56. Lahoti, P., et al.: Fairness without demographics through adversarially reweighted learning. NeurIPS 2020 (2020). http://alexbeutel.com/papers/NeurIPS-2020-fairness-without-demographics.pdf

The Foundational Ontology ThingFO:
Architectural Aspects, Concepts,
and Applicability

Luis Olsina[✉]

GIDIS_Web, Facultad de Ingeniería, UNLPam, General Pico, LP, Argentina
`olsinal@ing.unlpam.edu.ar`

Abstract. This work discusses the concepts, relationships, and constraints of the foundational ontology called ThingFO. Its concepts represent key aspects of the perceived or conceived world, including particular things (classes and individuals/instances), universal things (classes of classes), and assertions (expression classes) about both kinds of things and relations. Furthermore, ThingFO is placed at the top (foundational) level in the framework of a five-tier ontological architecture. Types of ontologies are placed in this architecture according to the level of generality/specificity. Therefore, depending on the goal and scope of a developed ontology, it can be placed in the architecture at the foundational, core, top-domain, low-domain, or instance layer. ThingFO is the single ontology at the top level, so ontologies at lower levels must reuse and specialize its concepts and relationships to ensure harmonization and interoperability. To show the applicability of ThingFO, this paper analyzes enriched concepts and specialized relationships for two core ontologies, particularly, for situation and process ontologies, where their concepts are in turn reused and extended by domain ontologies.

Keywords: Ontological architecture · Foundational ontology · ThingFO · core ontology · Domain ontology · Ontology reuse

1 Introduction

The term ontology in ISO/IEC 21838–1 [17] is defined as a "collection of terms, relational expressions and associated natural-language definitions together with one or more formal theories designed to capture the intended interpretations of these definitions". This standard is devoted to define the terminology of a top-level ontology –also known in the literature as foundational, formal, generic, upper level, or high level. Regarding the level of generality/specificity of the terminology, [17] recognizes two types, namely, top-level and domain ontologies. While other researchers like Ruy et al. [30] identify three types viz. Foundational, core and domain ontologies. Also, Scherp et al. [31] indicate that core ontologies are "situated in between the two extremes of foundational ontologies and domain ontologies… As foundational ontologies serve as a good modelling basis for core ontologies, so do core ontologies for domain ontologies".

© The Author(s), under exclusive license to Springer Nature Switzerland AG 2023
A. Fred et al. (Eds.): IC3K 2021, CCIS 1718, pp. 73–99, 2023.
https://doi.org/10.1007/978-3-031-35924-8_5

There is full agreement that the terminology or concepts of a foundational ontology must be independent of any domain. Or, in other words, it must be a domain-neutral ontology. In principle, a foundational ontology should be a useful reference conceptualization for any science. Even core ontologies like situation, process, and event ontology, among others, should be domain-independent reference conceptualizations closer to domain-dependent ontologies as stated by Scherp et al. In any case, they should semantically extend or reuse foundational elements [31].

It is worth noting that domain-dependent ontologies are the most widespread conceptualizations developed to date for most fields of the sciences. Unfortunately, most of the existing domain ontologies are not based on core and/or foundational ontologies. Or, if they do, there is often no clear separation of concerns regarding the ontological levels that an explicitly represented ontological architecture must provide. As indicated by Horsch et al. [16], top-level ontologies are becoming increasingly important for interoperability by integrating heterogeneous knowledge bases coming from different sources and domains of sciences.

Although many domain or application ontologies have been developed to date, around a dozen well-known foundational ontologies have been built in the last three decades. Among them are: Cyc (abbreviated from the term encyclopedia) [19], Basic Formal Ontology (BFO) [1], Descriptive Ontology for Linguistic and Cognitive Engineering (DOLCE) [21], General Formal Ontology (GFO) [15], Sowa [33], and Unified Foundational Ontology (UFO) [12], to name just a few.

D'Aquin et al. [5] indicate that a good practice for designing lower-level ontologies is that they should be based on a foundational ontology. As a benefit to knowledge reuse, a large number of lower-level ontologies can fall under the umbrella of a top-level ontology. For those who have been developing domain or application ontologies over time and wish to enhance and harmonize the work done with higher-level terminologies, the decision to select the most suitable existing higher-level ontology to adopt or adapt, or to create a new one, represents a great challenge.

Some principles and quality criteria –a couple taken from [5, 32]- that should be considered for the potential adoption or construction of a foundational ontology are, namely: formal simplicity and transparency promoting also the use of graphical representations for the conceptualization; coverage completeness but, at the same time, conciseness (minimum set of high-level concepts) and self-intuitiveness of the elements included; balanced representation of both taxonomic (generic and partitive hierarchical) and non-taxonomic (associative) relationships; clear delegation of responsibilities to core ontologies under the principle of modularity and loose coupling; and, explicit specification of an ontological architecture as well as guides and rules that promote the appropriate use of different levels of generality that must be taken into account when conceiving and placing ontologies.

In our research group, we have been developing domain ontologies, mainly for metrics and indicators [25], and processes, since the beginning of 2000 without integrating them into any higher-level ontology. More recently, when considering this enhancement, we have been faced with the dilemma of adapting existing high-level ontologies to harmonize our previously developed terminologies, or conceiving a new foundational ontology that takes into account some of the best features of existing ones in the context of an ontological architecture. After analyzing the cited foundational ontologies and their features, none of them simultaneously satisfied all the above principles and criteria, as we see later on. Therefore, we decided to build not only ThingFO but also the ontological architecture called Foundational, Core, Domain, and instance Ontological Architecture (FCD-OntoArch) with some guidelines and rules for placing ontologies.

The contributions of this paper are to discuss the key features of ThingFO and the proposed architecture. Regarding ThingFO, its terms designated Thing, Property, and Power represent the concept for particulars, the term named Thing Category represents the concept for universals, and Assertion is the key concept to represent the statements that arise when a human agent describes and models intentionally elements of the world corresponding to both particular things (Assertion on Particulars) and universal things (Assertion on Universals). Regarding FCD-OntoArch, it is a five-tier ontological architecture based on ideas of modularization, reuse, and specialization of concepts and relationships on lower levels. Additionally, to show the applicability of ThingFO, this paper illustrates enriched concepts and specialized relationships for two core ontologies –i.e., for situation and process–, where their concepts are in turn reused and extended by domain ontologies.

It is important to indicate that the current work is an extended version of the [23] paper. Unlike this cited conference paper of some 5,000 words, this chapter describes an abridged review of ontology types according to levels of generality in a multi-tier architecture, as well as guidelines and rules to follow for locating and harmonizing ontologies in FCD-OntoArch. In addition, a description of aspects of a meta-ontology that will serve as a formal theory for ThingFO is addressed, although it will be discussed in-depth in another manuscript. On the other side, it includes non-taxonomic relationship verification matrixes between SituationCO/ProcessCO and ThingFO that show the consistency between both ontologies. Finally, more details of the applicability of ThingFO than in [23] are given.

The remaining sections are organized as follows: Sect. 2 provides details of FCD-OntoArch, in which ThingFO and lower-level ontologies are placed. In addition, it describes concepts of a meta-ontology useful to better understand the elements of ThingFO. Section 3 discusses the proposed foundational ontology. Section 4 illustrates the usefulness of ThingFO for enriching terms and relationships of a couple of lower-level ontologies. Section 5 provides related work and a discussion about top-level ontologies. Finally, Sect. 6 summarizes conclusions and outlines future work.

2 Placement of ThingFO in an Ontological Architecture

Any newly built or adapted ontology should not be conceived and developed in isolation from an explicit representation of a multi-tier ontological architecture, as we argue below. A principle in our proposal is that a multi-tier ontological architecture should encourage modularity, extensibility, and reuse of ontology elements, i.e., concepts and relationships, at different architectural levels.

In Subsect. 2.1, we sum up the types of ontologies described in the literature concerning generality levels. Then, in Subsect. 2.2, we describe the FCD-OntoArch levels, also addressing guidelines, and rules to follow in order to locate and harmonize ontologies in them. Lastly, in Subsect. 2.3, we describe aspects of a syntactic and semantic meta-layer over FCD-OntoArch, in which a meta-ontology will be formally represented to serve as ontology theory.

2.1 Types of Ontologies According to Generality Levels in an Architecture

The ontology engineering community has conceived ontologies with different levels of generality to ease reuse and to also layer ontologies upon each other. There are documented classifications of ontologies that focus mainly on levels of generality or abstraction, as in Haller et al. [14], and Ruiz et al. [29]. Next, we quote some works that intend to propose, use or mention this type of categorization for ontologies, sometimes in conjunction with an ontological architecture. Considering the intentionality of the authors, we represent the types of ontologies according to the level of generality or abstraction in Fig. 1.

Recently, ISO/IEC 21838–1 includes in its terminology two types of ontologies, viz. Top-level ontology, and domain ontology. The former is defined as an "ontology that is created to represent the categories that are shared across a maximally broad range of domains", and the latter as an "ontology whose terms represent classes or types and, optionally, certain particulars (called 'distinguished individuals') in some domain". The ground is that a top-level ontology can be used in conjunction with domain ones at lower levels to support information/data exchange, retrieval, discovery, integration, and analysis. Nevertheless, this standard does not propose an explicit ontological architecture.

Haller et al. have recently recognized that there is no agreed ontological hierarchy. Then, adapting the ontology classification of Guarino [11], they propose an ontological architecture by largely distinguishing four different levels of abstraction in ontology design, namely: i) Upper Ontologies; ii) Mid-level Ontologies; iii) Domain Ontologies; and, iv) Use-Case Ontologies. Then, they give examples of existing ontologies placing them in the corresponding architectural layer.

Ruy et al. proposed the Software Engineering Ontology Network (SEON) [30], which is an architecture that relates a collection of ontologies located in layers of generality. SEON embraces three explicit layers. As per the authors, "the foundational ontology offers the ontological distinctions for the core and domain layers, while the core layer offers the SE [Software Engineering] core knowledge for building the domain networked ontologies. This way of grounding the ontologies in the network is helpful for engineering the networked ontologies, since it provides ontological consistency and makes a number of modeling decisions easier". It is worth mentioning that they do not model more specific sub-domain layers, but recognize that lower-level ontologies can be conceived based on more general domain ontologies. Also, it is important to remark that foundational and core layers contain ontological elements neutral from any domain. However, the core level in the authors' work is dedicated to SE, so the knowledge is not general enough for other scientific fields.

Other previous classifications of ontologies according to levels of generality or abstraction are those of Fensel [7], and Guarino et al. [10]. The former author identifies the following types: i) Generic or common-sense ontologies; ii) Representational ontologies; iii) Domain ontologies; and, iv) Method and Task ontologies. Whereas the latter authors identify: i) High-level ontologies; ii) Domain ontologies; iii) Task ontologies; and iv) Application ontologies.

Ultimately, as shown in Fig. 1, ontologies can be placed in domain-independent and domain-dependent layers. FCD-OntoArch adheres to this approach, which will be explained below.

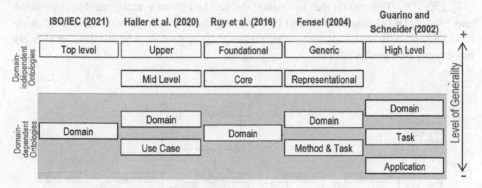

Fig. 1. Kinds of ontologies according to the generality level.

2.2 Levels, Guidelines, and Rules for FCD-OntoArch

FCD-OntoArch is a multitier ontological architecture that represents different levels of generality that must be considered when conceiving and developing ontologies. There is a set of guidelines and rules that must be followed in the development and location of ontologies in some of the levels of this architecture.

- Guideline #1: Any ontology conceptualization/formalization developed as an artifact cannot be conceived in isolation from an explicit specification of a layered ontological architecture. For example, a foundational ontology must be found at the top level (Foundational Ontological Level in Fig. 2) in this ontological architecture.
- Guideline #2: At the Foundational Ontological Level of the ontological architecture, in order to fulfill the principle of completeness and conciseness together with the principle of delegation of concerns, only one foundational ontology must be found.

As depicted in Fig. 2, FCD-OntoArch is a five-tier architecture, which considers foundational, core, top-domain, low-domain, and instance ontological levels. To provide an identification of the ontological components in the diagram, ontologies that belong to a specific level of generality have a denomination associated with their location within the architecture. For example, ontologies at the foundational level are called Foundational Ontologies (FO for short); ontologies at the core level are called Core Ontologies (CO); ontologies at the top-domain level are called Top-Domain Ontologies (TDO), and so forth.

On the left side of Fig. 2, the five proposed levels of generality are shown. It also presents the domain-independent and domain-dependent layers. The components located on the right side of the figure correspond to the ontologies already included in the architecture. At the foundational level, and following Guideline #2, Olsiña [23] proposed a unique ontology called ThingFO instead of other proposals such as UFO [13], which is made up of three ontologies at this level. At lower levels of the architecture, the ontologies already included are: i) at the core level: ProcessCO [2], GoalCO, SituationCO, PEventCO (Particular Event) [3], and ProjectCO; ii) at the top-domain level: TestTDO [34], FRsTDO (Functional Requirements), NFRsTDO (Non-Functional Requirements), and MEvalTDO (Measurement and Evaluation); and iii) at the low-domain level: MetricsLDO and IndicatorsLDO. Note that components or packages highlighted in grey are not exemplified in this paper.

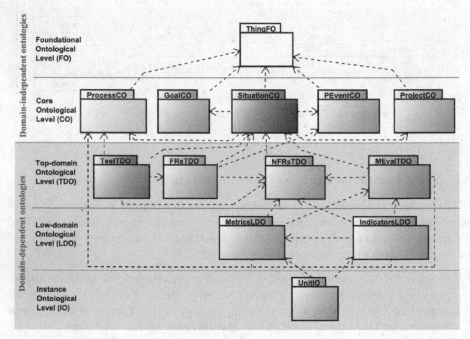

Fig. 2. Representation of the five-tier architecture of FCD-OntoArch that considers the ontological levels Foundational, Core, Top-Domain, Low-Domain, and Instance. Ontological components are depicted at the corresponding level. Note that NFRs stands for Non-Functional Requirements, FRs for Functional Requirements, MEval for Measurement and Evaluation, and PEvent for Particular Event. Also, note that this figure is adapted from [23], in which components shaded in grey will not be covered in this paper.

Using the ontological levels above, the consistent placement of ontologies within the architecture must be established by rules, namely:

- Rule #1: Any new ontology located at level CO, TDO, or LDO of the ontological architecture represented in Fig. 2 must guarantee correspondence of its elements (concepts and relationships) with the elements defined at the immediately higher level. For example, to introduce a new ontology at the Core Ontological Level, it must be guaranteed that its elements have correspondence with the elements defined at the Foundational Ontological Level. This allows the concepts of the lower level ontologies to be semantically enriched with the concepts of the higher level ontologies. Additionally, non-taxonomic relationships (associations) at lower levels must have a correspondence with non-taxonomic relationships defined at higher levels.

- Rule #2: Ontologies of the same level –except at the FO and IO levels– can be related to each other, but it must be guaranteed that their joint definition (as a whole) does not violate the principles of the next higher level. This implies that, if a core-level ontology uses elements from another ontology of the same level, together both models must guarantee a correct definition with respect to the foundational ontology. This allows the concepts and relationships of the ontologies of the same level to complement each other, maintaining correspondence with the definitions of the ontologies of the higher levels.

- Rule #3: At the Instance Ontological Level, only individuals of particular concepts can be found. A particular concept (concrete/particular class) represented at the foundational level by the term Thing, or any of its subclasses at lower levels results in instances. Therefore, an individual is an instance of a particular class at higher levels.

At this point, for instance, what does it mean that the concepts of an ontology at one level can be semantically enriched by other higher-level ontology concepts? It means, according to Rule #1, that the concepts (usually designated by terms) of an ontology at a certain level (e.g. top-domain or core) can reuse or 'inherit' the semantics of the corresponding more general concepts. For example, Artifact is a core term in ProcessCO, then Test Case in TestTDO is semantically enriched by it. That is, Test Case is an Artifact, or inherits the semantics, or is semantically enriched by the term Artifact. Moreover, Artifact has the semantics of Thing, which is a term (particular concept) in ThingFO.

Therefore, the definition of the term Test Case must be defined according to the test domain, but the designer already has the advantage of knowing the holistic meaning of the term Artifact, as it is explicitly defined in the ProcessCO ontology. In other words, these core terms provide a semantic basis that gives support to better defining and understanding more specific domain terms.

2.3 Aspects of a Layer and Meta-ontology on Top of FCD-OntoArch

As per Gruber [9], p. 199: "A body of formally represented knowledge is based on a conceptualization … An ontology is an explicit specification of a conceptualization. The term is borrowed from philosophy, where an ontology is a systematic account of Existence. For knowledge-based systems, what 'exists' is exactly that which can be represented."

In a nutshell, a conceptualization –built by human beings– includes concepts and relations in addition to constraints usually expressed in some formal notation. Concepts represent key aspects of the perceived or conceived world. Relationships link the specified concepts, and constraints remove ambiguity from the often implicit aspects of concepts and relationships, making them explicit and consistent for interpretation.

This paper discusses in the following sections mainly ThingFO, which specifies three key concepts, such as Thing, Thing Category, and Assertion. But what a concept is, what kinds of concepts there are, what elements the terms designate, etc., are not explicitly expressed in ThingFO. Moreover, what notational constructs are used to represent concepts and relationships (e.g. the ones used in Fig. 4) are not expressed in ThingFO nor in the FCD-OntoArch architecture. Therefore, at least one more layer is needed on top of the architecture presented in Subsect. 2.2. This theoretic meta-layer must embrace syntactic and semantic constructs and definitions, among other aspects.

Figure 3 depicts the proposed holistic ontological architecture in the context of the Model Driven Architecture (MDA) initiative. MDA was standardized by the Object Management Group (OMG) [27], among other complementary standards such as Meta-Object Facility (MOF), and Unified Modeling Language (UML). MDA and its four-layer architecture provide a robust basis for defining meta-models of any modeling language, so it is the straight choice to define an ontology-modeling language in MOF as well [6].

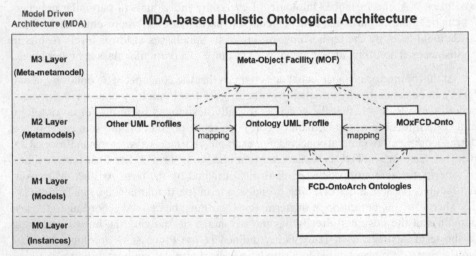

Fig. 3. Holistic ontological architecture in the context of MDA's four-layer MOF-based metadata architecture. Note that MOxFCD-Onto stands for Meta Ontology for Foundational, Core, Domain, and instance Ontologies

In this direction, since 2004 several initiatives have emerged to represent ontology architectures in the context of MDA, such as Duric et al. [6], and Lee et al. [18]. Even OMG issued the Ontology Definition Metamodel initiative. Following their approaches to ontology meta-modeling in the framework of MDA, we will formally represent the Meta Ontology for Foundational, Core, Domain, and instance Ontologies (MOxFCD-Onto), as well as review the Ontology UML Profile, which is a UML Profile that supports UML notation for ontology definition. Figure 3 represents on the left, the four layers of MDA, and on the right, our proposal. The details of these representations are outside the scope of the current chapter; however, below are some descriptions of the MOxFCD-Onto primitives.

Any ontology at the M1 layer includes Concepts, Relations, and Constraints. A Concept of something can be of four types, namely: Particular Concept, Universal Concept, Assertion Concept, or Individual Concept. In the ontology UML profile, Class corresponds to that of Concept, but two types of classes are required, such as a particular (concrete) class for the Particular Concept, and a universal (categorical) class for the Universal Concept. A Particular Concept as a concrete class represents and implies individuals or instances. Therefore, an Individual Concept represents a unique individual (in layer M0) of a particular class. Instead, a Universal Concept as a categorical class does not represent individuals but a class of particular classes useful for classification and abstraction purposes. Lastly, an Assertion Concept, also like a concrete class, represents the statement and specifications that somebody can make about aspects of particulars and universals.

A Concept has two Concept Attributes as class attributes. There is a class attribute that represents the constituent parts of something, whereas there is a class attribute that represents the capability or behavior.

It is important to know that a Concept must be designated by a Term and semantically clarified by its Definition; likewise, for the Concept Attribute. For this purpose, there is an Expression, which is a word or group of words in a given natural language or the corresponding symbols that can be used to name a Term and state its Definition.

A Relation is a key element of any ontology. Relations link Concepts. There are two general types of relationships, namely: taxonomic (generic and partitive hierarchical) relationships, and non-taxonomic (associative) relationships. All these kinds of relationships are supported by the UML notation. An associative relation usually requires a designation by a Term and should be clarified by its Definition in natural language.

Finally, a Constraint can be specified for a Concept or set of concepts, as well as for a Relation or a set of relationships. UML gives some support to constraints. Furthermore, Constraints (e.g. axioms) can be formalized using, for example, the Object Constraints Language (OCL), first-order logic, among other formal notations or expressions.

Ultimately, the primitives described above are essential to specify MOxFCD-Onto as an ontological theory at the M2 layer and to clarify the semantics and constraints of the key elements for all ontologies in the lower layers.

3   Concepts, Relationships, and Constraints of ThingFO

Developing a top-level ontology requires transdisciplinary knowledge. This is so because ontologists deal with the mental representations as subjects, who make explicit claims about the essentials of objects and their links between them in particular and universal situations in the world. To put it nicely, to represent a foundational ontology, the subject's mind's eye must be at the highest level. Schneider [32] indicates that building a top-level ontology involves challenges that are unusual for the effort to represent concrete knowledge for specific domains. On the one hand, the need for descriptive adequacy requires a considerable subtlety of conceptual grounds and analysis based on various disciplines such as Information Systems Engineering, Artificial Intelligence, Cognitive Sciences, and Philosophy. On the other hand, the usefulness of a foundational ontology depends on the greatest possible formal simplicity and transparency, as well as the completeness and conciseness of the elements included.

Foundational ontologies are representations of domain-independent concepts such as a Particular Thing and a Universal Thing, as well as human Assertions that deal with them and their relationships. Therefore, the main requirement to conceive such an ontology is to have a minimum set of particular and universal concepts, that is, key concepts, relationships, and constraints that represent the world so that they can be reused and specialized, and ultimately can be useful and easy to adopt or adapt in all domains of different sciences.

Next, in Subsect. 3.1, we discuss the concept of Thing, its relationships, and axioms. Likewise, in Subsect. 3.2, we analyze the Thing Category concept. Finally, in Subsect. 3.3, we present the concept of Assertion and its subtypes. Figure 4 depicts the ThingFO conceptualization in UML. Tables 1 and 2 present the definition of concepts and relations that will be used in Sect. 4. The full documentation of ThingFO is at http://arxiv.org/abs/2107.09129.

We use the following text convention: concepts begin with capital letters, concept attributes are italicized, and relations are underlined.

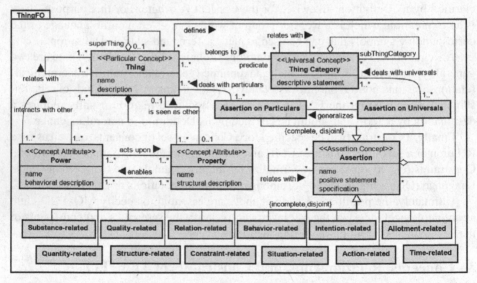

Fig. 4. Concepts, concept attributes, and relationships of the Thing Foundational Ontology. Note that this figure is adapted from [23].

Table 1. Definitions of those concepts included in ThingFO that semantically enrich terms in SituationCO (Fig. 5) or ProcessCO (only those shown in the fragment of Fig. 6).

Term	Definition
Thing (synonym: **Particular Thing,** **Object,** **Entity,** **Instance,** **Individual**)	Class or type of a perceivable or conceivable object, or its individuals of a given particular world Note 1: The term Thing has the semantics of Particular Concept Note 2: A Thing as a class represents and implies unique individuals or instances, not a universal category. Therefore, a particular Thing results in instances, whereas a universal Thing (i.e., a Thing Category) does not result in instances, at least with the valuable meaning of individual in a given particular world Note 3: A Thing is not a particular Thing without its properties and its powers, so things, properties, and powers all emerge simultaneously to form a unity. Or, in other words, they are necessary and sufficient for the existence of this unity Note 4: A subclass of a particular Thing as a particular class can be represented at any lower level of the ontological architecture (depicted in Fig. 2) except at the Instance Ontological Level, where only particular individuals are or exist. See Rule #3, in sub-Sect. 2.2
Thing Category (synonym: **Universal Thing,** **Entity Category**)	Class or type that represents a category that predicates on particular Things conceived by a human being's mind for abstraction and classification purposes Note 1: The term Thing has the semantics of Universal Concept Note 2: A Thing Category does not exist, is, or can be in a given particular world as a Thing does. Conversely, it may only be formed or developed mentally by human beings Note 3: A Thing Category as universal does not result in instances –at least with the valuable meaning of individual– but rather can be represented by more specific sub-categories of universal Things

(continued)

Table 1. (*continued*)

Term	Definition
Assertion (synonym: **Human Expression**)	Class or type that represents a positive and explicit statement or expression that somebody makes about something concerning Things, or their categories, based on thoughts, perceptions, facts, intuitions, intentions, and/or beliefs, conceived with an attempt to provide current or subsequent evidence Note 1: The term Thing has the semantics of Assertion Concept Note 2: The part of the previous definition that indicates "… *statement or expression that somebody makes…*" means that a concrete human being –as a particular Thing– defines or conceives Assertions Note 3: Regarding a particular Thing or category, a positive statement refers to what it is, was, or will be, and contains no indication of approval or disapproval Note 4: ISO/IEC [17] defines expression as "*word or group of words or corresponding symbols that can be used in making an assertion*"
Assertion on Particulars	It is an Assertion that somebody makes about something of one or more particular Things
Assertion on Universals	It is an Assertion that somebody makes about something of one or more Thing Categories
Constraint-related Assertion	It is an Assertion related to the specification of restrictions or conditions imposed on Things, Thing's attributes, relationships, interactions, or Thing Categories that must be satisfied or evaluated to be true in given situations or events
Situation-related Assertion	It is an Assertion related to the combination of circumstances, episodes, and relationships/events between target Things and context entities that surround them, or their categories, which is of interest or meaningful to be represented or modeled for an intended agent Note: A Situation can be represented statically or dynamically depending on the intention of the agent

Table 2. Definitions of those terms for non-taxonomic relationships included in ThingFO that are specialized in SituationCO or ProcessCO.

Relationship	Definition
belongs to	Particulars Things may belong to none or more Thing Categories Note: In other words, a Thing Category predicates about a set of particular Things and their instances

(continued)

Table 2. (*continued*)

Relationship	Definition
deals with particulars	An Assertion on Particulars deals with particular Things, both classes/subtypes and instances
deals with universals	An Assertion on Universals deals with Universal Things, which are Categories
defines	A Thing defines none or many Assertions Note: For example, a particular Thing such as a Human Agent defines or conceives Assertions, such as goals, events, and situations, among many others
generalizes	An Assertion on Universals abstracts none or more Assertions on Particulars
interacts with other	Due to the power of a Thing, particular Things interact with each other Note: Note that this relationship represents actions on other Things, not on the same Thing. This constraint is specified by an axiom in the ThingFO documentation
relates with (x2)	A Thing relates to other particular Things An Assertion may be related to other Assertions

3.1 The Concept of Particular Thing

The term Thing represents a particular, tangible or intangible, perceivable or conceivable object in the given world, but not a universal category, which is modeled by the term Thing Category. A particular entity represents and implies unique individuals or instances. Therefore, a particular Thing results in instances, whereas a universal Thing, i.e., a Thing Category does not result in instances. The Particular Concept named Thing can be represented by the concrete UML class and supports subtyping by inheritance at lower layers, except at the Instance Ontological Level (see Rule #3 in Subsect. 2.2).

A Thing is not a particular entity without its *Properties* and its *Powers*, so according to Fleetwood [8] "things, properties and powers all emerge simultaneously to form a unity … Things, properties and powers are necessary and sufficient for the existence of this unity". Note that the terms *Property* and *Power* have the semantics of Concept Attribute in MOxFCD-Onto, in which for a Particular Concept both must be mandatory. This must be expressed by an axiom in MOxFCD-Onto, and is reflected by the UML composition relationship in the ThingFO conceptualization. In addition, a Thing cannot exist or be in spatiotemporal isolation from other Things. This principle of non-isolation is represented among Things in Fig. 4 through the associative relation relates with, in which the cardinality is at least one. Note that cardinality is a Constraint that can be easily visualized in the UML graphical representation as well.

Thus, in a Particular Situation of the represented world, one or more Things in the role of the target is always surrounded by other Things in the role of the environment. These concepts are modeled in SituationCO in Fig. 5, by including the terms Target Entity and Context Entity, as we will describe in sub-Sect. 4.1. Note, however, that under the principles of simplicity and conciseness, we tried to delegate most of the responsibilities to the core ontologies so as not to overload ThingFO with derivable concepts, relationships, and axioms. This lack of conciseness often occurs in other related work, as we will discuss in Sect. 5.

Property has a *structural description* that refers to the intrinsic constitution, structure, or parts of a Thing, whereas Power has a *behavioral description* that refers to what a particular Thing does, can do, or behave. Thus, the *behavioral description* portrays the Power of a Thing in terms of responsibilities, operations, or actions.

Additionally, Fleetwood says that "Powers are the way of acting of a things' properties; powers are a things' properties in action ... Things have properties, these properties instantiate [...] acting powers, and this ensemble of things, properties and powers cause any events that might occur". These Fleetwood's statements are represented in the following relationships. One or more *Properties* enable one or more *Powers*. In turn, *Powers* act upon *Properties*, just as they can interact with other Things. Furthermore, we have represented Particular Events in the PEventCO ontology.

For ThingFO to be actionable at lower levels, three explicit axioms were defined. They are specified in first-order logic in the linked documentation referenced above, so only the textual description follows:

- All *Property* of a Thing enables only its *Powers*;
- The *Power* of a Thing only acts upon its *Properties*;
- The *Power* of a Thing only interacts with other *Things*.

Finally, note that a *Property*, which is a mandatory part of a Thing, most of the time, is seen as other Thing outside of it, with its own *Properties* and *Powers*.

3.2 The Concept of Universal Thing

The term Thing Category has the semantics of Universal Concept from MOxFCD-Onto. It represents a universal from a set of particular entities conceived by the human being's mind for abstraction and classification purposes. In other words, a Thing Category as a categorical class (class of classes) does not represent individuals but a class of particular classes useful for classification and abstraction purposes. Whereas a Thing is modeled by the concrete class, which implies unique instances, a Category of Thing is modeled by the abstract or categorical class in which the instances do not have the valuable meaning of an individual. Therefore, a Thing Category does not exist, is, or can be in a given particular world as individuals of a Thing does. On the contrary, it can only be mentally formed or developed by human beings as an abstract or generic construct, which in turn, hierarchies of partitive sub-categories can be developed.

Ultimately, a Thing Category is the `predicate` about particular Things. In other words, a Thing Category abstracts some common essence or concept attributes of Things. Therefore, Things belong to the intended Thing Category.

3.3 The Concept of Assertion

The third main concept in ThingFO is Assertion. This term –semantically enriched with the primitive Assertion Concept from MOxFCD-Onto– has a great conceptual impact when a human agent intentionally represents and models particular and universal Things and situations of the world in question.

The term Assertion is defined in Table 1 as "Class or type that represents a positive and explicit statement or expression that somebody makes about something concerning Things, or their categories, based on thoughts, perceptions, facts, intuitions, intentions and/or beliefs, conceived with an attempt to provide current or subsequent evidence".

Regarding a Particular or Universal Thing, a *positive statement* refers to what it is, was, or will be. Therefore, it contains no indication of approval (e.g. I like it) or disapproval (e.g. I dislike it). Assertions are conceptualized consequences of persons' mental models of the observed and represented world, phenomenon, or situation at hand. Considering the part of the previous phrase that says *"... statement or expression that somebody makes..."* means that a concrete human being –as an individual of a particular Thing– conceives and <u>defines</u> Assertions. And the part of the same phrase that indicates *"... about something concerning Things, or their categories ..."* means, for instance, about the substance, structure, behavior, relation, situation, quantity, quality, intention, and constraint, among other aspects of Things or Thing Categories.

In order to be valuable, actionable, and ultimately useful for any science, an Assertion should largely be verified and/or validated by theoretical and/or empirical evidence. Assertions can be expressed by informal, semiformal, or formal specification languages. Thus, a *specification* can include textual Expressions in a given natural language, mathematical and logical Expressions, or well-formed models and diagrams, among other modeling representations.

There is a term called Assertion on Particulars for Things, and another called Assertion on Universals for Thing Categories. Notice the UML constraint with the label `{complete, disjoint}` set in the inheritance relationship in Fig. 4. Hence Assertion on Particulars <u>deals with particulars</u> (Things), whereas Assertion on Universals <u>deals with universals</u> (Thing Categories).

Also, Fig. 4 shows 12 subtypes of Assertions that permit specifying and modeling the substance, relation, structure, intention, situation, and constraint, among other aspects of Things or Thing Categories. Notice also in the figure, that the UML constraint with the Expression `{incomplete, disjoint}` is set in the inheritance relationship. Because the `incomplete` tag is used in this expression, for example, a subtype termed Space-related Assertion can be added.

Next, we describe the subset of Assertion subtypes listed above. The reader can look at all the definitions at http://arxiv.org/abs/2107.09129. As an example, the reader can assume that a conceptualization of an ontology as an artifact (e.g. the ThingFO UML diagram in Fig. 4, plus the linked document with definitions of concepts, non-taxonomic relationships, and axioms) represents a combination of Substance-, Relation-, Structure-, Intention-, Situation- and Constraint-related Assertions.

A Substance-related Assertion deals with the ontological significance and essential import of a Thing as a whole entity or a set of Things. Substance aspects can be specified for Particular Things and can also be abstracted for Universal Things.

A Relation-related Assertion refers to logical relationships or natural associations between two or more Things or their categories. As mentioned above, a Thing cannot exist or be spatiotemporally isolated from other Things in a given particular world and situation. As a consequence, a Thing is related to other Things. In addition, it can be specified for Particular Things and can also be represented for Universal Things.

A Structure-related Assertion is related to the *Property* term, which represents the intrinsic constitution, structure, or parts of a Thing. An Intention-related Assertion addresses the aim to be achieved by some agent. The *statement* of an Intention-related Assertion considers the propositional content of a goal purpose in a given situation and time frame. It can be specified for both Particular and Universal Things.

A Situation-related Assertion deals with the combination of circumstances, episodes, and relationships/events between target Things and context entities that surround them, or their categories, which are of interest or meaningful to be modeled by a given agent. A situation can be represented statically or dynamically depending on the intention of the agent. The conceptualization of an ontology implies a static representation.

Lastly, a Constraint-related Assertion is related to the specification of restrictions or conditions imposed on concept elements, relations, and interactions that must be satisfied or evaluated to be true in given situations or events. It can be specified for both Particular and Universal Things.

4   Applicability of ThingFO to Semantically Enrich Ontologies at Lower Levels

To show the applicability of ThingFO, this section analyzes semantically enriched concepts and specializations of non-taxonomic relationships for two ontologies at the core level such as SituationCO and ProcessCO, where their concepts are in turn cross-cutting concerns mainly for domain terminologies. Hence, we illustrate the usefulness of ThingFO together with these two core ontologies, in which the domain ontologies not only extend the core concepts and relationships but also reuse some conceptual blocks or patterns.

It should be noted that this work uses stereotypes as a mechanism to semantically enrich and harmonize concepts. Considering the procedural way of enriching a given concept from a higher-level concept, Becker et al. [2] stated that stereotypes are, in some situations, a more appropriate mechanism than inheritance relationships, since they generate a weak coupling between a lower-level ontological component and a higher-level ontological component. In addition, they indicate that stereotypes can reduce the complexity of models, promoting understandability and communicability.

In the sequel, in Subsect. 4.1, we describe how ThingFO concepts are stereotyped in SituationCO to semantically enrich their more specific concepts, following Rule #1 stated in Subsect. 2.2. In Subsect. 4.2, we do an analogous description for ProcessCO. Also, we test how some ThingFO non-taxonomic relationships are consistently specialized, following Rule #2. To do this, we address aspects of the ProcessCO/SituationCO vs. ThingFO non-taxonomic relationship verification matrixes. Then, in Subsect. 4.3, we outline how these foundational and core concepts are extended and conceptual patterns are reused by domain ontologies, as in the case of TestTDO.

It is important to note that we are not going to discuss the content of the SituationCO and ProcessCO ontologies, but rather the enrichment and reuse mechanism of some of their concepts and relationships. The reader interested in these ontologies can look further at the entire SituationCO and ProcessCO documentation at http://arxiv.org/abs/2107.10083 and http://arxiv.org/abs/2108.02816, respectively.

4.1 ThingFO Semantically Enriches SituationCO

Figure 5 shows the UML conceptualization of the SituationCO ontology with most of its elements reused from ThingFO. SituationCO is placed at the Core Ontological Level in the framework of the architecture outlined in Subsect. 2.2. It deals with Particular and Generic Situations for a given Goal and problem at hand.

The term Situation is defined as a Situation-related Assertion that explicitly states and specifies the combination of circumstances, episodes, and relationships/events embracing particular entities and their surroundings, or categories of entities and their related generic context, which is of interest and relevant to be represented by a Human Agent/Organization with an established Goal.

Most of the SituationCO concepts extend directly from ThingFO. But it also borrows some core concepts from the GoalCO, ProcessCO, and ProjectCO ontologies, which in

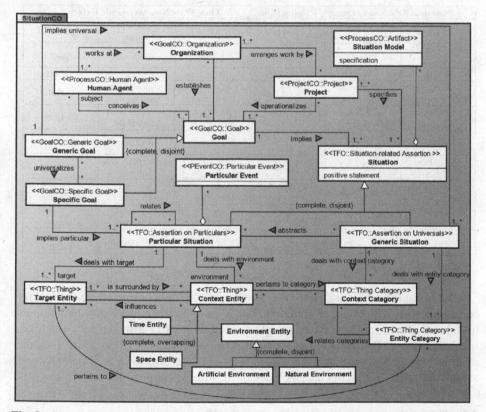

Fig. 5. Concepts, concept attributes, and relationships of the SituationCO ontology enriched from ThingFO (TFO). Note that GoalCO, among other packages, is represented in Fig. 2. Also, note that this figure is adapted a bit from [23].

turn are enriched by the foundational concepts. The term Thing semantically enriches the terms Target Entity and Context Entity (and its subtypes), as well as the completely reused terms of the core ontologies mentioned above, such as Project, Organization, and Human Agent. The term Thing Category semantically enriches the term Entity Category and Context Category. So concrete Target Entities pertain to the Entity Category, whereas Context Entities pertain to category Context Category, as depicted in Fig. 5.

Furthermore, the term Situation has the semantics of Situation-related Assertion. Therefore, a Particular Situation has also the semantics of Assertion on Particulars, while a Generic Situation has the semantics of Assertion on Universals. In addition, Goal –a term reused from GoalCO– has the semantics of Intention-related Assertion.

For the sake of brevity, we can say that a Human Agent/Organization conceives/establishes a Goal, which implies a Situation, which is represented by a Situation Model. A Project operationalizes Goals and specifies a Situation.

Table 3. An excerpt from the verification matrix of SituationCO non-taxonomic relationships that are specializations of ThingFO non-taxonomic relationships, correspondingly.

SituationCO's Non-taxonomic Relationships			ThingFO's Non-taxonomic Relationships		
Term 1	Relationship name	Term 2	Term 1	Relationship name	Term 2
Human Agent	conceives	Goal	Thing	defines	Assertion
Goal	implies	Situation	Assertion	relates with	Assertion
Particular Situation	deals with target	Target Entity	Assertion on Particulars	deals with particulars	Thing
Particular Situation	deals with environment	Context Entity	Assertion on Particulars	deals with particulars	Thing
Target Entity	is surrounded by	Context Entity	Thing	relates with	Thing
Context Entity	influences	Target Entity	(Power of) Thing	interacts with other	Thing
Generic Situation	abstracts	Particular Situation	Assertion on Universals	generalizes	Assertion on Particulars
Generic Situation	deals with entity category	Entity Category	Assertion on Universals	deals with universals	Thing Category
Target Entity	pertains to	Entity Category	Thing	belongs to	Thing Category

Following Rule #1, the SituationCO non-taxonomic relationships were verified for correspondence with those of ThingFO, which are represented in Fig. 4 and defined in Table 2. Table 3 exhibits a fragment of the SituationCO associations, which are specializations of the ThingFO ones, correspondingly. The complete non-taxonomic relationship verification matrix is found at the end of the document at http://arxiv.org/abs/2107.10083. This matrix also includes verification of cardinalities.

4.2   ThingFO Semantically Enriches ProcessCO

Figure 6 depicts a fragment of the UML conceptualization of the ProcessCO ontology with some enriched concepts and specialized relationships from ThingFO. ProcessCO is placed at the Core Ontological Level –like SituationCO. This ontology, which deals primarily with human work processes rather than natural processes, was first developed in the late 1990s, and recently updated to harmonize its concepts with ThingFO in the context of the FCD-OntoArch architecture.

The term Thing semantically enriches, for example, the term Work Entity and, consequently, subtypes the terms Work Process, Activity, and Task. Also, the reader can see that the term Work Product has the semantics of Thing, the same as Outcome, Artifact, and Service. Furthermore, a Work Entity consumes Product Entities, and produces Work Products. These two relationships are specializations of the interacts with other relation from ThingFO, as shown in Table 4. Note that all non-taxonomic relationships were verified with those of ThingFO, whose verification matrix can be found completely at the end of the document at http://arxiv.org/abs/2108.02816.

The term Thing Category enriches for instance the terms Product Category and Process Category. The latter has a subcategory termed Work Entity sub-Category, so Work Entities pertain to (this) category, where this underlined non-taxonomic relationship is specialized from the ThingFO belongs to relationship, as shown in Table 4. Also, the term Assertion on Particulars enriches the term Process Perspective.

We would like to illustrate the Process Perspective concept, which allows us to represent the functional, behavioral, and informational, among other views, for Work Entities and related concepts. Thus, the functional view entails the Work Entities' structure and Work Products as inputs and outputs. The behavioral perspective represents the dynamic view of Work Entities, such as iterations, sequences, and parallelisms.

In summary, a Process Perspective is an Assertion on Particulars, which depending on the particular Situation at hand may be a Behavior-related Assertion, an Action-related Assertion, or some other type of Assertion as commented in Subsect. 3.3. For example, Fig. 7 models the Functional and Behavioral Perspectives for the "Extract Data from a Sample of Documents" Activity in the context of conducting a Systematic Literature Review [24]. Furthermore, ProcessCO in Fig. 6 shows that a Process Perspective is represented by one or more Process Model *specification*. Note that *specification* is part of the term Assertion in ThingFO.

Consequently, each Assertion can be represented by at least a model in a given language. Figure 7 shows a concrete Process Model specified in the Software & Systems Process Engineering Meta-Model Specification (SPEM) language [26], in which concepts and relations of ProcessCO give support to the semantics of the SPEM icons. For example, Fig. 7 shows the Activity, Task, and Artifact icons. Also, we see the "Extract Data from Sample" Task, which consumes and produces Artifacts modelled by arrows.

Ultimately, a Process Model, a Situation Model (term included in Fig. 5), or any model made by a Human Agent has the semantics of Artifact. The *specification* of an Assertion –initially conceived in a person's mental representation– can be materialized in a model, which represents a produced Artifact of utility for a certain scientific problem and/or situation.

Finally, note that Rule #2 (Subsect. 2.2) holds for SituationCO and ProcessCO non-taxonomic relationships. For example, looking at the relation deals with particulars of ThingFO at the foundational level, this is specialized by refinement at the core level into

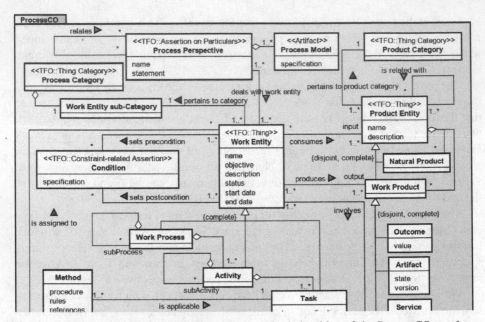

Fig. 6. Fragment of concepts, concept attributes, and relationships of the ProcessCO ontology enriched from ThingFO (TFO). Note that this figure is adapted from [2].

Table 4. An excerpt from the verification matrix of ProcessCO non-taxonomic relationships that are specializations of ThingFO non-taxonomic relationships, correspondingly.

ProcessCO's Non-taxonomic Relationships			ThingFO's Non-taxonomic Relationships		
Term 1	Relationship name	Term 2	Term 1	Relationship name	Term 2
Work Entity	consumes	Product Entity	(Power of) Thing	interacts with other	Thing
Work Entity	produces	Work Product	(Power of) Thing	interacts with other	Thing
Process Perspective	deals with work entity	Work Entity	Assertion on Particulars	deals with particulars	Thing
Process Perspective	relates	Process Perspective	Assertion on Particulars	relates with	Assertion on Particulars
Work Entity	pertains to category	Work Entity sub-Category	Thing	belongs to	Thing Category

three related but different terms (see Tables 3 and 4), so both semantic models together guarantee a correct definition with respect to the foundational ontology.

4.3 Foundational and Core Ontologies Benefit Those at the Domain Level

As commented at the beginning of Sect. 4, foundational and core concepts and relationships are extended, and conceptual blocks or patterns are reused by top-domain and

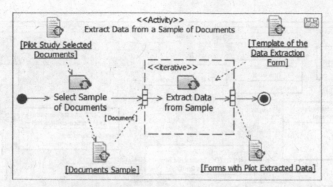

Fig. 7. Functional and behavioral perspectives for the Activity "Extract Data from a Sample of Documents" specified in SPEM. Note that this figure is taken from [24].

low-domain ontologies. For example, TestTDO [34] is a top-domain ontology for software testing activities, methods, and projects, which is terminologically benefited from the concepts of ThingFO, SituationCO, and ProcessCO. For reasons of space, we focus only on a couple of conceptual blocks for TestTDO. However, the descriptions below also apply to other domain ontologies, such as MEvalTDO, shown in Fig. 2.

Firstly, the term Particular Situation included in SituationCO (Fig. 5) semantically enriches the term Test Particular Situation represented in Fig. 8. Moreover, TestTDO includes the Particular Situation conceptual block or pattern, because it not only specializes SituationCO three terms but also reuses and redefines its four relationships. Considering the three terms specialized in TestTDO, they are now named Test Particular Situation, Testable Entity (with the semantics of Target Entity in FRsTDO and NFRsTDO), and Test Context Entity. Regarding the redefined SituationCO relationships, they have now termed <u>deals with test target</u>, <u>deals with test environment</u>, <u>surrounded by</u>, and <u>influences</u>.

Secondly, TestTDO extends from ProcessCO, the consumes/produces pattern, which specifies that all Work Entity <u>consumes</u> one or more Product Entities and <u>produces</u> one or more Work Products. For example, in Fig. 8, Design Testing (that has the semantics of Activity, which is a type of Work Entity and, in turn, of Thing) <u>consumes</u> Test Basis (that has the semantics of Artifact, which is a type of Work Product and, in turn, of Thing) and <u>produces</u> Test Specifications such as Test Case or Test Suite, which are Artifacts as well.

Thirdly, another reused conceptual block from ProcessCO is the work breakdown pattern, which indicates that a Work Process is composed of subProcesses and Activities, and the latter, by subActivities and Tasks (see in Fig. 6 the aggregation relationships between these terms). TestTDO considers this pattern since Testing with the semantics of Work Process aggregates at least three Testing Activities, i.e., Design Testing, Perform Testing, and Analyze Test Results.

Lastly, the Project pattern (Fig. 5) is also reflected in TestTDO, in which a given Test Project <u>operationalizes</u> a Test Goal and <u>defines</u> a Test Particular Situation.

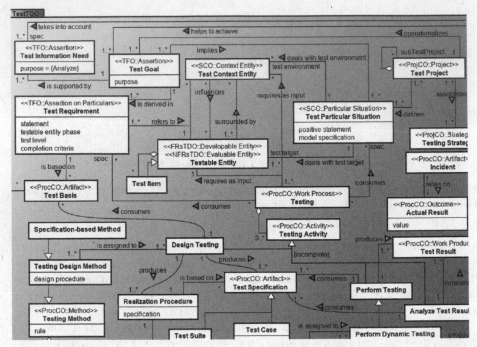

Fig. 8. Fragment of concepts, concept attributes, and relationships of the TestTDO ontology mainly enriched from core ontologies. Note that TFO stands for ThingFO, SCO for SituationCO, ProcCO for ProcessCO, and ProjCO for Project Core Ontology. Also, note that this figure is adapted from [34].

5   Related Work and Discussion

In this section, we cite related work and provide an abridged discussion on requirements and criteria to adopt, adapt, or conceive foundational ontologies. As commented in the Introduction Section, thousands of domain ontologies have been built to date, but no more than a dozen foundational ontologies have been developed in the last few decades, with some impact on academia or industry.

Mascardi et al. [20] provide in 2007 a description and comparison of 7 upper ontologies, namely: BFO [1], Cyc [19], DOLCE [21], GFO [15], PROTo ONtology (PROTON) [4], Sowa [33], and Suggested Upper Merged Ontology (SUMO) [19], which were the most referenced within the research community at the time of their study. To synthetize information for the comparison, they designed a template with a set of feature fields. Additionally, they also provided a summary of existing comparisons drawn among subsets of the top 7 cited ontologies previously made by other authors.

An upper ontology whose first version appeared in 1999 is Yet Another More Advanced Top Ontology (YAMATO) [22], which was not included in [20]. According to Mizoguchi [22], at that time there was some room for improvement in a couple of aspects of DOLCE, BFO, GFO, SUMO, and CYC, in particular, in the description of quality, representation, and process/event aspects.

Additionally, Guizzardi developed UFO in 2005 [12]. UFO is made up of three ontologies [13]: UFO-A (which deals with endurants), UFO-B (which deals with perdurants or events), and UFO-C (which deals with social entities). This ontology was not selected in Mascardi et al.'s study surely for chronological reasons. UFO incorporates previous developments mainly from the GFO and DOLCE ontologies adding new features.

Another contemporary initiative is COmmon Semantic MOdel (COSMO), which is an upper ontology that can serve to enable broad general semantic interoperability. The development of COSMO started as a merger of basic elements from Cyc, SUMO, and DOLCE adding new features as well. Note that all the documentation of this open project can be accessed at http://micra.com/COSMO/.

As per Mizoguchi [22], "Ontology design is a kind of design activity which necessarily has some design rationale that largely influences the resulting ontology". For example, ISO/IEC 21838-1 [17] establishes a set of requirements or design rationale for top-level ontologies (TLO). Among these are: i) TLO as textual artifact, ii) Relations between textual artifact and axiomatizations, iii) Documentation of the purpose of the TLO, iv) Documentation demonstrating breadth of coverage, and v) Domain neutrality, among others. Furthermore, ISO/IEC 21838-2 is dedicated to BFO, which is an ontology that meets the requirements set by ISO/IEC 21838-1.

Some other principles, criteria, and requirements –some listed in [5, 32]- that should be considered for the potential adoption or construction of a foundational ontology can be mentioned, such as: i) formal simplicity and transparency, ii) use of graphical representations for the conceptualization, iii) coverage completeness but, at the same time, conciseness (minimum set of top-level concepts), iv) self-intuitiveness of the elements included, v) balanced representation of both taxonomic and non-taxonomic relationships, vi) clear delegation of responsibilities to core ontologies under the principle of modularity and loose coupling, and vii) explicit specification of an ontological architecture as well as guides and rules that promote the appropriate use of different levels of generality that must be taken into account when conceiving and placing ontologies.

A partial characterization of existing foundational ontologies is briefly presented below. Note that documentation of a comprehensive characterization and comparison is beyond the scope of this section and would require an additional manuscript.

As for the numbers, the smallest are Sowa (with 30 classes, 5 relations, and 30 axioms), and BFO (36 classes linked through the taxonomic relationship 'is_a', making it a taxonomy rather than an ontology). While the Cyc figures are approximately 300,000 concepts, 3,000,000 assertions (facts and rules), and 15,000 relations, including in these numbers micro-theories. COSMO's numbers are also huge as it has 24,059 types (OWL classes), over 1,300 properties, and over 21,000 restrictions.

The foundational ontology in which its conceptualization is fully graphically represented is UFO, which is also in the framework of a layered ontological architecture (SEON [30]). Most of the rest use other logic-based formal representations, which are often not as easy to convey to many stakeholders, and are not explicitly represented in an ontological architecture.

On the other hand, a clear delegation of concerns to core ontologies is often not observed. For example, among the BFO 36 classes, are terms such as Process, Quality, and Temporal region that ThingFO delegates to lower levels. Similarly, UFO is made up of three ontologies at the upper level, however, ThingFO is the single ontology at that level and delegates the Process, Event, and Situation concerns at the core level.

Considering the terms, there is often a lack of consensus on semantic correspondence. For example, the DOLCE distinction between 'endurant' and 'perdurant' does not fully correspond to that established in GFO. Moreover, COSMO's great effort began as a way to tackle the problem of semantic interoperability by merging basic elements of Cyc, SUMO, and DOLCE, and adding new ones.

As commented in the Introduction Section, we have been developing domain ontologies since the beginning of 2000 without integrating them into any top-level ontology. More recently, when considering this improvement, we have been faced with the dilemma of adapting existing top-level ontologies to harmonize our previously developed ontologies, or conceiving a new foundational ontology that takes into account some of the best features of existing ones, and also the framework of a holistic ontological architecture.

When developing ThingFO, we have taken into account most of the principles, criteria and requirements mentioned above, e.g. the use of the UML graphical representation for the conceptualization of ThingFO, which is in the framework of a holistic ontological architecture based on MDA (see Fig. 3). In addition, we have considered the criterion of completeness of coverage but, at the same time, conciseness in representing the world through three key concepts, namely, Particular Thing, Universal Thing, and Assertion. It is worth remarking that the types of Assertions dealing with particulars and universals shown in Fig. 4 are not represented in this way in any of the quoted ontologies at the upper level. Lastly, ThingFO promotes a clear delegation of concepts such as those mentioned above (Process, Situation, and Event) to core ontologies under the principle of modularity and loose coupling.

In summary, the figures for the current version (v1.3) of ThingFO are 17 defined terms for Concepts, 15 defined terms for Concept Attributes, 3 specified axioms in first-order logic (plus those that should reuse from MOxFCD-Onto), and 12 defined terms for non-taxonomic relationships that are well balanced with the taxonomic relationships.

6   Conclusions and Future Work

This chapter has discussed the architectural aspects, concepts, relationships, and constraints of ThingFO, as well as its applicability.

Taking into account the architectural aspects, we have described FCD-OntoArch as the five-tier ontological architecture based on principles of modularization, reuse, and specialization of concepts and relationships at lower levels, which also include guidelines and rules to be followed in order to locate and harmonize both adapted and conceived ontologies in its layers. This multitier architecture promotes a clear separation of concerns by considering the ontological levels that allow the allocation of components appropriately. Furthermore, in Subsect. 2.3, we have discussed the need for a syntactic and semantic meta-layer on top of FCD-OntoArch, in which a meta-ontology must be formally represented to serve as a theory of lower-level ontologies. In this direction, it is proposed to reuse the MDA architecture, which is made up of recognized standards and languages in Information Systems and Software Engineering.

Regarding the concepts, relationships, and constraints of ThingFO, this foundational ontology is at the highest level of FCD-OntoArch, therefore lower-level ontologies benefit from reuse or specialization of its three key concepts, such as Thing (for particulars), Thing Category (for universals), and Assertion (for statements and representations of diverse aspects of both). So the main requirement to conceive ThingFO was to have a minimum set of particular and universal concepts that represent the world so that they can be reused and specialized, and ultimately can be useful and easy to adopt or adapt in all domains of different sciences. In a nutshell, the main aim is to have a large number of core and domain ontologies accessible under the umbrella of a complete but concise foundational ontology. For example, situation, process, event, quality, and quantity concerns, among others, are not represented in the ThingFO concepts as they usually are in all the other upper ontologies mentioned above. Thus, in our proposal, quality issues are represented in NFRsTDO (see Fig. 2), quantity issues are mainly represented in MetricsLDO and IndicatorsLDO, the dynamic aspect of particular events are represented in PEventCO, and so forth.

Concerning the applicability aspects of ThingFO, this chapter has illustrated the semantically enriched concepts of the SituationCO and ProcessCO ontologies, where their elements are, in turn, cross-cutting concerns primarily for top-domain or low-domain terminologies of any science. Particularly, to show the applicability of ThingFO alongside these two core ontologies, we have also dealt with the mechanism to not only enrich terms but also to reuse and specialize non-taxonomic relationships for a top-domain software testing ontology as well as addressing the benefit of reusing conceptual blocks or patterns. Furthermore, the non-taxonomic relationships of the SituationCO and ProcessCO ontologies were verified for their correct joint correspondence considering them as refinements –not as subsets– of those of ThingFO, following Rule #2 established in Subsect. 2.2.

It is worth mentioning some limitations of the present work. Some constructs used in ThingFO remain so far implicit and semi-formal. As noted at the end of Subsect. 2.3, the Concept, Particular Concept, Universal Concept, Assertion Concept, Individual Concept, Concept Attribute, Relation, and Constraint primitives, among others, are essential to specify MOxFCD-Onto as an ontological (formal) theory in the M2 layer and clarify the semantics and constraints of the key elements for all ontologies in the M1/M0 layers. This is a work in progress and will be documented in a follow-up manuscript. Additionally, in light of this effort, the current OWL implementation of ThingFO should also be reviewed.

Last but not least, ThingFO and FCD-OntoArch were validated by a couple of external experts, outside of the GIDIS_Web research group members, and based on their recommendations, some improvements were made. We are aware that further validation efforts are needed. Ultimately, if, as a produced artifact, the ThingFO ontology were adopted step by step by academia and industry, this would be a promising fact of its usefulness and validity.

Acknowledgments. This line of research is supported partially by the Engineering School at UNLPam, Argentina, in the project coded 09/F079. We warmly thank Maria Julia Blass and Silvio Gonnet (both CONICET researcher and professor at the National University of Technology, Santa Fe, Argentina) for the validation and feedback provided. Last but not least, I would like to thank

Pablo Becker and Guido Tebes (both GIDIS_Web research members at the Engineering School, UNLPam, Argentina) for the close collaboration on ThingFO.

References

1. Arp, R., Smith, B., Spear, A.D.: Building Ontologies with Basic Formal Ontology. The MIT Press (2015). https://doi.org/10.7551/mitpress/9780262527811.001.0001
2. Becker, P., Papa, M.F., Tebes, G., Olsina, L.: Analyzing a process core ontology and its usefulness for different domains. In: Springer Nature Switzerland AG book, CCIS 1439: International Conference on the Quality of Information and Communication Technology, A. C. R. Paiva et al. (Eds.): QUATIC'21, pp. 183–196, (2021)
3. Blas, M.J., Gonnet, S., Tebes, G., Becker, P., Olsina, L.: Ontology definition for the representation of behaviors based on events (in Spanish). In: ASSE'21, Argentine Symposium on Software Engineering, vol: 50 JAIIO, pp. 38–51, held virtually in Oct. 2021, Salta, Argentina, ISSN: 2451–7593 (2021)
4. Casellas, N., Blázquez, M., Kiryakov, A., Casanovas, P., Poblet, M., Benjamins, R.: OPJK into PROTON: legal domain ontology integration into an upper-level ontology. In: Meersman, R., Tari, Z., Herrero, P. (eds.) OTM 2005. LNCS, vol. 3762, pp. 846–855. Springer, Heidelberg (2005). https://doi.org/10.1007/11575863_106
5. D'Aquin, M., Gangemi, A.: Is there beauty in ontologies? Appl. Ontol. 6(3), 165–175 (2011)
6. Duric, D., Gasevic, D., Devedzic, V.: Ontology modeling and MDA. J. Object Technol. 4(1), 109–128 (2005)
7. Fensel, D.: Ontologies: A Silver Bullet for Knowledge Management and Electronic Commerce, 2nd edn. Springer-Verlag, Berlin, Heidelberg (2004)
8. Fleetwood, S.: The ontology of things, properties and powers. J. Critical Realism 8(3), 343–366 (2009)
9. Gruber, T.R.: A translation approach to portable ontologies. Knowl. Acquis. 5(2), 199–220 (1993)
10. Guarino, N., Schneider, L.: Ontology-driven conceptual modelling: advanced concepts. In: Spaccapietra, S., March, S.T., Kambayashi, Y. (eds.) ER 2002. LNCS, vol. 2503, pp. 12–12. Springer, Heidelberg (2002). https://doi.org/10.1007/3-540-45816-6_6
11. Guarino, N.: Semantic matching: formal ontological distinctions for information organization, extraction, and integration. In: Information Extraction A Multidisciplinary Approach to an Emerging Information Technology, Springer, Berlin Heidelberg, pp. 139–170 (1997). https://doi.org/10.1007/3-540-63438-X
12. Guizzardi, G.: Ontological foundations for structural conceptual models. PhD thesis, University of Twente, Enschede, The Netherlands (2005). ISBN 90–75176–81–3
13. Guizzardi, G., Falbo, R., Guizzardi, R.: Grounding software domain ontologies in the unified foundational ontology (UFO): the case of the ODE software process ontology. In: 11th Conferencia Iberoamericana de Software Engineering (CIbSE'08), pp. 127–140 (2008)
14. Haller, A., Polleres, A.: Are we better off with just one ontology on the Web? Semantic Web J. 11(1), 87–99 (2020)
15. Herre, H.: General formal ontology (GFO): A foundational ontology for conceptual modelling. In: Poli, R., Healy, M., Kameas, A. (eds.) Theory and Applications of Ontology: Computer Applications, pp. 297–345. Springer Netherlands, Dordrecht (2010). https://doi.org/10.1007/978-90-481-8847-5_14
16. Horsch, T., et al.: Pragmatic interoperability and translation of industrial engineering problems into modelling and simulation solutions. TR. No. 2020–A, 2nd Revised Version (2021). https://doi.org/10.5281/zenodo.4749106

17. ISO/IEC: International organization for standardization. Information technology - Top-level ontologies (TLO) - Part 1: Requirements. ISO/IEC Standard 21838–1, 1st Ed. 2021–08 (2021)
18. Lee, J., Chae, H., Kim, C., Kim, K.: Design of product ontology architecture for collaborative enterprises. Expert Syst. Appl. **36**(2 Part 1), 2300–2309 (2009). https://doi.org/10.1016/j.eswa.2007.12.042
19. Lenat, D., Guha, R. V.: CYC: A idterm Report. AI Mag. **11**(3), 32 (1990)
20. Mascardi, V., Cordì, V., Rosso, P.: A comparison of upper ontologies. WOA **2007**, 55–64 (2007)
21. Masolo, C., Borgo, S., Gangemi, A., Guarino, N., Oltramari, A., Schneider, L.: The Wonder-Web library of foundational ontologies (D17) (2002). http://wonderweb.man.ac.uk/deliverables.shtml
22. Mizoguchi, R.: YAMATO: yet another more advanced top-level ontology. In: Proceedings of the 6th Australasian Ontology Workshop, Adelaide, pp. 1–16 (2010)
23. Olsina, L.: Applicability of a foundational ontology to semantically enrich the core and domain ontologies. In: 13th International Joint Conference on Knowledge Discovery, Knowledge Engineering and Knowledge Management, Vol. 2: KEOD (Knowledge Engineering and Ontology Development), Portugal, pp. 111–119, ISBN 978–989–758–533–3 (2021)
24. Olsina, L., Becker, P., Peppino, D., Tebes, G.: Specifying the process model for systematic reviews: an augmented proposal. J. Softw. Eng. Res. Dev. (JSERD) **7**, 1–23 (2019). https://doi.org/10.5753/jserd.2019.460
25. Olsina, L., Martín, M.: Ontology for Software Metrics and Indicators, Journal of Web Engineering, Rinton Press, USA, vol. 2, no. 4, pp. 262–281, ISSN 1540–9589 (2004)
26. OMG, Object Management Group, SPEM: Software & Systems Process Engineering Meta-Model Specification, version 2.0 (2008)
27. OMG, Object Management Group, MDA: Model Driven Architecture Guide rev. 2.0 (2014)
28. Pease, A.: Ontology: A Practical Guide. Articulate Software Press, Angwin, CA (2011)
29. Ruiz, F., Hilera, J.R.: Using Ontologies in Software Engineering and Technology. Chapter 2, In: Ontologies in Software Engineering and Software Technology, Calero, C., Ruiz, F., Piattini, M., (Eds). Springer Berlin Heidelberg, pp . 49–102 (2006). https://doi.org/10.1007/3-540-34518-3_2
30. Ruy, F.B., Falbo, R.A., Barcellos, M.P., Costa, S.D., Guizzardi, G.: SEON: a software engineering ontology network. In: Blomqvist, E., Ciancarini, P., Poggi, F., Vitali, F. (eds.) EKAW 2016. LNCS (LNAI), vol. 10024, pp. 527–542. Springer, Cham (2016). https://doi.org/10.1007/978-3-319-49004-5_34
31. Scherp, A., Saathoff, C., Franz, T., Staab, S.: Designing core ontologies. Appl. Ontol. **6**(3), 177–221 (2011)
32. Schneider, L.: How to build a foundational ontology. In: Günter, A., Kruse, R., Neumann, B. (eds.) KI 2003. LNCS (LNAI), vol. 2821, pp. 120–134. Springer, Heidelberg (2003). https://doi.org/10.1007/978-3-540-39451-8_10
33. Sowa, J.: Knowledge Representation: Logical, Philosophical, and Computational Foundations. Brooks Cole Publishing, Pacific Grove (1999)
34. Tebes, G., Olsina, L., Peppino, D., Becker, P.: Specifying and analyzing a software testing ontology at the top-domain ontological level. J. Comput. Sci. Technol. **21**(2), 126–145 (2021). https://doi.org/10.24215/16666038.21.e12

Evidence in Policymaking: A Systematic Approach

Daniel Guzman Vargas[1,2]([✉]), Jente Versigghel[1,2], and Sidharta Gautama[1,2]

[1] Department of Industrial Systems Engineering and Product Design, Ghent University, Technologiepark 46, 9052 Gent-Zwijnaarde, Belgium
{Daniel.GuzmanVargas,Jente.Versigghel,Sidharta.Gautama}@UGent.be
[2] Flanders Make, B-3920 Lommel, Belgium

Abstract. Complexity in policymaking challenges policymakers in the design of the best policy alternative, and the consequent policy implementation strategy, to tackle complex social problems. In this paper, we explore a methodology for a Decision Support System that could help policymakers cope and incorporate the problems' complexity during the design and implementation of their policies. The methodology is based upon a systematic exploration of the problem space supported by expert knowledge and case study research to define the parameters that describe a given policy process. The relevance of the methodology in the context of the literature in policy failure and evidence-based policymaking is discussed. A small-scale experiment is set in the frame of Urban Vehicle Access Regulations in Europe where an application of the methodology suggests that the methodology could facilitate case data analysis, the identification of alternative policy configurations and key implementation aspects of the policy strategy, and the drafting of alternative scenarios based on possible configurations and strategies.

Keywords: Decision support systems · Urban vehicle access regulations · Wicked problems · Evidence-based policymaking

1 Introduction

Policymakers have the crucial task to develop innovative solutions to increasingly complex policy problems which requires of sophisticated analysis on the facts with strong foundations on logic, knowledge and experience rather than on political interests or the bargaining of conflicting interest groups [1, 2]. Ideally, a policymaker that has to make, wants to make or, is able to make a decision about a given problem should not only select the 'best policy alternative but also, the best political strategy for the adoption and implementation of this alternative' [3]. A very difficult task, nonetheless, considering the "genuine uncertainty" inherent to complex social problems and the "bounded rationality" policymakers face in the policymaking process [4–11].

In contrast with most of the problems in science or engineering, complex social problems, sometimes referred as "wicked" problems, generally lack clarity in their problem definition, present conflicting perspectives, and may not have an associated optimal solution [6, 12, 13]. Considering the rather discouraging characteristics of wicked problems,

A. Fred et al. (Eds.): IC3K 2021, CCIS 1718, pp. 100–117, 2023.
https://doi.org/10.1007/978-3-031-35924-8_6

how should one deal with wicked problems? a general conclusion seems to be that "the methods for problem handling appropriate to pacified conditions do not transfer to more turbulent and problematic environments" generally ascribed to wicked problems [14]. Work in [14] suggests that when dealing with "wicked" problems, decision-makers are more likely to use a method and find it useful if it:

- accommodates multiple alternative perspectives,
- can facilitate negotiating a joint agenda,
- functions through interaction and iteration,
- generates ownership of the problem formulation and its action implications through transparency of representation.

These requirements outline the specifications of a decision support system (DSS) appropriate to wicked problems. According to [14] the technical attributes of such a system are the following:

- **Representing problem complexity graphically** rather than algebraically or in tables of numerical results will aid participation.
- **Systematic exploration of the solution space.** "Lay people can generally express their judgments more meaningfully by choosing between discrete alternatives rather than across continuous variables."
- **Identification of relevant possibilities** rather than estimation numerical probabilities.
- **Alternative scenarios** instead of future forecasts.

We study in this paper a methodology for a DSS that, making use of the requirements presented in [14], feeds from expert knowledge and policy-related evidence to support decision-makers in the policy-making process. This paper extends the work of the authors in [15] with an extended data set of case studies and discussions on the relevance of the methodology in the context of policy failure and the role of evidence in policymaking.

The reminder of this paper consists of 5 parts. First, we frame the methodology in the context of the literature in policy failure and policy success. Next, we present the methodology as described in [15]. Then we describe an application use case for the methodology: the development and implementation of *Urban Vehicle Access Regulations* (UVARs) in Europe. We perform a small-scale experiment of 11 city case implementations. Finally, we present the conclusions to our findings and prospects for further research.

2 Policy Failure, Policy Success, and the Role of Evidence in Policymaking

2.1 On Policy Failure and Success

The definition of policy failure (and by analogy of policy success) is contested by two main schools of thought. "Purely relativists" argue that policy failure and success in policymaking are inherently subjective "interest'"-inspired assessments of different policy actors thus lacking the minimum requirements to achieve an objective classification [16, 17]. Other kind of work, however, rejects this relativistic approach, focusing on describing and analyzing different kinds of policy "success" and "failure". This "rationalistic" stream of literature deals with policy failure as the opposite to policy success: "whatever does not succeed is a failure" [16]. In this line of research, we can, for instance, define policy success as a policy "that achieves the goals that proponents set out to achieve and attracts no criticism of any significance and/or support is virtually universal" [18].

Furthermore, scholars of policy failure have found that "clearly identifiable policy failures have tended to occur only in very specific circumstances and have little to do with the psychological propensities of policy participant" [19]. Table 1 presents a synthesis of the sources of policy failure as found by academics of policy failure.

Table 1. Sources of policy failure.

Source of policy failure	Bibliography
Overreaching government attempting to address "unaddressable" or "wicked" problems, without properly identifying neither a cause of nor a solution to such problems	[20, 21]
Governments failing to properly anticipate (adverse) policy consequences or risk of system failures	[22–24]
Implementation failures often due to a lack of effective oversight over implementers on the part of decision-makers (e.g., funding, legitimacy issues, etc.)	[25–27]
Governments and policymakers failing to learn the appropriate lessons from their own and other government's previous experiences due to ineffective or inappropriate policy monitoring and/or feedback processes and structures	[28, 29]

2.2 Coping with Failure and the Role of Evidence in Policymaking

Proponents of evidence-based policymaking suggest that better information management in policymaking can lead to improvements in the policy process that can help policymakers cope with each of these sources of failure (Table 1) [11, 13, 17, 19, 30–32].

Similarly, scholars of policy transfer propose that the experience of other governments can be used as a source of ideas and evidence that could spark the decision-making process and contribute to the development of successful and more effective policies, as long as the differences in political systems and environments are understood and assimilated into the transfer process [33–35]. This trend continues in the field of policy learning, where it is suggested that governments could withdraw lessons from their counterparts involved in similar problems, which would help them find solutions and deal with their own problems. This in such a way that "if the lesson is positive, a policy that works is transferred, with suitable adaptations. If it is negative, observers learn what not to do from watching the mistakes of others" [36].

These similar, yet different, approaches to evidence in policymaking suggest that evidence-driven policymaking could contribute to more effective policy designs through the provision of greater amounts of evidentiary policy-relevant data collected by means of rigorous research and evaluation of both one's own and similar programs [13, 19,

33]. However, the role that this information may have on the design of effective policies is constrained by the policymakers' "policy analytical capacity", i.e., the ability to perform applied research and data modeling methods, as well as data analysis techniques, such as trend analysis and forecasting methods, to anticipate future policy impacts and developments [19]. As such, these ideas help us frame the relevance of the methodology described in [15] and analyzed in this paper as a tool for evidence-driven policymaking that could facilitate the analysis of the collected policy-relevant data thus increasing the "policy analytical capacity" of policymakers.

3   Methodology

In this section, we briefly present the methodology presented in [15]. This methodology "aims to support policymakers in the understanding of the complexity of the policy problems. Helping them through with a broader notion of the solution space and an easier visualization of the problem's complexity" through a systematic approach that combines expert knowledge and policy-relevant information.

The methodology consists of a twofold coding process that "could facilitate the identification of patterns in the description of empirical evidence [...] and work as a rubric for the collection of case data."

3.1   Parametrization of the Solution Space

Here the relevant factors that interact in the development of a policy solution to a specific policy problem are identified and defined. For this, three types of parameters should be considered:

- *Contextual Parameters*: These parameters define the context in which the policy problems take place. They reflect the environment in which the policy problem is framed, the factors that can influence governmental decisions, and the elements that policymakers aim to influence with their decisions.
- *Control Parameters*: These parameters shape the overall policy from a strategic point of view. They correspond to all the relevant factors that policymakers could control in order to implement their policies.
- *Time*: Time helps define the dynamics of the policy process, providing coherence and logic to its narrative [37]. Additionally, time and timing in politics are a big deal. Timing can be a strategic tool [38]; it can constraint the opportunity for the development of a policy – "policy window" [39]; and it defines the life-span of a policy – policy cycle [17, 40]. Policymakers make decisions that affect and mold social systems, and consequently, this new state of the affairs demands a reaction from policymakers. This never-ending series of discrete events describes both the path taken by the policymakers in solving a policy problem (policy strategy) and its implications and effects on the system.

The definition of the parameters is achieved through expert knowledge. A commission of experts on the specific policy provides the first input to the framework. Academics, policy consultants, and other practitioners immerse in the implementation and development of such policies are put together to find a consensus on the parameters relevant to the policy process. Their input consists of the set of categorical parameters that best describe the policy context (contextual parameters) and the elements of the policy strategy (control parameters). The quality of the outcome of the methodology is therefore dependent on the quality of the expert's commission.

3.2 Definition of the Policy Life Cycle

In the process of defining the parameters of the solution space, the group of experts should be asked to think about the different stages that comprise the development of the policy strategy from its conception until after its implementation. For this, the participants are referred to the policy cycle for inspiration. The policy cycle intends to simplify the policy process by deconstructing it into discrete stages that describe the chronology of the policy process. The policy cycle helps dive into the complexity of policymaking and in spite of its drawbacks, such as its excessive generality ("practice varies from problem to problem"), the policy cycle framework is a good heuristic in policymaking for the answer to the question "what to do now?" [41].

The policy cycle consists of five discrete stages used to describe the chronology of the policy process; these are [40]:

- Agenda setting. Here a problem is defined and recognized, and the need for intervention is expressed.
- Policy formulation. At this stage, the objectives of a subsequent policy are defined and alternatives for action are considered.
- Decision-making. Here the final adoption, i.e., a final course of action, is formally set.
- Implementation. At this stage, the policy adopted is executed or enforced.
- Evaluation. Here the effects, both intended and unintended, of the implemented policy are assessed in relation with the objectives previously set and the current problem perception (agenda). Outcome of the evaluation may lead to a continuation, a termination or a re-design of the policy.

The framework relies on the policy cycle only as a source of inspiration. Participants should be allowed to modify the stages, or even define new ones, in the way their experience find it more suitable. With this new, "customized" definition of the policy cycle (hereinafter *policy life cycle*), the participants can trigger the discussion on the parameters, both *contextual* and of *control*, that may play a role at each policy stage.

The policy life cycle is then used as a "custom" tool in the parametrization process that contributes to the definition of detailed elements that are part of a policy strategy and that may have been difficult to foresee at a higher level. Additionally, the linear temporality of the process provides streamlined thinking, and a conception of the parameters as changing elements in a policy as a sequence of discrete events that describes the change of state of a (set of) parameter(s) as the policy matures. During this process, relationships between the parameters may arise and their use in finding new parameters not yet defined should be encouraged. However, participants should be asked to focus on the identification of the parameters only: the magnitude and characteristics of these relationships albeit relevant should not be discussed here.

4 A Systematic Look at Urban Vehicle Access Regulations in Europe

In this section we investigate the application of the methodology to the case of Urban Vehicle Access Regulations (UVARs) in Europe.

UVARs are measures to regulate the access of urban vehicles to urban infrastructure in order to cope with societal challenges that markets alone cannot address [42]. The objective of such policies is generally dealing with the negative externalities generated by traffic: pollution, congestion, traffic-related accident rates, infrastructure costs, liveability and quality of urban space [42–45]. Given the range of objectives, magnitude of the problems, urban contexts, and political landscapes, UVARs may take many forms:

- *Low emission zones* (LEZs), for example, are designated areas where the access of polluting vehicles is restricted or penalized [42].
- *Congestion charging* (CC) refers to the imposition of a fee to access congested downtown areas during a specified time frame [46].
- *Vehicle access bans* - partially or total - such as the *limited traffic zones* (commonly known in Italy as *Zona a traffico limitato*) or pedestrian zones [47].
- Traffic cell architecture where traffic between cells is limited by design [47], e.g., *Superblock Scheme* in Barcelona.
- *Hybrid*. UVARs can be implemented independently or be designed as a combination (hybrid) of them, e.g., CC with differential "emission" fees [47].

The negative externalities caused by traffic are significantly harmful in urban areas due to the high concentration of people. With over 200 LEZs in place across Europe [48], the widespread of UVARs highlights the intention of decision makers across Europe in dealing with such externalities by implementing UVARs.

However, the implementation of restrictive and prohibitory policies, as in the case of UVARs, is generally accompanied by strong public and political controversy. Therefore, public acceptability of a proposed UVAR plays a major role in determining whether the public accepts or rejects the scheme, or in other words, whether or not the proposed measure survives the policy process [42, 46].

The methodology here presented was applied to the case of UVARs in the frame of the European Commission H2020 project *ReVeAL* - Regulating Vehicle Access for improved Liveability (grant agreement No. 815008). ReVeAL is an R&I project which mission is to enable cities to optimize urban space and transport network usage through new and integrated packages of urban vehicle access policies and technologies. With this goal in mind, an expert commission consisting of academics, practitioners, and consultants with ample European experience on urban planning, transport planning, quality assurance, drafting and development of urban mobility projects was put together in a series of workshops to follow the methodology, i.e., to define the Policy (UVAR) Life Cycle and perform the parametrization of the solution space (Fig. 1).

4.1 The Policy Life Cycle of UVARs

The UVAR life cycle was defined by the experts' commission as consisting of four phases:

- *Ideation phase:* Timespan in which problems come to the attention of governments (Agenda-setting) and a set of solutions emerges in response. It is characterized by the identification and the incomplete definitions of the problem. This stage only ends when a problem is re-conceptualized or redefined in such a way that a range of feasible solutions becomes imaginable. The solutions in the stage can be found in a conceptual stage, the details of the scheme (Use of technology, communication strategy, etc.) are not necessarily discussed in this phase.

- *Design phase:* Time span by which UVAR measure's designs are developed in more detail. In this stage, the UVAR measure's initial concept is worked out. Multiple

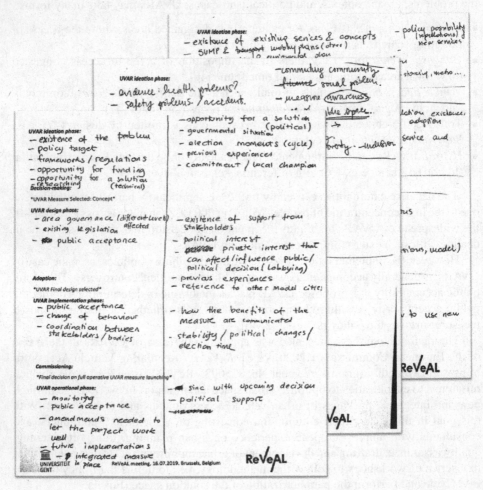

Fig. 1. Example of workshop notes collected.

designs may be considered here; alternative enforcement technologies, different communication strategies, etc. The alternative assessment results in a proposal for the technical and strategic design of the UVAR measure.

- *Implementation phase:* Involves executing the policy option selected at the decision-making phase. This involves all the necessary action to put the UVAR measure into practice – if applicable: pilots, demos, referendum, establishing of communication channels, legal permits, etc.
- *Operation phase:* Here all the activities following the launching of the UVAR measure (full scale) take place. This may include the monitoring and evaluation of the measure, the coupling with new (future) UVAR measures, feedback collection and design fine-tuning, etc.

Additionally, from the definition of the policy life cycle for UVARs, three "policy gates" where identified. These "gates" are specific points in time defined by a set of specific events that determine the end of a phase and/or the beginning of a new one. The "gates" are:

- *Decision-making gate:* The actual decision on a particular course of action to follow is made here – selection of the UVAR measure at a conceptual level.
- *Adoption gate:* The legitimization of the UVAR measure takes place here. In this gate, the final design is approved for implementation. The outcome of this stage is affected by the technical feasibility of the design and/or the political feasibility of implementing the measure.
- *Commissioning gate:* Final decision needed for the full-scale implementation/operation is made here.

Together, the four phases and the three gates define the policy life cycle of an UVAR. Figure 2 is a representation of the UVAR life cycle as depicted by the expert's commission. Making use of their own depiction of the Policy life cycle, participants continued to perform the parametrization of the solution space.

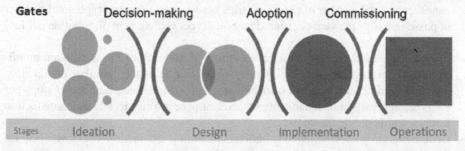

Fig. 2. Policy life cycle of an urban vehicle access regulation. Taken from [15].

4.2 Parametrization of the UVAR Solution Space

Participants found inspiration in the work of [49] on the monitoring of sustainable mobility in cities for the definition of the *contextual parameters*. Through a review of relevant and scientifically sound indicators applicable in different social and economic contexts, [49] identified a set of indicators that could be applied for the purposes of self-evaluation of a city's mobility system, monitoring, policy assessment, bench-marking assessment between cities and back-casting.

Participants were familiar with the set of indicators defined in [49] from the application of such indicators by the European Commision (cf. EC SUMI) and the World Business Council for Sustainable Development (cf. SiMPlify mobility tool). Based on their experience with this indicator set, however, the group of experts found it more appropriate to focus on the set of parameters used for the calculation of such indicators rather than on the indicator set perse. This to avoid further assessment and discussions on the validity of each indicator as a metric, methodological issues in their determination and pre-assessment of the raw data. Additionally, by doing so, the data collected allows for the calculation of this or any other set of indicators when performing an analysis, or to work with the granular information if appropriate. Subsequently, participants reached consensus on a total of 35 *contextual parameters*. These parameters can be grouped into five clusters that could later be used to monitor and evaluation of a city context, UVAR assessment and between-city benchmarking. The clusters that group the *contextual parameters* correspond to:

- *General information:* A set of parameters that includes GDP, surface of target area, distribution of direct land use for mobility (roads, railways, inland ports and waterways, bus lanes, etc.), distribution of indirect land use for mobility (public and private parking, service areas, logistic centers, stations, etc.), and availability of functional activities in target area (business, energy resources, hospitals, schools, etc.).
- *Demographic information:* This set accounts for number of inhabitants, gender and age distribution of population, distribution of inhabitants by employment status, distribution of the average monthly income per inhabitant, and average household size.
- *Transport information:* This set of parameters covers the total length of the road network and its distribution according to use (30 km/h zones, bike lanes, pedestrian zones, etc.), total number of passenger trips per year per transport type, total number of passenger trips per year per shared mobility type, vehicle fleet distribution per fuel type.
- *Effects on inhabitants:* 7 parameters capturing availability of PT and shared mobility modes, average monthly ticket price for public transport, number of ticketing machines and offices, size and distribution of PT vehicle fleet, number of stops per PT type, distribution of inhabitants by level of accessibility to PT, user satisfaction levels towards public transport.
- *General mobility information:* 8 parameters including satisfaction level towards noise level, quality of air, and public spaces, traffic accident rate, average distance work-home, main mode of transport work-home, average travel time to work and back home.

For the *control parameters*, the process yielded a total of 23 parameters. These parameters arose from the experience of the participants gained through their academic and research background, through the development, implementation and evaluation of

UVARs in different cities across Europe, and through their participation on the development, implementation and audit of (sustainable) urban mobility plans in several cities across Europe, as well as other relevant experience. This set of parameters can be used to describe the policy process of UVARs across its *Policy Life Cycle* (Fig. 2). The set of parameters can be grouped into four thematic clusters, these are:

- *System design/technology:* Here the focus is on the availability, functionality, and status of UVAR-related systems – and the technologies that make up these systems – in a city throughout the UVAR life cycle. It covers aspects directly related to the way in which an UVAR operates (enforcement technology, and when applicable systems for application, issuing and payment of permits), the technological options used for monitoring of externalities caused by traffic and evaluation of UVAR (e.g., quality of air, congestion), communication channels used during the deployment (broadcasting vs tailored, online vs traditional) of UVARs and for the provision of UVAR-related information to users (e.g., variable message signs, car navigation systems).

- *Governance:* This set of parameters relates to the availability and types of legal frameworks, political instruments, and planning instruments that can support the development of different UVAR types. Details on participatory and transparency issues such as the availability and types of communication endeavors and public consultation processes. Additionally, some of the parameters in this clusters intend to capture the actors and/or institutions that shape, influence and/or make decisions, and provide or facilitate funding for UVARs.

- *User needs:* The focus here is on whether the different relevant user groups (frequent and non-frequent users, transport mode specific users, goods traffic) and stakeholders have been identified at any given point of the process. The parameters also intend to describe whether user needs have been included (taken into account) during the life cycle, the existence (and types) of stakeholder engagement processes, and which design aspects and/or adaptation relate to specific user needs. Additionally, this set of indicators intents to capture events along the policy life cycle that directly address different stakeholders, classifying stakeholder groups into interest groups (car lobbyists, citizen or environmental groups, political parties, etc.) and vulnerable groups (age, disability, gender, ethnicity, socio-economic, etc.). Finally, some of the parameters in this cluster intend to monitor the tone of the general opinion, the level of acceptability towards the measure, and the main arguments for and against the measure.

- *Mobility services and concepts:* This set of parameters focuses on the types of activities/development, and the status of such activities, in the city related to improvements in public transport (e.g., fleet renewal to reduce emissions, increase of the service), enhancement of soft mobility (e.g., extension of pedestrian networks, provision of bike facilities), changes in the parking system (e.g., improvement of enforcement capacity, modification of on-street/off-street parking supply), enhancement of shared mobility (e.g., bike, car, van sharing systems), improvements in urban logistics (e.g., last mile delivery projects and promotion, urban logistics infrastructure/platforms/hubs), and low emission vehicles and ITS (intelligent transportation system) developments (e.g., charging network for EVs, introduction of platforms to combine multiple mobility modalities, enhancement or promotion of cleaner taxis and private hire vehicles).

These parameters, both contextual and of control, in combination with the *policy life cycle* (Fig. 2) should facilitate the description of the UVAR process and the identification of the main variables in the process.

4.3 UVAR City Cases

To visualize the possibilities of our approach, we make use of a set of 11 different case studies covering 11 European cities that have implemented different UVAR measures (Table 2). Case study researchers have been given the set of parameters and the *policy life cycle* as a rubric for the collection of policy-relevant data. In this way, researchers were asked to use the definition of the different stages of the UVAR life cycle and the different parameter categories to focus and direct their research.

Table 2. List of city case studies and respective UVAR measure.

City	UVAR Measure	Geographical Scope	Description
Milan, Italy	CC applied to a perimeter	City center	If a vehicle enters the charging zone at defined moments, it needs to pay the congestion charge. Exemptions are foreseen for low pollutant vehicles
Barcelona, Spain	Superblock strategy	Neighborhood (Multiple neighborhoods)	Limiting motorized vehicle access within a combination of various building blocks in the city into one superblock of around 400mx400m
Bologna, Italy	LTZ	City center	LTZ with access enabled through purchase of permits and time periods, and with limited exemptions
La Rochelle, France	Delivery regulations	City center	Polluting (delivery) vehicles are gradually restricted

(continued)

Table 2. (*continued*)

City	UVAR Measure	Geographical Scope	Description
Ghent, Belgium	Traffic circulation plan	City center	Limiting through traffic and increasing accessibility by sustainable transport modes by dividing the city in nonconnected sectors and car-free areas
Gr. London, Great Britain	Pollution charge	City center	Polluting vehicles entering the zone must pay the pollution charge
Mechelen, Belgium	Cycling zone	City center	City center is converted to a cycle zone, where cyclists have priority and motorized vehicles are considered guests
Amsterdam, The Netherlands	Low emission zone	City	Limited circulation for certain polluting vehicle types
Groningen, The Netherlands	Traffic circulation plan	City center	Limiting through traffic and increasing accessibility by sustainable transport modes by dividing the city in nonconnected sectors and car-free areas
Oslo, Norway	Limited parking availability	City center	Removing on-street parking spaces, transforming those spaces to public space
Stuttgart, Germany	Low emission zone	City	Limited circulation for certain polluting vehicle types

Before the beginning of the documentation, case study researchers were presented with the third parameter: time. Researchers were asked to focus on the chronology of the events that describe the process, making note of the time of occurrence of each event. Accounting for time as one of the relevant parameters means that the outcome of the data collection process will yield a timeline of data points containing the main events that describe the process (hereinafter process timeline), alongside changes in contextual parameters.

Finally, researchers had the task of reporting for each event the source of their information, e.g., academic papers, interviews, emails, etc. Thus, each event should be backed entirely by one (or a combination) of these sources and be independent of the researcher's understanding of the process.

5 Discussion

The identification of the events in the *process timeline* that correspond to the "policy gates" helps us define the *policy life cycle*. Figure 3 shows the *policy life cycle* for each of the 11 city cases.

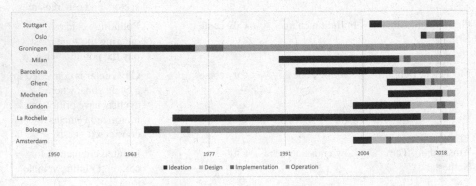

Fig. 3. Policy *life cycle* of city case studies.

From Fig. 3 we can see, for instance, that a constant throughout all the cases is the short span of the *implementation phase* (followed behind by the *design phase*) with respect to the *ideation phase*. This falls in line with the findings in [15]. The short span of the *implementation phase* seems to be a strategic choice which allows decision-makers to redirect the public and political debate away from mere assumptions on the impacts the measure may have once implemented towards the real impacts and perceptions of a "tangible" scheme. The rapid implementation process is again a motivation for the support of policymakers in the quick design of robust policy strategies.

Figure 4 illustrates the *parameterized instance* of the case study for the city of Ghent, i.e., a depiction of the data parametrization and categorization of the data collected by the case study researchers for the case of Ghent, Belgium on the circulation plan implemented in 2017. This *parameterized instance* facilitates the visualization and identification of patterns in the data in a simpler manner. Here, each row corresponds to an UVAR-related event, and each black box corresponds to the "activation" of a *control* parameter triggered in a given event. This could be, for instance, the renovation of public transport infrastructure in the *ideation* phase (See event (a) in Fig. 4), a call for a referendum from part of citizen groups opposing the UVAR measure in the *design* phase (See event (b) in Fig. 4), the allocation of *Park and Ride* (P + R) locations to complement the UVAR measure in the *implementation* phase (See event (c) in Fig. 4), or the beginning of participatory workshops to gather citizen feedback on the measure in the *operation* phase (See event (d) in Fig. 4).

From a between city analysis of the parameterized instances we can see, for instance, that monitoring activities, whether monitoring of air quality or traffic, are a common

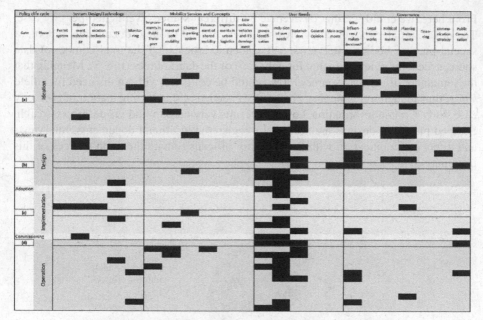

Fig. 4. Parameterized *instance* - Case study Ghent. Taken from [15].

theme in the *ideation* phase. Its occurrence is directly linked to the problem identification and definition. Other common themes include plans, research, communication and participation activities, changes in legal frameworks, formation of political alliances, and the implementation of initial (complementary) measures to tackle the defined problems. The number of complementary measures implemented generally increases as we approach the commissioning gate. For instance, we can see how improvements in public transport linked to an increase of supply and/or economic incentives for the use of public transport, appear mainly in Bologna, Amsterdam, Milan, and London. This finding aligns with the notion that this kind of interventions are of special importance in restrictive and prohibitory measures such as LEZs, LTZs, or CCs in order to provide an alternative to private vehicles [50].

Additionally, we could observe that the conception of an UVAR is commonly one of the components of a major political instrument, instead of a stand-alone measure, this seems to help provide a context and a purpose to the measure, aligning it with the goals of the city and showcasing the UVAR measure as a part of a "consistent" and carefully crafted vision of the city.

Finally, since the outcome of the coding process (*contextual* and *control* parameters, and *policy life cycle*) can be used as a rubric that highlights the important factors case study researchers should consider during the data collection process, we should take a look at the implications of its utilization for this purpose. Based on the data collected, we could observe that case study researchers could find a major proportion of the information through desktop research, before going into the field to corroborate and complement their findings, e.g., through interviews or field visits. For the 11 city case studies, on average 46 events were registered in the *process timelines* for each city case study.

From here, we could see that on average 52 different sources were cited per city case. The different data sources cover press releases, official (policy) documents, reports of special-purpose bodies, interviews, and academic articles. Of the total number of data sources, field interviews account for only 20% of the data sources (Fig. 5). Meaning that the remainder of the data sources (80%) could be collected without the need for a field study, thus reducing the number of resources needed in the documentation of each city case study. Certain information, however, results very hard to find via desktop research. Scraped plans and designs are not usually registered in official documents. Interviews and direct communication with (former) city officials remain the main sources of this information.

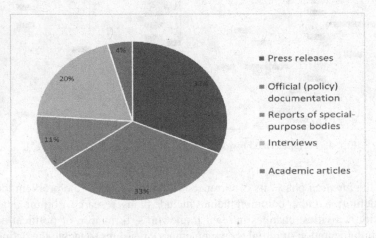

Fig. 5. Distribution of the different data sources across all the city case studies.

Additionally, it is remarkable that very few events rely on academic articles or other academic sources. Academic literature mostly focuses on well-studied, highly influencing measures, e.g., Milan, London. The gap in literature regarding UVARs was made evident during this study. An unexpected finding considering how frequent UVAR implementations are in the European landscape.

We can see how the proposed methodology could be used to identify patterns and common trends in the policy process that can give light into crucial aspects of a policy strategy, and thus support policymakers in the implementation and development of such policies. The methodology could thus benefit of an integration with advanced data analysis techniques (e.g., trend analysis and predictive models). The small sample size (number of case studies), however, limits the statistical significance of the results. This in combination with the heterogeneity of the sample (in terms of their urban landscapes, and UVAR types), hinders the identification of useful patterns among the *contextual parameters* that could help us support the validity of these parameters or assess the findings in [49]. We believe, nonetheless, that the findings here summarized can illustrate the potential of the methodology in the assessment of policy processes and inspire future research on the matter.

6 Conclusions and Future Work

In this paper, we have explored the methodology described in [15]. The methodology is based upon a systematic exploration of the problem space supported by expert knowledge and case study research to define the parameters that describe a given policy process, to provide non-binding guidance in the collection of case data, and to allow for a systematic interpretation of the empirical evidence collected in the case studies, facilitating the identification of patterns – and their underlying relationships in both within and across case analysis.

A small-scale application of the methodology to the case of Urban Vehicle Access Regulations (UVARs) in Europe was performed in the frame of the EC H2020 project ReVeAL (grant agreement No. 815008). The experiment suggests that the methodology could facilitate the identification of patterns and trends in the case data that could be otherwise hard to see given the amount of data and variables, the identification of possible policy configurations (i.e., configurations of control parameters) and the drafting of alternative scenarios based on the possible configurations. As such, the methodology could benefit of an integration with advance data analysis techniques (e.g., trend analysis and predictive models). However, given the small sample size and the number of parameters, more work should be done regarding the contextual parameters. A larger sample size and/or a more concise set of parameters could give light into a methodology for the trend analysis within-cities and bench-marking both within- and between cities.

Furthermore, the proposed methodology seems to facilitate the data collection process, supporting desktop research and reducing the time and effort needed for field research. The importance of field research, however, continues to be relevant in developing the case studies.

Finally, a limitation of the study relates to the type of implementations studied (case studies). It would be interesting to study the impact of the methodology when applied to unsuccessful UVAR implementations as this could help extend the validation of the methodology regarding its application in the identification of causes for failure (and not only to success as it was the case in this study).

Acknowledgements. The ReVeAL project (Regulating Vehicle Access for Improved Liveability) is a CIVITAS initiative funded by the European Union's Horizon 2020 research and innovation program under grant agreement No 815069. The project will help to add Urban Vehicle Access Regulations (UVAR) to the standard range of urban mobility transition approaches of cities across Europe.

References

1. Schneider, A.L., Ingram, H.: Public policy and democratic citizenship: what kinds of citizenship does policy promote? In: Handbook of Public Policy Analysis: Theory, Politics, and Methods (2017)
2. Howlett, M., Mukherjee, I., Woo, J.J.: From tools to toolkits in policy design studies: the new design orientation towards policy formulation research. Policy Polit., vol. 43, no. 2, (2015)
3. Behn, R.D.: Policy analysis and policy politics. Policy Stud. Rev. Annu. **7**(2), 199–226 (1981)

4. Ritchey, T.: Wicked Problems – Social Messes (2011)
5. Langlois, R.N., Everett, M.J.: Complexity, genuine uncertainty, and the economics of organization. Hum. Syst. Manag., **11**(2), (1992)
6. Weber, E.P., Khademian, A.M.: Wicked problems, knowledge challenges, and collaborative capacity builders in network settings. Public Adm. Rev., **68**(2), (2008)
7. Simon, H.A.: Bounded rationality and organizational learning. Organ. Sci. **2**(1), (1991)
8. Lindblom, C.E., Cohen, D.K., Warfield, J.N.: Usable knowledge, social science and social problem solving. IEEE Trans. Syst. Man Cybernet. **10**(5), (1980)
9. Nair, S., Howlett, M.: Policy myopia as a source of policy failure: adaptation and policy learning under deep uncertainty. Policy Polit., vol. **45**(1), (2017)
10. Dequech, D.: Bounded rationality, institutions, and uncertainty. J. Econ. Issues **35**(4), (2001)
11. Sanderson, I.: Complexity, 'practical rationality' and evidence-based policy making. Policy Polit. **34**(1), (2006)
12. Head, B.W., Alford, J.: Wicked problems: implications for public policy and management. Adm. Soc. **47**(6), (2015)
13. Head, B.W.: Toward more 'Evidence-Informed' policy making? Public Adm. Rev. **76**(3), (2016)
14. Rosenhead, J.: What's the problem? An introduction to problem structuring methods. Interfaces (Providence), **26**(6), (1996)
15. Guzman Vargas, D., Gautama, S.: Support in policymaking: a systematic exploration of the policymaking process. In: Proceedings of the 13th International Joint Conference on Knowledge Discovery, Knowledge Engineering and Knowledge Management, vol. 2: KEOD, ISBN 978–989–758–533–3, pp. 120–127 (2021). https://doi.org/10.5220/0010641600003064
16. Howlett, M.: The lessons of failure: learning and blame avoidance in public policy-making. Int. Political Sci. Rev. **33**(5), 539–555 (2012). https://doi.org/10.1177/01925121112453603
17. Howlett, M., Ramesh, M., Perl, A.: Studying Public Policy: Policy Cycles and Policy Subsystems, vol. 3. Oxford University Press, Oxford (2009)
18. McConnell, A.: Policy success, policy failure and grey areas in-between. J. Public Policy **30**(3), (2010)
19. Howlett, M.: Policy analytical capacity and evidence-based policy-making: Lessons from Canada. Can. Public Adm. **52**(2), (2009)
20. Churchman, C.W.: Wicked problems [Guest Editorial]. Manage. Sci. **14**(4), (1967)
21. Pressman, J.L., Wildavsky, A.B.: Implementation: how great expectations in Washington are dashed in Oakland. Oakl. Proj. Ser., (1973)
22. Bovens, M., Hart, P.: Frame multiplicity and policy fiascoes: limits to explanation. Knowl. Policy **8**(4), 61–82 (1995). https://doi.org/10.1007/BF02832230
23. Perrow, C.: Normal accidents : living with high risk technologies - Updated Edition. (1999)
24. Roots, R.I.: When laws backfire unintended consequences of public policy. Am. Behav. Sci. **47**(11), 1376–1394 (2004)
25. Kerr, D.H.: The logic of 'Policy' and successful policies. Policy Sci., **7**(3), (1976)
26. Lupia, A., Mccubbins, M.D.: Learning from oversight: fire alarms and police patrols reconstructed. J. Law, Econ. Organ. **10**(1), (1994)
27. McCubbins, M.D., Schwartz, T.: Congressional Oversight Overlooked: Police Patrols versus Fire Alarms. Am. J. Pol. Sci. **28**(1), (1984)
28. May, P.J.: Policy learning and failure. J. Public Policy **12**(4), 331–354 (1992). https://doi.org/10.1017/S0143814X00005602
29. Scharpf, F.W.: Policy failure and institutional reform: why should form follow function? Int. Soc. Sci. J. **38**, (1986)
30. Cartwright, N., Hardie, J.: Evidence-based policy: a practical guide to doing it better. J. Soc. Policy **42**(33), (2012)

31. Nam, T.: Do the right thing right! Understanding the hopes and hypes of data-based policy. Gov. Inf. Q., **37**(3), (2020)
32. Head, B.W.: Reconsidering evidence-based policy: key issues and challenges. Policy Soc. **29** (2), (2010)
33. Mossberger, K., Wolman, H.: Policy transfer as a form of prospective policy evaluation: challenges and recommendations. Public Adm. Rev., **63**(4), (2003)
34. Dolowitz, D., Marsh, D.: Who learns what from whom: a review of the policy transfer literature. Polit. Stud., **44**(2), (1996)
35. Dolowitz, D.P., Marsh, D.: Learning from abroad: the role of policy transfer in contemporary policy-making. Governance **13**(1), (2000)
36. Rose, R.: What is lesson-drawing? J. Public Policy, **11** (1), (1991)
37. Massey, D.: Politics and space/time. Theory and Methods: Critical Essays in Human Geography (2017)
38. Djourelova, M., Durante, R.: Media attention and strategic timing in politics: evidence from U.S. presidential executive orders. Econ. Work. Pap. (2019)
39. Kingdon, J.W.: Agendas, Alternatives, and Public Policy (2014)
40. Jann, W., Wegrich, K.: Theories of the policy cycle. Handbook of Public Policy Analysis: Theory, Politics, and Methods (2017)
41. Bridgman, P., Davis, G.: What use is a policy cycle? Plenty, if the aim is clear. Australian J. Public Adm. **62**(3), 98–102 (2003). https://doi.org/10.1046/j.1467-8500.2003.00342.x
42. Lopez, O.N.: Urban vehicle access regulations. In: Zeimpekis, V., Aktas, E., Bourlakis, M., Minis, I. (eds.) Sustainable Freight Transport: Theory, Models, and Case Studies, pp. 139–163. Springer International Publishing, Cham (2018). https://doi.org/10.1007/978-3-319-629 17-9_9
43. Elbert, R., Friedrich, C.: Simulation-based evaluation of urban consolidation centers considering urban access regulations. In: Proceedings - Winter Simulation Conference, vol. 2018-December (2019)
44. Carnovale, M., Gibson, M.: The effects of driving restrictions on air quality and driver behavior. 1–20 (2013)
45. Wachs, M.: Fighting traffic congestion with information technology. Issues Sci. Technol., **19** (1), (2002)
46. Morton, C., Lovelace, R., Anable, J.: Exploring the effect of local transport policies on the adoption of low emission vehicles: evidence from the London congestion charge and hybrid electric vehicles. Transp. Policy **60**, 34–46 (2017). https://doi.org/10.1016/j.tranpol.2017. 08.007
47. Goddard, H.C.: Using tradeable permits to achieve sustainability in the world's large cities. Policy design issues and efficiency conditions for controlling vehicle emissions, congestion and urban decentralization with an application to Mexico City. Environ. Resour. Econ. **10** (1), (1997)
48. Mudway, I.S., et al.: Impact of London's low emission zone on air quality and children's respiratory health: a sequential annual cross-sectional study. Lancet Public Heal. **4**(1), (2019)
49. Gillis, D., Semanjski, I., Lauwers, D.: How to monitor sustainable mobility in cities? Literature review in the frame of creating a set of sustainable mobility indicators. Sustainability (Switzerland) **8**(1). (2016)
50. Croci, E.: Urban road pricing: a comparative study on the experiences of London, Stockholm and Milan. Transp. Res. Procedia **14**, 253–262 (2016). https://doi.org/10.1016/j.trpro.2016. 05.062

BERT-Based Ensemble Learning Approach for Sentiment Analysis

Hasna Chouikhi[1]([✉]) [iD] and Fethi Jarray[2] [iD]

[1] LIMTIC Laboratory, UTM University, Tunis, Tunisia
hasna.chouikhi@fst.utm.tn
[2] Higher Institute of Computer Science of Medenine, Medenine, Tunisia
fethi.jarray@isim.rnu.tn

Abstract. Sentiment Analysis is a fundamental problem in social media and aims to determine the attitude of a writer. Recently, transformer-based models have shown great success in sentiment analysis and have been considered the state-of-the-art model for different NLP tasks. However, the accuracy of sentiment analysis for low resource Languages still needs improvements. In this paper, we are concerned with sentiment analysis for Arabic documents. We first applied data augmentation techniques on publicly available datasets to improve the robustness of supervised sentiment analysis models. Then we proposed an ensemble architecture of Arabic sentiment analysis by combing different BERT models. We validated these methods using three available datasets. Our results showed that the BERT-based ensemble method achieves an accuracy score of 96%.

Keywords: Arabic sentiment analysis · BERT models · Ensemble learning · Large scale dataset

1 Introduction

Sentiment Analysis (SA) is a Natural Language Processing (NLP) research field that handles people's opinions, sentiments, and emotions. SA techniques are categorized into symbolic and sub-symbolic approaches. The former use lexical and ontologies [2] to encode the associated polarity with words and multi-word expressions. The latter consist of supervised, semi-supervised and unsupervised machine learning techniques that perform sentiment classification based on word co-occurrence frequencies. Among all these techniques, the most popular are based on deep neural networks. Some hybrid frameworks leverage both symbolic and sub-symbolic approaches. SA can be seen as a multistep process including data retrieval, data extraction, data pre-processing, and feature extraction. The ultimate subtasks of sentiment classification allow three types of classification: polarity classification, intensity classification, and emotion identification. The first type classifies the text as positive, negative, or neutral, while the second type identifies the degree of polarity as very positive, positive, negative, or very negative. The third classification identifies emotions such as sadness, anger, or happiness. Practically, the Arabic language has a complex nature, due to its ambiguity and

A. Fred et al. (Eds.): IC3K 2021, CCIS 1718, pp. 118–128, 2023.
https://doi.org/10.1007/978-3-031-35924-8_7

rich morphological system. This nature associated with various dialects and the lack of resources represent a challenge to the progress of Arabic sentiment analysis research.

The major contributions of our present work are as follows:

- Create large-scale sentiment Arabic datasets (LargeASA) for Arabic sentiment analysis's task.
- Use an adjusted model ASA Medium BERT.
- Design a new staking approach (also known as Stacked Generalization) for Arabic Sentiment Analysis by combing three BERT based models (Arabic-BERT [3], AraBERT [4] and mBERT [5]).
- Perform data augmentation using a back-translation method by exploiting the pretrained English-Arabic translation model. Data are translated into English and back to Arabic to generate new augmented data.

2   Related Work

The learning based approaches of ASA can be classified into two categories: classical machine learning approaches and deep learning approaches.

Machine learning (ML) methods have been widely used for sentiment analysis. ML addresses sentiment analysis as a text classification problem. Many approaches such as the support vector machine (SVM), maximum entropy (ME), naive Bayes (NB) algorithm, and artificial neural networks (ANNs) have been proposed to handle ASA. NB and SVM are the most widely exploited machine learning algorithms for solving the sentiment classification problem [6] Al-Rubaiee et al. [7] performed polarity classification and rating classification using SVM, MNB, and BNB. They achieved 90% accuracy polarity classification and 50% accuracy rating classification.

The use of DL is less common in Arabic SA than in English SA. [8] proposed an approach based on RNN (recurrent neural network) which is trained on a constructed sentiment treebank and improved sentence-level sentiment analysis in English datasets. [9] used CNN model for SA tasks and a Stanford segmenter to perform tweet tokenization and normalization. They used Word2vec for word embedding with ASTD datasets. [10] used a LSTM-CNN model with only two unbalanced classes (Positive and negative) among four classes (objective, subjective positive, subjective negative, and subjective mixed) form ASTD.

Since its release in 2018, many pretrained versions of **BERT** [5] has been proposed for sequence learning, such as ASA. The recent trend in sentiment analysis is based on the BERT representation. Let us briefly describe and recall BERT and the different versions that handle Arabic texts. BERT (Bidirectional Encoder Representations from Transformers) is pre-trained by conditioning on both left and right context in all layers, unlike previous language representation models. Applying BERT to any NLP task requires only to fine-tune one additional output layer to the downstream task (see Fig. 1).

The multilingual BERT (**mBERT**) [5] model is trained in many languages, including Arabic, and serves as a universal language model. ElJundi et al. [12]

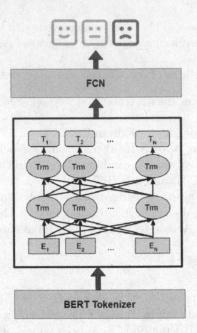

Fig. 1. BERT based architecture for ASA.

developed an Arabic specific universal language model (ULM), **hULMonA**. They fine-tuned mBERT ULM for ASA. They collected a benchmark dataset for ULM evaluation with sentiment analysis. Safaya, A et al. [3] proposed **ArabicBERT** which is a set of pre-trained transformer language models for arabic language. They used a base version of arabic BERT model (bert-base-arabic). Antoun, W et al. [4] created **AraBERTv02** based on the BERT model. It was trained on Arabic corpora consisting of internet text and news articles of (8.6B tokens). [13] introduced **GigaBERTv3** which is a bilingual BERT for English and Arabic. It was pre-trained on a large corpra (Gigaword, Oscar and Wikipedia). [14] designed **MARBERT** and ArBERT. Both are built on the basis of the BERT-based model, except for MARBERT. ArBERT was trained on a collection of Arabic datasets, mostly books and articles written in Modern Standard Arabic (MSA). While MARBERT trained both Dialectal (DA) and MSA tweets, it does not output the next sentence prediction (NSP) objective, as it is trained on short tweets. Additionally, MARBERT and ArBERT were experimented on the ArSarcasm dataset [15]. Finally, [16] trained **QARiB** (QCRI Arabic and Dialectal BERT) on a collection of Arabic tweets and sentences of text written on MSA.

3   Proposed Approach

In this paper, we design an ensemble learning model by stacking BERT models to address the Arabic sentiment analysis problem. More specifically, we combine the predictions of three BERT models dedicated to the Arabic language (Arabic-BERT, mBERT and AraBERT).

We follow three steps to design a sentiment analysis system:

– First, we split the input texts into tokens by tokenization. Figure 2 presents the result of Arabic-BERT and mBERT tokenizers applied to an example sentence (S). We observe that the Arabic-BERT tokenizer is more appropriate for Arabic because it considers the characteristic of Arabic morphology.
– Second, we convert each text to a BERT's format by adding the special [CLS] token at the beginning of each text and the [SEP] token between sentences and the end. Then we execute BERT to get the vector representation of each word.
– Finally, we add a classification layer on top of the [CLS] token representation to predict the text's sentiment polarity.

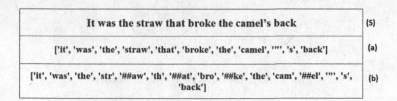

Fig. 2. Comparison between Arabic BERT (a) and mBERT (b) tokenizer.

3.1 Data Augmentation for ASA

Data augmentation (DA) consists of artificially increasing the size of the training data set by generating new data points from existing data. It is used for low-resource languages, such as Arabic, to avoid overfitting and create more diversity in the data set. Data augmentation techniques can be applied at the character, word, and sentence levels. There are various data augmentation methods, including Easy Data Augmentation (EDA) methods, Text Generation and Back Translation. This work uses a back-translation strategy [30] of translating Arabic sentences into English and back into Arabic. We have run back translation on all the available ASA data sets, including the AJGT, LABR, HARD, and LargeASA datasets.

3.2 Refine Tuning of Arabic BERT Model (ASA-Medium BERT)

In this section, we propose an ASA based on the Arabic BERT model. As mentioned in the original paper, Arabic BERT is available in four versions: bert-mini-arabic, bert-medium-arabic, bert-base-arabic, and bert-large-arabic. We applied a grid search strategy to find the best Arabic BERT version with the best hyperparameters [29]. Table 1 represents the hyperparameters of Arabic BERT for ASA used after our fine-tuning. We used the AJGT dataset [20] as a testing dataset.

Among all the works cited, the approach of Ali Safaya [3] is the closest to our approach. Figure 3 depicts the proposed architecture for arabic SA. Our architecture consists of three blocks. The first block describes the text preprocessing step, where we used an Arabic BERT tokenizer to split the word into tokens. The second block is the training model. Arabic BERT model is used with only 8 encoder (Medium case [3]). The outputs of the last four hidden layers are concatenated to get a fixed-size representation. The third block is about the classifier, where we used a dropout layer for some regularization and a fully connected layer for our output.

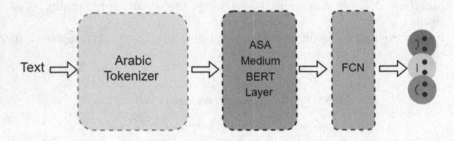

Fig. 3. ASA-medium BERT architecture.

Table 1. Hyper-parameters of ASA-medium BERT.

Hyper-parameters	Batch-size	dropout	Max length	Hidden size	learning rate
Value	16	0.1	128	512	2e-5

Table 1 displays the hyperparameters of the proposed model. The overall model is trained by the AdamW optimizer. We note that with hyperparameters optimization by grid search strategy, we outperform the approach of [3].

Table 2 explains the architectural difference between the ASA-medium BERT model [1], the Arabic BERT [3] and the AraBERT [4] model. It shows that with an Arabic tokenizer, the number of encoders in the Arabic BERT model influences the accuracy value.

Table 2. Architectural characteristics of **ASA-medium BERT**, AraBERT and Arabic BERT models.

Models	Batch-size	Epochs	Layers	Activation function	Tokenizer
ASA-medium BERT	16	5	8	Softmax	Arabic-BERT
Arabic BERT [3]	16/32	10	12	ReLU	Arabic-BERT
AraBERT [4]	512/128	27	12	Softmax	AraBERTV02-Base

3.3   Stacking BERT Based Model for ASA

A Stacking model is a hierarchical model ensemble framework in which the predictions, generated by using various machine learning base modes, are used as inputs for a meta-model. The objective of the meta-model is to optimally combine the base model predictions to form a new classifier. In this work, we used the medium Arabic BERT [3], AraBERT [4] and mBERT [5] as the base model and a fully connected layer as a meta-model (Fig. 4).

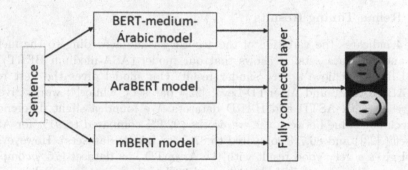

Fig. 4. Stacking of the BERT-baseds model for ASA.

In the experimental section, we imagine three stacking scenarios: automatic stacking of each BERT, pairwise stacking, and full stacking of three BERT models

4   Experiments and Results

4.1   Datasets

In this paper we perform experiments on three available datasets HARD, LABR and AJGT (Table 3) and a LargeASA constructed by merging the other datasets. All were split into two subsets: 80% for training, and 20% for testing.

- Hotel Arabic Reviews Dataset (HARD) [18] contains 93,700 reviews. Each one has two parts: positive comments and negative comments. It covers 1858 hotels contributed by 30889 users.
- Large-scale Arabic Book Reviews (LABR) [19] contains more than 63,000 book reviews in Arabic.
- Arabic Jordanian General Tweets (AJGT) [20] contains 1,800 tweets annotated as positive and negative.
- Large-scale Arabic Sentiment Analysis (LargeASA). We aggregate the HARD, LABRR, and AJGT datasets into a large corpus for ASA. This dataset is publicly available upon request.

Table 3. Statistics of the datasets used.

Dataset	Samples	Labels	Dialect
LABR	63,000	P/N	MSA/DA
HARD	93,700	P/N	MSA/DA
AJGT	1,800	P/N	DA (Jordan)
LargeASA	158,500	P/N	MSA/DA

4.2   Refine Tuning Results

Table 4 indicates the variation of the accuracy value according to the method used and the data sets. It shows that our model (ASA-medium BERT) and AraBERT [4] achieve a very similar result. Our model gives the best result for LABR, AJGT and ArsenTD-Lev ([22]) datasets; while [4] works give the best result with ASTD and HARD datasets. We found a slight difference in the accuracy value between the two works (92,6% compared to 91% for ASTD dataset ([23]) and 86,7% compared to 87% for LABR datasets). However, our model gives a very good result with the ArsenTD-Lev dataset (75% compared to an accuracy value that does not exceed 60% with the other models).

Table 4. ASA-medium BERT accuracy vs previous ASA approaches.

Model \ Dataset	AJGT	LABR	HARD	ASTD	ArsenTD-Lev
Arabic-BERT base	-	-	-	71.4%	55.2%
hULMonA [12]	-	-	95.7%	69.9%	52.4%
AraBERT	93.8%	86.7%	**96.2%**	**92.6%**	59.4%
mBERT	83.6%	83%	95.7%	-	-
ASA-medium BERT	**96.11%**	**87%**	95%	91%	**75%**

The first row block of Table 5 shows a comparison between the three base models that are used in the stacking approach. It shows that Medium Arabic BERT is the most performant and mBERT is the less performant. We will envisage different stacking strategies for these base models to strengthen them.

4.3   Stacking Results

The second row block of Table 5 shows the performance of stacking each model with its own. By cross comparing the first and second row blocks of Table 5 , we conclude that performance of the model did not improve by auto stacking a model with itself. This is may be due to the fact that we have only a small number of classes; positive and negative, and it may be interesting to check the efficiency of auto stacking for large number of classes such as the sentiment

Table 5. Comparison between accuracies of BERT stacking strategies.

Stacking	Model \ Dataset	AJGT	LargeASA	LABR	HARD
Base models	ASA-medium BERT	**96.11%**	90%	87%	95%
	mBERT	83.6%	83%	85%	95.7%
	AraBERT	93.8%	85%	86.7%	**96.2%**
Auto stacking	ASA-medium BERT x2	94%	90%	90%	96%
	mBERT x2	83%	86%	87%	95%
	AraBERT x2	77 %	87 %	86%	96%
Pairwise stacking	ASA-medium BERT+ mBERT	94%	90%	90%	96 %
	ASA-medium BERT+ AraBERT	90%	90%	88%	96%
	mBERT + AraBERT	78 %	88%	88%	95%
Full stacking	ASA-medium BERT+ mBERT +AraBERT	93%	91%	88%	95%
	ASA-medium BERT+ mBERT +AraBERT+DA	**93.03%**	**91.09%**	**88.02%**	**95.07%**

Table 6. Effect of data augmentation on accuracy values.

Method	Models	AJGT	LargeASA	LABR	HARD
Without DA	ASA-medium BERT x2	**94%**	90%	90%	**96%**
	AraBERT x2	77%	87%	86%	**96%**
	mBERT x2	83%	86%	87%	95%
	ASA-medium BERT+ mBERT	**94%**	90%	90%	96%
	ASA-medium BERT+ AraBERT	90%	90 %	88%	96%
	mBERT + AraBERT	78 %	88%	88%	95%
With DA	ASA-medium BERT x2	**96%**	93%	93%	**97%**
	AraBERT x2	**96%%**	88%	89%	96%
	mBERT x2	**96%**	92%	90%	**97%**
	ASA-medium BERT+ mBERT	**96%**	**95%**	**94%**	**97%**
	ASA-medium BERT+ AraBERT	**96%**	94%	93%	**97%**
	mBERT + AraBERT	95%	94 %	92%	96%

analysis with intensity. The third row block of Table 5 details the results obtained by pairwise stacking of different models. It shows that the BERT based models can be strengthened by stacking them with ASA-medium BERT. The last row block of Table 5 shows the results of fully stacking the three base models: Arabic BERT, AraBERT and mBERT. From all stacking scenarios, we conclude that the best way is to autostack ASA-medium BERT with itself.

4.4 Effect of Data Augmentation

Table 6 shows the impact of data augmentation on accuracy measures. As can be seen from the table with data augmentation, the ensemble learning model perform better as the number of training samples will increase.

5 Conclusion

In this paper, we proposed a BERT based ensemble learning for Arabic sentiment analysis. We used medium Arabic BERT, AraBERT, and mBERT as base models. First, we proved that by refine tunig Arabic BERT model we outperform the state-of-the-art for ASA. Second, the experiment results showed that the stacking strategy improves the accuracy. As a continuation of this contribution, we plan to generalize our results to the sentiment analysis with intensities case and investigate more data augmentation techniques.

References

1. Chouikhi, H.; Chniter, H. and Jarray, F.: Stacking BERT based models for Arabic sentiment analysis. In Proceedings of the 13th International Joint Conference on Knowledge Discovery, Knowledge Engineering and Knowledge Management - KEOD, ISBN 978-989-758-533-3; ISSN 2184-3228, pp. 144-150 (2021). https://doi.org/10.5220/0010648400003064
2. Dragoni, M., Poria, S., Cambria, E.: OntoSenticNet: a commonsense ontology for sentiment analysis. IEEE Intell. Syst. **33**(3), 77–85 (2018)
3. Safaya, A., Abdullatif, M., Yuret, D.: KUISAIL at SemEval-2020 task 12: BERT-CNN for offensive speech identification in social media. In: Proceedings of the Fourteenth Workshop on Semantic Evaluation, pp. 2054–2059 (2020)
4. Antoun, W., Baly, F., Hajj, H.: AraBERT: Transformer-based model for Arabic language understanding. arXiv preprint arXiv:2003.00104 (2020)
5. Devlin, J., Chang, M. W., Lee, K., Toutanova, K.: BERT: pre-training of deep bidirectional transformers for language understanding. arXiv preprint arXiv:1810.04805 (2018)
6. Imran, A., Faiyaz, M., Akhtar, F.: An enhanced approach for quantitative prediction of personality in Facebook posts. Int. J. Educ. Manag. Eng. (IJEME) **8**(2), 8–19 (2018)
7. Al-Rubaiee, H., Qiu, R., Li, D.: Identifying Mubasher software products through sentiment analysis of Arabic tweets. In: 2016 International Conference on Industrial Informatics and Computer Systems (CIICS), pp. 1–6. IEEE (2016)
8. Socher, R., et al.: Recursive deep models for semantic compositionality over a sentiment treebank. In: Proceedings of the 2013 Conference on Empirical Methods in Natural Language Processing, pp. 1631–1642 (2013)
9. Rangel, F., Rosso, P., Charfi, A., Zaghouani, W., Ghanem, B., Sánchez-Junquera, J.: Overview of the track on author profiling and deception detection in Arabic. Working Notes of FIRE 2019, vol. 2517, pp. 70–83 (2019). CEUR-WS. org
10. Alhumoud, S., Albuhairi, T., Alohaideb, W.: Hybrid sentiment analyser for Arabic tweets using R. In: 2015 7th International Joint Conference on Knowledge Discovery, Knowledge Engineering and Knowledge Management (IC3K), vol. 1, pp. 417–424. IEEE (2015)
11. Zahran, M.A., Magooda, A., Mahgoub, A.Y., Raafat, H., Rashwan, M., Atyia, A.: Word representations in vector space and their applications for Arabic. In: Gelbukh, A. (ed.) CICLing 2015. LNCS, vol. 9041, pp. 430–443. Springer, Cham (2015). https://doi.org/10.1007/978-3-319-18111-0_32

12. ElJundi, O., Antoun, W., El Droubi, N., Hajj, H., El-Hajj, W., Shaban, K.: hUL-MoNA: the universal language model in Arabic. In: Proceedings of the Fourth Arabic Natural Language Processing Workshop, pp. 68–77 (2019)
13. Lan, W., Chen, Y., Xu, W., Ritter, A.: An empirical study of pre-trained transformers for Arabic information extraction. arXiv preprint arXiv:2004.14519 (2020)
14. Abdul-Mageed, M., Elmadany, A., Nagoudi, E.M.B.: ARBERT & MARBERT: deep bidirectional transformers for Arabic. arXiv preprint arXiv:2101.01785 (2020)
15. Farha, I.A., Magdy, W.: From Arabic sentiment analysis to Sarcasm detection: the ArSarcasm dataset. In: Proceedings of the 4th Workshop on Open-Source Arabic Corpora and Processing Tools, with a Shared Task on Offensive Language Detection, pp. 32–39 (2020)
16. Abdelali, A., Hassan, S., Mubarak, H., Darwish, K., Samih, Y.: Pre-training BERT on Arabic tweets: practical considerations. arXiv preprint arXiv:2102.10684 (2021)
17. Grave, E., Bojanowski, P., Gupta, P., Joulin, A., Mikolov, T.: Learning word vectors for 157 languages. arXiv preprint arXiv:1802.06893 (2018)
18. Elnagar, A., Khalifa, Y.S., Einea, A.: Hotel Arabic-reviews dataset construction for sentiment analysis applications. In: Shaalan, K., Hassanien, A.E., Tolba, F. (eds.) Intelligent Natural Language Processing: Trends and Applications. SCI, vol. 740, pp. 35–52. Springer, Cham (2018). https://doi.org/10.1007/978-3-319-67056-0_3
19. Aly, M., Atiya, A.: LABR: a large scale Arabic book reviews dataset. In: Proceedings of the 51st Annual Meeting of the Association for Computational Linguistics, (Volume 2: Short Papers), pp. 494–498 (2013)
20. Alomari, K.M., ElSherif, H.M., Shaalan, K.: Arabic tweets sentimental analysis using machine learning. In: Benferhat, S., Tabia, K., Ali, M. (eds.) IEA/AIE 2017. LNCS (LNAI), vol. 10350, pp. 602–610. Springer, Cham (2017). https://doi.org/10.1007/978-3-319-60042-0_66
21. Joulin, A., Grave, E., Bojanowski, P., Mikolov, T.: Bag of tricks for efficient text classification. arXiv preprint arXiv:1607.01759 (2016)
22. Baly, R., Khaddaj, A., Hajj, H., El-Hajj, W., Shaban, K.B.: ArSentD-LEV: a multi-topic corpus for target-based sentiment analysis in arabic levantine tweets. arXiv preprint arXiv:1906.01830 (2019)
23. Nabil, M., Aly, M., Atiya, A.: ASTD: Arabic sentiment tweets dataset. In: Proceedings of the 2015 Conference on Empirical Methods in Natural Language Processing, pp. 2515–2519 (2015)
24. Ghanem, B., Karoui, J., Benamara, F., Moriceau, V., Rosso, P.: IDAT at fire2019: overview of the track on irony detection in Arabic tweets. In: Proceedings of the 11th Forum for Information Retrieval Evaluation, pp. 10–13 (2019)
25. Shoukry, A., Rafea, A.: Sentence-level Arabic sentiment analysis. In 2012 international conference on collaboration technologies and systems (CTS), pp. 546–550. IEEE (2012)
26. Eskander, R., Rambow, O.: SLSA: a sentiment lexicon for standard Arabic. In: Proceedings of the 2015 Conference on Empirical Methods in Natural Language Processing, pp. 2545–2550 (2015)
27. Dahou, A., Elaziz, M.A., Zhou, J., Xiong, S.: Arabic sentiment classification using convolutional neural network and differential evolution algorithm. Comput. Intell. Neurosci. **2019**, 2537689 (2019)
28. Harrat, S., Meftouh, K., Smaili, K.: Machine translation for Arabic dialects (survey). Inf. Process. Manag. **56**(2), 262–273 (2019)

29. Chouikhi, H., Chniter, H., Jarray, F.: Arabic sentiment analysis using BERT model. In: Wojtkiewicz, K., Treur, J., Pimenidis, E., Maleszka, M. (eds.) ICCCI 2021. CCIS, vol. 1463, pp. 621–632. Springer, Cham (2021). https://doi.org/10.1007/978-3-030-88113-9_50
30. Ma, J., Li, L.: Data augmentation for Chinese text classification using back-translation. J. Phys. Conf. Ser. **1651**(1), 012039 (2020). IOP Publishing (2020)

An Ontology-Driven Approach to the Analytical Platform Development for Data-Intensive Domains

Viktor S. Zayakin[1,2] , Lyudmila N. Lyadova[1]([⊠]) , Viacheslav V. Lanin[1] ,
Elena B. Zamyatina[1] , and Evgeniy A. Rabchevskiy[2]

[1] HSE University, Studencheskaya Str. 38, 614070 Perm, Russia
`{LLyadova,VLanin,EZamyatina}@hse.ru`
[2] SEUSLAB LLC, Shosse Kosmonavtov Str. 111 (Building 27), 614066 Perm, Russia
`E.Rabchevskiy@seuslab.ru`

Abstract. The development and support of knowledge-based systems for experts in the field of social network analysis is complicated by the problems of viability maintenance inevitably emerging in data intensive domains. Largely this is the case due to the properties of semistructured objects and processes that are analyzed by data specialists using data mining techniques and other automated analytical tools. In order to be viable a modern knowledge-based analytical platform should be able to integrate heterogeneous information, present it to users in an understandable way and support tools for functionality extensibility. In this paper we introduce an ontological approach to analytical platform development. Common requirements for analytical platform have been identified and substantiated. Theoretical basis of the proposed approach is described. General structure of the knowledge base is designed. The core of the platform is the multifaceted ontology including data ontologies describing data sources and data types and structures, problem ontologies describing specific user's tasks, domain ontologies. Ontology-based domain-specific modeling tools are the part of analytical platform software too. The information integration method, design patterns for developing analytical platform core functionality such as ontology repository management, domain-specific languages generation and source code round-trip synchronization with DSL-models are proposed. Diagrams and schemes are included to paper to illustrate approach description.

Keywords: Open data · Social media · Social network · Information · Integration · System viability · Knowledge bases · Multifaceted ontology · Domain specific modelling · Design patterns

1 Introduction

In the modern dynamically changing world, the problem of the operational development of new information systems, corresponding to user needs, reflecting the specifics of their activities, as well as the tasks of updating existing systems and settings for

A. Fred et al. (Eds.): IC3K 2021, CCIS 1718, pp. 129–149, 2023.
https://doi.org/10.1007/978-3-031-35924-8_8

changing conditions, are pointed. This problem is especially relevant when performing interdisciplinary studies related to search and analysis of data in the Internet, in which specialists in various fields are involved. Often, an analytical system is created for a specific project, which makes it impossible to use it in other projects and even when the conditions for solving the same research task change (for example, when connecting to new data sources, when changing the requirements for the presentation of results, to the user interface or to methods for solving problems). Thus, the development of technology for creating systems that adapt to changing conditions and user needs becomes an urgent task of software engineering.

Information and analytical platforms provide prompt access to information (search, collection and consolidation of data from disparate sources), transformation and analysis of data, visualization of results. Universal platforms allow to solve common data management tasks, as well as configure systems based on them to take into account the characteristics of working in specific conditions based on data analysis. Nowadays the tasks of applying knowledge-based methods in software engineering have already been set. However, there is a need to expand research aimed at adapting software engineering methods to the requirements of developing data-dependent software in order to increase the productivity of developers.

Modern architectures must support "on-the-fly" IT infrastructure, self-service environments, contain resource inventory tools, and include automated deployment factories for applications, sources, and data replicas. One of the main features of the platform is support for dynamic reconfiguration of applications: assembly/disassembly "on-the-fly" of target functions supported by a set of ready-made basic components included to the platform; support for the creation and execution of specific scenarios of researches, etc. Thus, platform users need "control panel" that allows them to form resource policies and to describe scripts. To meet the requirements, it is necessary to implement an application and information integration strategy based on the appropriate software infrastructure of the intermediate layer, which should allow to assemble individual applications into a unified system.

Mass media (in particular, social networks) attract the attention of analysts working in various research fields as a rich source of information [21].

From the user's point of view any social network is an interactive multi-user website, the content of which is filled by the network participants themselves. It is an automated social environment that allows a group of users to communicate about their common interests. Communication is carried out via different tools (for example a web service of internal mail or instant messaging, and so on). On the one hand, social networks help solve many tasks, but on the other hand, they might become a source of problems. This fact has motivated a large number of researchers to study social networks. The greatest interest is caused by the problems of dissemination of information on the network, issues of community formation, etc. The methods of static analysis of networks using graph models, statistical methods and machine learning methods are better developed. When analyzing social networks, economists receive information about transactions, the influence of others on human behavior, while political scientists investigate the formation of political preferences. Static and dynamic methods may be used for these purposes.

The creating analytical systems in data-intensive fields (such as mass media or social network analysis) inevitably is followed by challenges of maintaining the viability of these systems. Systems of analytics are characterized common features and common problems at process of development, maintenance, and support that lead to common design problems:

- The data from a variety of heterogeneous sources are extracted and processed. The logical models of databases and knowledge bases that describe the analyzed processes are intensively expanded and modified. As a result, information integration problems arise. These problems are largely due to the properties of the information being processed, which is semi-structured.
- Various categories of specialists (such as system analysts, software engineers and programmers, knowledge engineers, data analysts and domain experts, etc.) are involved into developing intelligent systems. Each of the listed groups of specialists can interpret the integrated information depending on their domain and specialization. So, for analytical platforms the data interpretation according to different domain models and tasks is important.
- The analytical platforms used in data-intensive domains are to be extensible and customizable. Users are needed to describe and implement algorithms of data processing themselves (including the use of data mining, process mining and machine learning techniques and so on). The end-users (in particular, domain experts) do not have skills in programming needed to solve these tasks. Thus, platform's extensibility problem requires providing users with domain-specific modeling (DSM) tools to describe research scenarios or to create new methods of analysis.

To develop a comprehensive solution of these problems, it is necessary to solve the following tasks:

1. Requirements analysis and clarification for analytical platforms for research in domains with intensive using data.
2. Creating formal model for knowledge base design and developing basic structure of knowledge base.
3. Developing knowledge-based approach to information integration.
4. Designing core architecture of the knowledge-based analytical platform.
5. Developing design patterns for creation of analytical platforms based on the core architecture.

Based on the obtained general decisions, analytical platforms for research of data-intensive domains can be designed.

2 Related Works: Requirement Analyses and Design Challenges

Let's consider approaches to solving the most interesting problems of social network analysis according to goal of the research presented in this paper and analyze the challenges in order to define requirements for analytical platform development tools.

Previous research works provide many examples of using social networks to distribute content among users. This is how marketers try to spread information about products in order to make profit [4, 17, 39, 43]. On the other hand, attackers try to spread malicious or fake information [8, 11, 16, 35]. Thus, it is necessary to develop algorithms or strategies that either contribute to the fastest possible dissemination of information, or, conversely, hinder dissemination. Developing such methods and researching their effectiveness are some of the most pressing tasks that can be solved using analytical platforms for the data-intensive domains.

For the analysis of social networks static methods (statistical methods, methods of graph theory etc.) and methods of dynamic analysis (simulation modeling) are widely used.

In the article [36], event logs are used to identify social connections between employees of a company, to build a sociogram that reflects the structure of social connections for users of the CRM system of the company. These tools are useful to study connections between users of mass media too. Process Mining tools also allows identify regularities of processes in social networks, in behavior of users and groups of users.

To use Process Mining tools, it is needed to get an event log. An overview of the technologies for extracting information on events from mass media is given in the paper [1, 32, 33, 42].Event logs can be built on the base of data stored in databases [5]. Event logs can be constructed with using data of network messages [6] and event data of different applications [28]. Methods of extracting data to generate event logs from unstructured or semistructured sources are also discussed. News events can be extracted from social media [30]. The article [40] describes a system that automatically identifies certain types of global events, such as natural disasters, epidemics, and military conflicts through the analysis of news sites and social networks. The article describes several experimental approaches to semantic integration of user content published in social networks with existing information systems. The development of a system used to automatically receive and categorize events based on user posts on Twitter is described in the article [31]. The author uses machine learning algorithms to work with publications and identifies various event groups from comments, including entities, events, dates, and categories.

Semantic technologies extend data pre-processing capabilities at preparing event logs for the analysis with process mining tools. These technologies have become the kernel for process analysis software developing [10] as they allow solve the tasks of information retrieval, data extraction and analysis, in particular, when searching for and analyzing facts [37].

Simulation methods, their capabilities and advantages are discussed in the articles [11, 26]. The results of application of various methods and tools of simulation modeling to solve problems of social networks analysis are presented. Simulation experiments with both artificial data formed in "virtual networks" and data obtained from real social networks allow to simulate behavior in time, investigate the repercussions of certain events, and predict their results.

The variety of data sources and methods of analysis, the need for their integration in analytical systems and necessitating operational adapting to changing conditions require to use of new approaches in the development of analytical systems. The most promising approach is to create knowledge-based analytical tools.

The heterogeneous information integration, support of changes traceability in data and knowledge models and interpretation of information according to the domain model is important for the data consumer. These tools are to be developed primarily at creating viable knowledge-driven systems [13]. The development of the analytical platform software is a challenging task for an ordinary developer since it requires creating methods for solving specific problems and designing different domain models. Therefore, the solution of such a complex task should be focused on creating basic tools invariant to the domains. These core tools could be used to implement base functionality of a platform supporting customization by developers and users [14].

The development tools for creating knowledge-driven analytical platforms for the data-intensive domains shall meet the following basic requirements:

1. Providing models extensibility to allow description of new information models (such as new data sources or new domain models) with automatic checking logical integrity of the integrated models.
2. Ensuring the domain data integration with results of their analysis at the automated data processing according to the multi-stage research scenario described with using different methods (e. g. data mining techniques or simulation experiments) by users.
3. Delivering tools for independent interpretation of data and results of their processing for end-users (analysts, domain experts) according to their different domain models.
4. Ensuring traceability of changes in models and metamodels to provide the relevance of semantic interpretation and annotation of stored and processed information.
5. Providing tools for declarative specification of data sources and data structures used to extract data from specified data sources as well as methods, algorithms, and research scenarios for data processing.
6. Ensuring tools for the customization of software components implementing data processing algorithms according to models of data and knowledge.

Related works dedicated to developing knowledge-driven analytical platforms focus on issues on creation of approaches to information integration and data pooling. The approaches proposed by many authors are based on ontologies [23, 32].

Existing approaches are focused on independent modeling and integrating various aspects of information and analytical systems (such as data sources and data structures, data processing tasks, domains, etc.). The information integration based on the ontologies are used to design event mining tools for monitoring global processes [1], to integrate spatial databases [15, 27], to construct or transform queries to distributed databases [3, 7, 38], to describe and form datasets for machine leaning tasks [20].

The approach to creating ontology-driven software development framework is proposed in [25]. The authors investigated limitations of the usability of software systems. These were tracked back to the developmental stages of software products and were attributed to the human aspects of organizational systems that are not captured. On the other hand, ontologies are explored and positioned as artefacts that can be used to capture these aspects. This paper presents a framework that positions ontologies as the core of the software development process. Ontology artefacts take the role of the software model that bridges the semantic and communication gap between the software development phases as well as among stakeholders in the development process. At the same time, it allows culture and social context, semantics and pragmatics to be maintained in the software products that run organizational information systems. The authors consider possible uses of ontologies in software development. They describe several types of ontologies (domain ontologies, method ontologies, status ontologies, intentional ontologies, social ontologies, process ontologies). Software development requirements, provided with ontology-driven approach, are described. The need and effectiveness of using the ontological approach are justified in the paper. The software development process requires an ontology-driven analysis model that is made up of domain, process or method ontologies to capture the domain, business and specification models of the system to be represented as a software model. This model should be stored and maintained in an ontology-driven repository. To address the requirements of the software development metrics improving schedule times and quality and reducing development costs, an ontology-driven software development environment should be implemented.

In the paper [18] ontology-driven software engineering approach with extended ontologies is proposed, in particular, DSLs (Domain Specific Languages) ontology and integration ontology are included into ontological framework. Using SPARQL patterns are described too.

An approach proposed in this paper also provides an extension of the integration model, allowing to embed new ontologies into multifaceted ontology [33] via describing axiomatic relations between elements of new ontologies and elements of previously created ontologies. Creating an effective mechanism for different ontologies integration into the unified multifaceted ontology and providing tools of domain specific modeling are required to implement this approach.

Based on the analysis of the related works the following common design challenges of the developing knowledge-driven analytical platforms should be stated and solved:

1. Integration of information at the level of source metamodels (descriptions of data sources, data processing tasks, domains) which are described independently of each other. The metamodels can be described by users (domain experts, analysts, and other specialists) or research teams, models can be imported and reused.
2. Automated interpretation of data (input data and results of data processing) based on models (formal descriptions of domain rules and constraints) to use single subsystem for restructuring data according to different models to reduce the volume of stored information.
3. Integration of DSM tools into analytical platform to specify data processing modules for gathering, preprocessing, analyzing and interpreting data. The DSM subsystem (language toolkits) provides users with tools to extend the functionality of the platform independently.
4. Integration of task solvers into analytical platform based on declarative specifications of the functional modules. Generating scripts with calls of solvers is provided with declarative descriptions of input data and results, and parametrized attributes of solvers.
5. Composition of data processing modules into pipelines based on the scenarios described with DSM tools and input and output data structures described in ontologies. The scenarios define the sequence of data processing modules execution and date flows.

The knowledge-driven analytical platform development should be started by creating a formal model to design the knowledge base.

3 Formal Model of Knowledge Base Design

Formally, let's define the ontology as a

$$O = < C, R, P, D, A, U >,$$

where C is the set of concepts (classes), R is the set of relations (object properties), P is the set of attributes of concepts (data type properties), D is the set of data types, A is the set of axioms, U is the set of instances (class objects).

The set of relations R is defined as the set of binary relations between concepts.

$$\forall R_1 \in R \exists C_1, C_2 \in C : R_1 \subseteq C_1 \times C_2.$$

A set of attributes P is defined as a set of binary relationships between concepts and data types.

$$\forall P_1 \in P \exists C_1 \in C, D_1 \in D : P_1 \subseteq C_1 \times D_1.$$

Instances of ontologies U are defined as some subset of objects, each of which corresponds to at least one ontology concept.

$$U \subseteq \bigcup_{C_i \in C} C_i, \forall a \in U \exists C_1 \in C : a \in C_1.$$

Let's define the set of axioms A as the set of statements regarding instances of ontology of the following types:

1. Instance a belongs to concept C_1.
2. Instances a and b are in relation R_1.
3. Instance a has a P_1 property value of d of data type D_1.

For the simplification of next definitions let's designations for these types of axioms in accordance with the following formal definitions:

$$C_1(a) \Leftrightarrow (a \in U, C_1 \in C, a \in C_1),$$

$$R_1(a, b) \Leftrightarrow (a, b \in U, R_1 \in R, aR_1b, (\exists C_1, C_2 \in C : R_1 \subseteq C_1 \times C_2)),$$

$$P_1(a, D_1(d)) \Leftrightarrow (a \in U, d \in D_1, P_1 \in P, aP_1d, (\exists C_1 \in C, D_1 \in D : P_1 \subseteq C_1 \times D_1)).$$

Any fact annotated with the ontology O is a collection of axioms. When developing ontologies, a small number of instances and facts relative to them are usually known, which may be incorporated into the ontology beforehand. The main part of the facts is formulated on the basis of domain data, which are uploaded into the fact base at the process of data collection, preprocessing, analysis and interpretation of information from various information sources.

Thus, set A is only a small fraction of the set of all axioms $\mathcal{A}$ that can theoretically be annotated using the ontology O. The fact base described by ontology O is denoted F and it is defined formally as a subset of set $\mathcal{A}$. As a result, we have.

$$\mathcal{A} = \bigcup_{C_i \in C} \{C_i(a) | a \in U\} + \bigcup_{R_j \in R} \{R_j(a, b) | a, b \in U\} +$$

$$+\bigcup_{P_k \in P, D_l \in D} \{P_k(a, D_l(d)) | a \in U, d \in D_l\},$$

$$A, F \subseteq \mathcal{A}, |F| \gg |A|.$$

Finally, the knowledge base K can be formally defined as a

$$K = < O, F > .$$

A set of production rules that define the relationship of elements of the O_1 ontology with elements of the O_2 ontology to determine the interpretation of data when the context of the subject area changes, let's name as the ontological mapping f and denote $f: O_1 \rightsquigarrow O_2$. Based on it lets determine the correspondence between the sets of axioms, which are described in terms of two ontologies, name it an interpretive mapping and denote $I(f)$. Denoting the set of all possible axioms annotated using the ontology O as $\mathcal{A}(O)$, we have $I(f) \subseteq 2^{\mathcal{A}(O_1)} \times 2^{\mathcal{A}(O_2)}$, where 2^X is the set of all subsets of the set X.

Let q be a query to the fact base corresponding to the ontology O, defined formally as the relation between subsets of possible values of the parameter set Q of the query and subsets of possible facts described with the ontology O. Also suppose that p is a procedure for processing subject data, which, based on a subset of subject data (axioms) described with ontology, matches it with a new subset of axioms described by the same ontology. Finally, let O_1, O_2, O_3 be ontologies, $f: O_1 \rightsquigarrow O_2$ and $g: O_2 \rightsquigarrow O_3$ be ontological mappings. Then the definition of the process of replenishing the knowledge base with new facts when applying the procedures for processing and interpreting subject data can be formally presented as a composition of relationships.

$$\left[I(g)\right] \circ p \circ \left[I(f)\right] \circ q \subseteq 2^Q \times 2^{\mathcal{A}(O_3)}, q \subseteq 2^Q \times 2^{\mathcal{A}(O_1)}, p \subseteq 2^{\mathcal{A}(O_2)} \times 2^{\mathcal{A}(O_2)}.$$

Here, q is a procedure for generating input data with structure described using the ontology O_1. Next, the interpretive mapping $I(f)$ is used to structure this data according to the ontology O_2, which declaratively describes the task of processing this data using the procedure p. Finally, the interpretive mapping $I(g)$ is an interpretation of the results of applying the data processing procedure for structuring according to the O_3 ontology.

The described model allows to determine the approach to ensuring traceability of changes. Between different versions of ontologies using production rules, one can define the corresponding ontological mappings $F_{ij}: O_i \rightsquigarrow O_j$, where i, j are versions of ontologies.

4   The Basic Structure of Knowledge Base

A diagram (see Fig. 1) shows data flows in the knowledge base and the relationships between mappings that integrate information in the form of ontologies structurally divided into three groups of ontologies:

1. Models describing data and data sources (*Data Ontologies* include information on data storage formats, data types and data structures, attributes, and arity of relations, etc.).

2. Models describing tasks of data processing (*Problem Ontologies* include information on the structure of input and output data for data processing procedures, on the functional modules, on the executed scripts, etc.). These descriptions can be extended with the descriptions of new research scenarios using domain-specific languages.

3. Domain models (*Domain Ontologies* include concepts of the domain and relations between concepts, as well as axiomatic statements modeling the constraints of the domains).

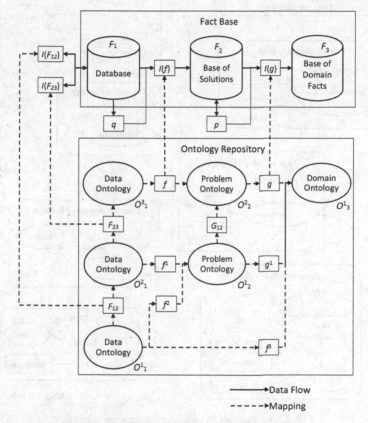

Fig. 1. The basic structure of knowledge base.

This multifaceted ontology is extensible. For example, to include a new data source into a knowledge base model, researcher can describe ontological mappings to associate the appropriate data ontology with a task ontology that describes the conceptual schema of the problem being solved.

An example of an ontology integration scheme for solving social network analysis tasks is shown in Fig. 2. Data extracted from two social networks (VKontakte and Facebook) is used for analysis. Each social network is described with separate ontologies (VK and FB). VK ontology collects data on friendship relations between users, facts of making several types of publications (text posts, videos, etc.) on the topic under study and some information from the user's profile. FB ontology collects facts about the subscription of users to each other, information from the profiles. Obviously, data from other social networks can be used for analysis, which demonstrates the extensibility of the approach.

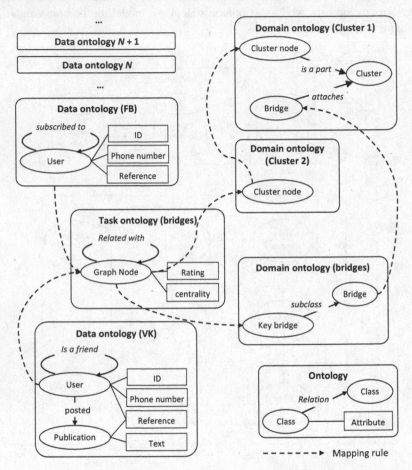

Fig. 2. An example of ontology integration scheme.

The results of solving the problem can be interpreted in different ways. For some experts, it may be important whether the user of the network is a bridge (the domain ontology (bridges) models this viewpoint), for others, which users are included in clusters within the network in question (the domain ontology (clusters) models this viewpoint). Depending on the desired context, these viewpoints can be described independently of each other by different ontologies and corresponding ontological mapping rules, ensuring the independence of expert interpretation of the data and the results of their analysis.

As a domain ontology, an ontology based on the extraction of common structural elements of various social networks, an ontology of events can be developed [21].

All social networks are characterized with user-oriented design. The interaction between users and recognition (individuality) of community members are the basic principles of user-oriented design [9]. These properties allow to solve the task of data extracting (for example to generate event logs with identification of the network events and objects). Seven main structural elements, characterizing social networks based on the principles of user-oriented design, are highlighted most often [19].

The identification of functional components for the selected structural components provides information need for analyzing events in social networks and their description. The event model of a social network is formed based on the information on the functional components relevant to the structural components of social networks [21].

The ontology of events can be expanded and supplemented with descriptions of events related to various domains (for example environmental disasters, events related to the Covid-19 pandemic, etc.). The constructed event ontologies allow the retrieval of information about various types of events in the described domains and the formation of event logs that can be included into fact base and can be used to identify patterns of processes in social networks with Process Mining tools [32, 33]. Event logs can be supplemented with data obtained from other sources described with data source ontologies (for example, news tapes, open databases, etc.). This allows studies to be performed on a wider dataset.

5 Functionality of Analytical Platform Core

In this section the basic functionality of the analytical platform core is described.

The core of a knowledge-driven analytical platform is multifaceted ontology. The knowledge engineer is responsible for managing the ontology repository (see Fig. 3) [41]. Ontologies are created in a form corresponding to the OWL 2 [29]. The ontology management tools are implemented in the system. Users can import ontologies created

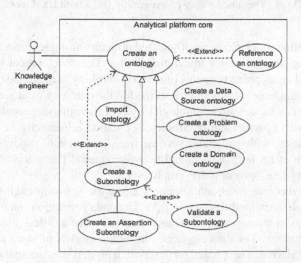

Fig. 3. The core functionality of the ontology managing tools.

with external editors (e.g., Protege). Implementing tools based on user interviewing will provide end users, who do not have specialized knowledge and skills of knowledge engineers, with adequate features to create ontologies.

According to the proposed approach to analytical platform development, the software architect can create DSLs with DSM tools integrated into platform (see Fig. 4). Language toolkits provides users with tools to specify data sources and data structures, functional modules and research scenarios in a declarative way using visual editors.

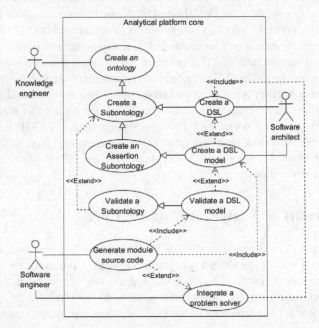

Fig. 4. The functionality of integrating DSLs with DSM tools.

Users can define which elements of selected domain ontologies form a concrete DSL metamodel using the pattern for integrating DSLs. The development of DSL can be automated based on mapping elements of domain ontology to metamodel selected from basic modeling language metamodels described in the ontology of modeling languages [23]. Mapping rules are defined as ontologies by experts with using ontology editor. The proposed approach provides the possibility of creating a hierarchy of interconnected modeling languages with automatic vertical transformation of models [24]. Experts can define the rules for horizontal model transformations. The theoretical basis of the language toolkits development is *HP*-graph [34].

In addition, the core functional modules allow the software engineer to generate source code of platform modules (see Fig. 5). The code generation can be implemented as horizontal model transformation. Transformation rules are described by users and stored in the ontology. The data engineer can define models of input and output data structure with DSLs too. Then, based on the created models the data analyst can describe dataset and extract data that is passed into a solver (to functional module) when task is being solved. He can validate the dataset according to the model that defines its structure. The result of data processing can also be validated when the data processing task is completed.

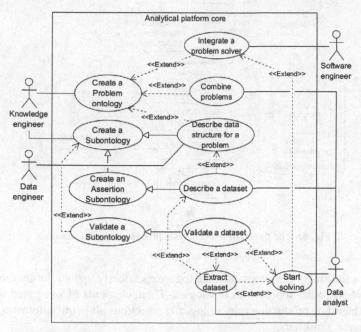

Fig. 5. The functionality of integrating DSLs and problem solvers.

The key users (data analytics) can extend functionality using DSM tools that reduce their dependence on developers (software engineers) and increase adaptability of the analytical system.

6 Information Integration Based on Ontological Approach

The information integration is the central task in the analytical platform development. Integration tools provide users with data extracted from various sources in a transparent and comprehensible to solve analysis tasks. In the data-intensive domains data sources and data models are extending and iteratively evolving. Therefore, developing an approach to information integration is important.

Existing approaches to information integration [1, 3, 7, 20, 27, 38] allow to describe data sources and integrate descriptions, but these approaches are limited in managing different versions of the same models. It is resulting in difficulties of changes traceability. An ontological approach to information integration helps to overcome this problem [41]. The proposed approach to information integration allows to organize information using knowledge of domain experts at the process of data analysis and interpretation (see Fig. 6).

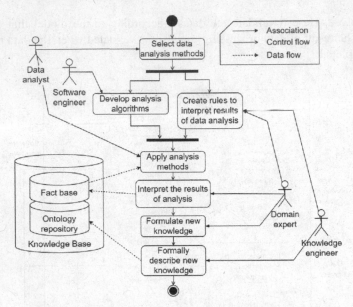

Fig. 6. The model of data analysis process and interpretation.

Various information sources are modeled independently using relevant terminology for the context of the source with ontologies. Then, elements of integrated ontologies are linked based on production rules or logical restrictions allowing automatic inference using semantic reasoners.

7   Description of Design Patterns

The core functionality of the analytical platform implements base modules for gathering, preprocessing, analyzing and interpreting data. Besides, it is possible to extend platform specifying new functionality by adapting its base modules [12].

An approach to analytical platform development is illustrated in Fig. 7.

The platform allows to describe new functional modules and research scenario, data sources and data structures using visual domain-specific languages generated on the base of domain ontologies [23]. Users who are not familiar with programming can describe new modules and functions of the platform adapting existing functionality to their specialized tasks with using generated DSLs [22, 24]. At the same time, DSL metamodels also are represented in ontologies to support the uniformity of descriptions.

An approach to information integration described above is used to specify data sources, structures of input data that could be queried from fact base and passed into platform modules for processing, and structures of output data (results of processing). Besides, analytical platform modules' ontologies describe base functionality of concrete analytical platform (for instance, platform for social network analysis) to be implemented using core functionality of a platform and could import, reuse, and extend integrated information ontologies as well.

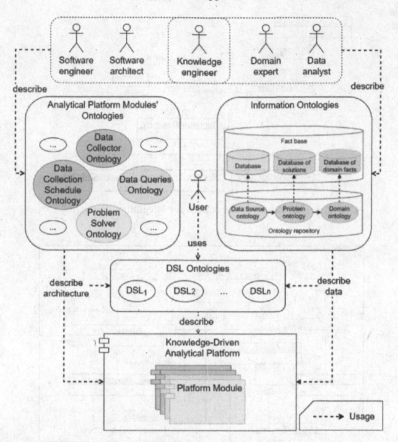

Fig. 7. An approach to analytical platform development.

The next task of the project is to develop design patterns for the common core of different analytical platforms which could be developed using this approach [41]. The specification of OWL 2 language [29] is used. Patterns are described as UML class diagrams.

The pattern for integrating ontologies (see Fig. 8) describes the integrated sources, as well as the types of logical constraints that can be used to link elements of several ontologies.

The pattern for ontology-based metamodeling (see Fig. 9) is intended to create metamodels defined as the ontologies for describing DSLs.

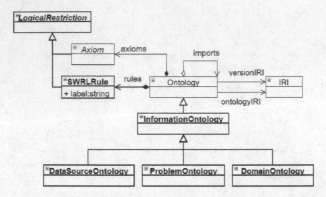

Fig. 8. The model of the pattern for integrating ontologies.

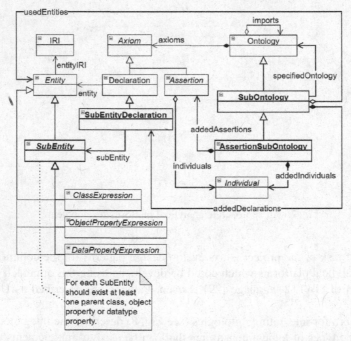

Fig. 9. The model of the pattern for ontology-based metamodeling.

The pattern for integrating DSLs (see Fig. 10) specifies the ontological metamodeling pattern for generating and integrating DSLs to create languages to specify data sources and data structures, to describe data processing modules and research scenarios. These tools allow to manage the architecture of the analytical platform.

The pattern for integrating problem solvers (see Fig. 11) describes the entities that are used to implement functional modules (data processing modules). These modules are describing using generated DSLs. The implementation of this pattern requires coordinating the processes of designing platform modules using DSL, implementing algorithms, modeling the input and output data for the solvers.

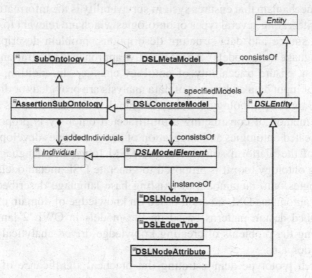

Fig. 10. The model of the pattern for integrating DSLs.

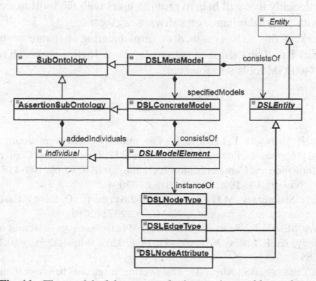

Fig. 11. The model of the pattern for integrating problem solvers.

8 Conclusion

An ontological approach to the development of an analytical platform is proposed, providing the ability to create analytical systems for data-intensive domains.

The main mechanism that ensures system survivability is the information integration that provides integrating several types of ontologies which are relevant to data-intensive domains (data source and data structure descriptions, problem descriptions, domain models and language metamodels). An interpretive approach to integration helps to avoid data duplication, ensure traceability of ontology changes. In addition, automatically interpretation of input data and results of data analysis are provided for different groups of users according to terminology that they are familiar and solved tasks specifics.

A flexible method of constructing a multifaceted ontology is proposed, allowing extension of created ontologies and integration of new ontologies developed by experts.

The core of the platform software is the DSM tools. The language toolkits are based on using ontology too. It is proposed to generate DSL metamodels via mapping domain ontologies onto metamodel of existing base language described in ontology. This approach automates DSL creation based on knowledge of domain experts.

The described design patterns based on the models in OWL 2 language are the basis for solving the problems of creating knowledge-driven analytical platforms for data-intensive domains.

The research prototype demonstrating the practical significance of the proposed approach has been developed.

It is expected that the developed models will be used to implement analytical platform core functionality that will help to provide users with the tools to extend platform functionality with minimal reliance on software engineers.

Further work in this field is aimed at implementing software of the platform's core functionality based on described patterns and ontological approach to information integration and to DSM tools development.

References

1. Abrosimova, P., Shalyaeva, I., Lyadova, L.: The ontology-based event mining tools for monitoring global processes. In: Proceedings of the IEEE 12th International Conference on Application of Information and Communication Technologies (AICT), pp. 108–113. IEEE, Almaty (2018). https://doi.org/10.1109/ICAICT.2018.8747094
2. Alizadeh, M., Shahrezaei, M.H., Tahernezhad-Javazm, F.: Ontology Based Information Integration: a Survey. arXiv preprint, arXiv:1909.12372 (2019)
3. Asfand-E-Yar, M., Ali, R.: Semantic integration of heterogeneous databases of same domain using ontology. IEEE Access **8**, 77903–77919 (2020). https://doi.org/10.1109/ACCESS.2020.2988685
4. Bindu, P.V., Thilagam, P.S., Ahuja, D.: Discovering suspicious behavior in multilayer social networks. Comput. Hum. Behav. **73**, 568–582 (2017). https://doi.org/10.1016/j.chb.2017.04.001
5. Calvanese, D., Montali, M., Syamsiyah, A., van der Aalst, W.M.P.: Ontology-driven extraction of event logs from relational databases. In: Reichert, M., Reijers, H.A. (eds.) BPM 2015. LNBIP, vol. 256, pp. 140–153. Springer, Cham (2016). https://doi.org/10.1007/978-3-319-42887-1_12

6. Carrasquel, J.C., Chuburov, S.A., Lomazova, I.A.: Pre-processing network messages of trading systems into event logs for process mining. In: Kalenkova, A., Lozano, J.A., Yavorskiy, R. (eds.) TMPA 2019. CCIS, vol. 1288, pp. 88–100. Springer, Cham (2021). https://doi.org/10.1007/978-3-030-71472-7_7

7. Chuprina, S., Nasraoui, O.: Using ontology-based adaptable scientific visualization and cognitive graphics tools to transform traditional information systems into intelligent systems. Sci. Visualization 8(1), 23–44 (2016)

8. Dang-Pham, D., Pittayachawan, S., Bruno, V.: Applications of social network analysis in behavioural information security research: concepts and empirical analysis. Comput. Secur. 68, 1–15 (2020). https://doi.org/10.1016/j.cose.2017.03.010

9. Dawot, N.I.M., Ibrahim, R.: A review of features and functional building blocks of social media. In: Proceedings of the 8th Malaysian Software Engineering Conference (MySEC), pp. 177–182. IEEE, Langkawi. (2014). https://doi.org/10.1109/MySec.2014.6986010

10. De Medeiros, A.K.A., Van der Aalst, W., Pedrinaci, C.: Semantic process mining tools: Core building blocks. In: Proceedings of the 16th European Conference on Information Systems, pp. 15–23. Galway, Ireland (2008)

11. Dmitriev, I., Zamyatina, E.: How to prevent harmful information spreading in social networks using simulation tools. In: van der Aalst, W.M.P., et al. (eds.) AIST 2019. CCIS, vol. 1086, pp. 201–213. Springer, Cham (2020). https://doi.org/10.1007/978-3-030-39575-9_21

12. Gribova, V.V., Kleshchev, A.S., Moskalenko, F.M., Timchenko, V.A., Shalfeeva, E.A.: Extensible toolkit for the development of viable systems with knowledge bases. Softw. Eng. 9(8), 339–348 (2018). https://doi.org/10.17587/prin.9.339-348

13. Gribova, V.V., Moskalenko, F.M., Timchenko, V.A., Shalfeeva, E.A.: Viable intelligent systems development with controlled declarative components. Inf. Math. Technol. Sci. Manage. 3(11), 6–17 (2018). https://doi.org/10.25729/2413-0133-2018-3-01

14. Gribova, V., Shalfeeva, V.: Ontological Approach to Creating Viable Intelligent Systems. In: International Symposium on Knowledge, Ontology, and Theory (KNOTH), pp. 110–114 (2021). https://doi.org/10.1109/KNOTH54462.2021.9685030

15. Hasani, S., Sadeghi-Niaraki, A., Jelokhani-Niaraki, M.: Spatial Data Integration Using Ontology-Based Approach. Int. Arch. Photogramm. Remote Sens. Spatial Inf. Sci., XL-1/W5, pp. 293–296 (2015). https://doi.org/10.5194/isprsarchives-XL-1-W5-293-2015

16. Ilieva, D.: Fake news, telecommunications and information security. Int. J. "Information Theories and Applications" 25(2), 174–181 (2018)

17. Kang, H., Munoz, D.: A dynamic network analysis approach for evaluating knowledge dissemination in a multi-disciplinary collaboration network in obesity research. In: 2015 Winter Simulation Conference (WSC), pp. 1319–1330 (2015). https://doi.org/10.1109/WSC.2015.7408256

18. Katasonov, A.: Ontology-driven software engineering: beyond model checking and transformations. Int. J. Semantic Comput. 6(2), 205–242 (2012). https://doi.org/10.1142/S1793351X12500031

19. Kietzmann, J.H.: Social media? get serious! understanding the functional building blocks of social media. Bus. Horiz. 54(3), 241–251 (2011). https://doi.org/10.1016/j.bushor.2011.01.005

20. Kumar, V.S., Cuddihy, P., Aggour, K.S.: NodeGroup: a knowledge-driven data management abstraction for industrial machine learning. In: Proceedings of the 3rd International Workshop on Data Management for End-to-End Machine Learning, pp. 1–4 (2019). https://doi.org/10.1145/3329486.3329497

21. Lanin, V., Lyadova, L., Zamyatina, E., Vostroknutov, N.: An ontology-based approach to social networks mining. In: Proceedings of the 13th International Joint Conference on Knowledge Discovery, Knowledge Engineering and Knowledge Management, vol. 2: KEOD, pp. 234–239. SciTePress, Lisbon. (2021). https://doi.org/10.5220/0010716600003064

22. Lubyagina, A., Lyadova, L., Sukhov, A.: Business processes modelling with DSM platform at integrated systems development. ITHEA Int. J. "Inf. Content Process." 1(4), 372–389 (2014)
23. Lyadova, L., Sukhov, A., Nureev, M.: An ontology-based approach to the domain specific languages design. In: Proceedings of the 15th International Conference on Application of Information and Communication Technologies (AICT), pp. 1–6. IEEE, Baku (2021). https://doi.org/10.1109/AICT52784.2021.9620493
24. Lyadova, L.N., Sukhov, A.O., Zamyatina, E.B.: An integration of modeling systems based on DSM-platform. In: Proceedings of the 18th International Conference on Computers (part of CSCC '14). Advances in Information Science and Applications, vol. 2, pp. 421–425. CSCC, Santorini Island (2014)
25. Mavetera, N., Kroeze, J.H.: An ontology-driven software development framework. In: Proceedings of the 14th International Business Information Management Association Conference (14th IBIMA), pp. 13–24. Istanbul, Turkey (2010)
26. Mikov, A., Zamyatina, E., Kozlov, A., Ermakov, S.: Some problems of the simulation model efficiency and flexibility. In: Proceedings of the 8-th EUROSIM Congress on Modelling and Simulation EUROSIM, pp. 532–538. Cardiff, Wales, United Kingdom (2013)
27. Morocho, V., SaltorLluís, F., Pérez-Vidal, L.: Schema integration on federated spatial DB across ontologies. In: DBLP Conference: Engineering Federated Information Systems: Proceedings of the 5th Workshop EFIS 2003, pp. 63–72. Coventry, UK (2003)
28. Mukala, P., Buijs, J., Leemans, M., van der Aalst, W.: Learning analytics on coursera event data: a process mining approach. In: Proceedings of the 5th International Symposium on Data-driven Process Discovery and Analysis (SIMPDA 2015): CEUR Workshop Proceedings, vol. 1527, pp. 18–32. Vienna, Austria (2015)
29. OWL 2 Web Ontology Language Structural Specification and Functional-Style Syntax (Second Edition). https://www.w3.org/TR/2012/REC-owl2-syntax-20121211. Accessed 07 Apr 2022
30. Peña-Araya, V.: Galean: visualization of geolocated news events from social media. In: Proceedings of the 38th International ACM SIGIR Conference on Research and Development in Information Retrieval (SIGIR '15), pp. 1041–1042. ACM, New York (2015). https://doi.org/10.1145/2766462.2767862
31. Ritter, A.: Open domain event extraction from twitter. In: Proceedings of the 18th ACM SIGKDD International Conference on Knowledge Discovery and Data Mining, pp. 1104–1112 (2012). https://doi.org/10.1145/2339530.2339704
32. Shalyaeva, I., Lyadova, L., Lanin, V.: Events Analysis Based on Internet Information Retrieval and Process Mining Tools. In: Proceeding of the 10th International Conference on Application of Information and Communication Technologies (AICT), pp. 168–172. IEEE, Baku (2016). https://doi.org/10.1109/ICAICT.2016.7991678
33. Shalyaeva, I., Lyadova, L., Lanin, V.: Ontology-driven system for monitoring global processes on basis of internet news. In: Proceedings of IEEE 11th International Conference on Application of Information and Communication Technologies (AICT2017), pp. 385–389. IEEE, Moscow (2017). https://doi.org/10.1109/ICAICT.2017.8687086
34. Suvorov, N.M., Lyadova, L.N.: HP-graph as a Basis of a DSM Platform Visual Model Editor. Proc. Inst. Syst. Programm. RAS 32(2), 149–160 (2020). https://doi.org/10.15514/ISPRAS-2020-32(2)-12
35. Tumbinskaya, M.V.: Protection of information in social networks from social engineering attacks of the attacker. J. Appl. Inf. 12(3(69)), 88–102 (2017)
36. Van der Aalst, W.M.P., Reijers, H., Song, M.: Discovering social networks from event logs. Comput. Support. Coop. Work 14, 549–593 (2005). https://doi.org/10.1007/s10606-005-9005-9

37. Vokhmintsev, A., Melnikov, A.: The knowledge on the basis of fact analysis in business intelligence. In: Kovács, G.L., Kochan, D. (eds.) NEW PROLAMAT 2013. IAICT, vol. 411, pp. 354–363. Springer, Heidelberg (2013). https://doi.org/10.1007/978-3-642-41329-2_34

38. Xiao, G., Hovland, D., Bilidas, D., Rezk, M., Giese, M., Calvanese, D.: Efficient ontology-based data integration with canonical IRIs. In: Gangemi, A., et al. (eds.) ESWC 2018. LNCS, vol. 10843, pp. 697–713. Springer, Cham (2018). https://doi.org/10.1007/978-3-319-93417-4_45

39. Yang, D., Liao, X., Shen, H., Cheng, X., Chen, G.: Dynamic node immunization for restraint of harmful information diffusion in social networks. Phys. A Stat. Mech. Appl. **503**, 640–649 (2018). https://doi.org/10.1016/j.physa.2018.02.128.

40. Zavarella, V.: An Ontology-Based Approach to Social Media Mining for Crisis Management. In: SSA-SMILE@ ESWC, pp. 55–66 (2014)

41. Zayakin, V.S., Lyadova, L.N., Rabchevskiy, E.A.: Design patterns for a knowledge-driven analytical platform. Proc. Inst. Syst. Programm. RAS **34**(2), 43–56 (2022). https://doi.org/10.15514/ISPRAS-2022-34(2)-4

42. Zhan, L., Jiang, X.: Survey on event extraction technology in information extraction research area. In: Proceedings of the IEEE 3rd Information Technology, Networking, Electronic and Automation Control Conference (ITNEC), pp. 2121–2126. IEEE, Chengdu, China (2019). https://doi.org/10.1109/ITNEC.2019.8729158

43. Zhao, N., Cheng, X., Guo, X.: Impact of information spread and investment behavior on the diffusion of internet investment products. Phys. A Stat. Mech. Appl. **512**, 427–436 (2018). https://doi.org/10.1016/j.physa.2018.08.075

How to Design a Business-Oriented Digitalized Innovation Environment: A Multi-perspective Approach

Lukas Hellwig[1,2](✉) [iD], Jan Pawlowski[1,2] [iD], and Michael Schäfer[2]

[1] University of Jyväskylä, Seminaarinkatu 15, 40014 Jyväskylä, Finland
{lukas.hellwig,jan.pawlowski}@hs-ruhrwest.de
[2] Ruhr West University of Applied Science, Lützowstraße 5, 46236 Bottrop, Germany
michael.schaefer@hs-ruhrwest.de

Abstract. The present study is based on the need of companies to increase their innovation capacity and promote the digital competencies of their employees. In the private and academic context, digitized innovation environments have been identified as a promising concept. The transfer of these potentials to the business context has so far only been partially successful and rarely studied scientifically. Based on preliminary studies and a complementary literature review, a total of 19 factors could be identified that influence a projection of the DIE approach also for the business context. For this purpose, an approach as holistic as possible was chosen and factors from different perspectives were considered: Business, Employee, Technology, and Process. The factors range from technical requirements such as "Functionality" to social issues of the "Stakeholder Mindset". The range of factors identified thus also reflects the complexity of the DIE phenomenon. Further mapping and analysis were also able to identify correlations between the individual factors and derive initial recommendations for action. Thus, the study makes a valuable contribution to both practice and science by providing the basis for concept designs in practice and interventions in science.

Keywords: Digitalized innovation environment · Fabrication laboratory · Fablab · Makerspace · Concept design · Influencing factor · Business orientation · Multi-perspective approach

1 Introduction

The digital transformation as an irreversible process is in full progress and meanwhile permeates all areas of daily life, fundamentally influencing structures and processes [1]. Extensive changes can be observed both in the private sphere and in the business context, so it is not surprising that this phenomenon is also frequently the subject of scientific research [2–5]. Due to the comprehensive areas of influence and the multitude of manifestations, a wide variety of disciplines are dealing with digital transformation and examining it from different perspectives.

A. Fred et al. (Eds.): IC3K 2021, CCIS 1718, pp. 150–171, 2023.
https://doi.org/10.1007/978-3-031-35924-8_9

In this paper, we look at the specific phenomenon of digitalized innovation environments in the context of the disciplines of information systems and business information systems. These environments are becoming increasingly popular, especially in academic and private contexts, but are also being noticed more and more by companies [6]. In recent years, a separate movement and community have developed around DIEs: The Makers. They have evolved from the former DIY community but are now increasingly using digital systems and technologies to realize their ideas. In doing so, the members of the Maker community resort to new approaches to innovation, such as Open Innovation [7], User Innovation, or Digital Innovation [8, 9]. Whereas, according to Schumpeter's model [10], innovation used to come from a single inventor and was driven to the point of commercialization, innovation in these communities and institutions takes place in an iterative and collaborative process [11, 12]. These developments in the nature of innovation can also already be seen in companies:

Innovation processes are already being opened up and external players are being involved to obtain new stimuli. As a result, innovation is no longer the exclusive task of research and development departments in companies; instead, interdisciplinary innovation teams are increasingly being formed. This development is already being researched under the term "open innovation" and is a frequent subject of research. On the other hand, there is the increased use of digital technologies and methods in innovation processes, which is generally known as digital innovation. The results and products of innovation processes are also becoming increasingly digital in nature, enabling enormous growth potential due to their scalability. For example, many of the world's most valuable companies are based on digital innovation (e.g. Amazon, Apple, Microsoft, Alphabet, Alibaba, and Facebook [13]). Digital innovation and the comparatively low investment costs associated with it mean that even smaller companies can act as innovation drivers. Disruptive innovations are no longer the preserve of financially strong concerns but are frequently developed by more flexible start-ups. The pressure to innovate has increased in recent decades, and shorter and shorter iteration cycles are necessary to keep up with the competition for innovation leadership. For this purpose, it is necessary to understand the potentials known from other contexts and to develop them systematically.

Based on the conference paper by Hellwig et al. [14], this paper supplements the previous state of knowledge by taking a more detailed look and also considers the corporate perspective as well as technology and process aspects. For this holistic approach, a complementary case study is used for evaluation and a solid basis for an action-oriented bussiness-oriented DIEs design is laid. In this paper, we focus on the business perspective and examine the potentials for companies that arise from the digital transformation and the development around DIEs and identify relevant factors that influence the use of these potentials. So far, only superficial efforts have been made to identify these factors [15]. For this purpose, we look at developments in other contexts and systematically project the findings onto the business context. In the private and academic sectors, there are already environments that specifically promote open innovation and digital innovation and are characterized by their interdisciplinary innovation teams [16]. These processes are often supported by digital technologies to implement ideas in the minimum amount of time [17]. There are several names for comparable facilities such as Coworkingspace, FabLab, Makerspaces, living Labs, innovations laboratory, or innovation hubs [18]. In this paper, we use the term Digitalized Innovation Environments (DIE) as an umbrella to summarize these facilities, as they are all characterized by the use of digital technologies and methods to support innovation while providing open access to a wide range of players [19]. This combination leads to faster iteration cycles through the quick realization of initial prototypes by using digital manufacturing technologies like 3D printing and CNC milling [20]. The users of such facilities are often very heterogeneous, which enables an interdisciplinary exchange among them while at the same time maintaining democratic standards. In the academic environment, these facilities are mostly used to teach applied sciences according to the hands-on principle [21]. In the private context, such DIEs are often organized in the form of clubs whose users have a passion for do-it-yourself and an affinity for technology [22, 23]. These users name themselves Makers.

The potential of these facilities has so far only been recognized or taken up by companies to a very limited extent. Only in a few cases have DIEs been integrated directly into corporate processes [24]. Larger corporations occasionally maintain their own innovation environments, but these are usually reserved for the research and development departments and do not meet the requirement of open and interdisciplinary knowledge exchange. As a result, the potential for innovation and the knowledge of other employees usually remain unexploited [25].

Even more extensive collaborations between external DIEs and companies have rarely been the subject of research in the scientific community, although the fundamental potentials have certainly already been considered [26, 27]. These are also seen as promising drivers of innovation in companies but have not yet been structurally opened up [28]. So far, however, no specific focus has been placed on how these potentials can be tapped or which factors play a role in this. This is certainly also due to the low level of empirical data available since comprehensive cooperations or integrations of DIEs have been very rare so far.

Against this background, the paper attempts to derive a structured framework for the successful integration of DIEs into business innovation processes based on a variety of different research approaches. In particular, the paper focuses on the influencing factors but also discusses the underlying framework conditions. A multi-perspective approach will be used to obtain as comprehensive a picture as possible. In addition to the company perspective, the employee, the process, the product, and the technology perspectives will also be taken into account. The starting point for this is the investigation of the usage behavior of employees in one of the few company-internal DIEs. This data basis is supplemented by further investigations of the company's potential and processes as well as the comprehensive consideration of the innovation and development processes within DIEs. In summary, the research approach can be formulated in the following research question:

RQ: What factors influence the design of a business-centered Digitalized Innovation Environment?

This explorative approach tries to structure the puzzle pieces around the topic of DIEs in the business context and combine them into a larger picture. At the same time, it is intended to make an important contribution to practice, in that the intended results can be applied to the implementation of new types of innovation environments in the business context. But also for science, this study represents an important contribution to better understanding the phenomenon of DIEs and their underlying mechanisms. Especially in the information systems discipline, the findings can be used as a basis for further investigations. For example, subsequent action design science research approaches could be realized in the form of concrete interventions [29]. This would also create the opportunity to make a significant contribution to theory building [9].

2 Digitalized Innovation Environments

In the private and academic context, environments in which innovations are targeted and offer a platform for the exchange of knowledge and equipment are already well-known instruments [27, 30]. However, isolated attempts can also be observed in the business sector in the form of coworking spaces and LivingLabs [6, 31]. LivingLabs are characterized by their realistic environment and the user as co-creator, and their underlying innovation methods have already been identified as an element of user innovation [32]. The ever-increasing use of a wide variety of digital components and tools has become a new type of innovation in recent years. For example, 3D printers and CNC mills paired with in-house electronics development allow the production of functional prototypes without having to be skilled in craftsmanship [33]. Thus, new user groups can help create the innovation process and even external actors can be involved via digital communication channels. Based on these technologies, a variety of different innovation environments have developed under different names. Makerspaces, Hackerspaces, Fablabs, InnovationLabs, and Cocreation Laboratory are just a few common names. These environments have evolved from different contexts and differ in their focus, orientation, and user groups [34]. However, the names do not allow for a clear delineation, as there is no common understanding of the terms. Alone a Fab Charter, which defines some very generic requirements for a FabLab defines some criteria [35]. There have already been attempts to create a clear understanding in science, but this has only achieved insufficient separation and the digital aspect has been excluded [36, 37]. Each innovation environment is individually adapted to its specific context and contains characteristics from the different streams. For this study, the totality of these comparable facilities with all their facets will be considered. Therefore, the term "digitized innovation environment" is adopted as an umbrella term for these facilities. These environments are physical spaces that use a variety of different digital technologies to support innovation but are not themselves digital. Thus, unlike a virtual reality environment, these are digitalized rather than digital/digitized innovation environments. For this study, use the following definition of "Digitalized Innovation Environments":

"Digitalized Innovation Environments are physical spaces that provide both traditional and digital tools and state-of-the-art technologies to support collaborative and interdisciplinary innovation and knowledge transfer" [38].

Sporadically, the potential of such DIEs has already been recognized by companies and various efforts have been made to integrate them into their innovation processes [24, 39]. However, collaboration has so far mostly been limited to supporting research and development departments [40]. Some large companies provide their own DIEs to their development teams, but even these have so far mostly been reserved for a very limited circle of users and are neither organized in an interdisciplinary way nor do they encourage open knowledge transfer. As a result, the potentials of the DIE known from the private and academic contexts are not exploited [25]. Previous studies have already identified the potentials and functions that a DIE could assume within a company [38], but there is a lack of concrete implementation scenarios. Accordingly, empirical data on the integration of DIEs and companies is very limited, so the previous findings have to be located on a meta-level, which does not support a concrete application so far. In a logical next step, the development of a precise concept for the use, instruction, communication, and networking of such facilities is necessary [28]. Initial framework conditions have already been identified that influence the use of a DIE opportunity. However, so far these only cover the employee perspective. To enable successful implementation, however, the company perspective is also of crucial importance, as is the influence on the innovation products. Only when integration into existing structures is made possible can empirical data be collected on the impact on companies' innovation capabilities. In the next step, this can lead to inductive theory building, which represents a far-reaching contribution to the IS research landscape as well as to practice.

3 Methodological Approach

Although DIEs are a well-known phenomenon, most scientific studies consider them in an academic or private context. Empirical data on DIEs in a business context are so far very limited. It is therefore not possible to refer to a large number of existing best-practice examples to tackle the research question. Therefore, it is to a certain extent a chicken-and-egg problem: Without viable concepts and studies on the embedding of DIEs in established companies, the possible potentials will not be leveraged, but without functioning symbioses, it is also difficult to develop appropriate and sound concepts. This paper attempts to contribute to breaking this deadlock by using existing data from various related research fields to derive a theoretical concept in a systematic analysis process. This must then be empirically tested and validated in further steps.

To be able to develop a concept that is as far-reaching as possible, it is necessary to take into account the complexity of the construct and view it from different points of view. Only if all the players involved are taken into account can a DIE be sustainably integrated into existing business structures and processes and generate added value. This paper will therefore base its identification of relevant factors and framework conditions on the following four dimensions: Company perspective, employee perspective, process aspects, and technology aspects.

The business perspective forms the foundation of the study, as it defines the context in which implementation can take place at all. Thus, the integration of a DIE must represent added value for the company and fulfill several basic requirements. For example, such a project must be economical or have other positive effects on the company. Based on the initial research question, further guiding questions (GQ) are formulated in the following to specify the perspectives:

GQ1.1: Which company factors influence the integration of a DIE?

GQ1.2: Which framework conditions must be fulfilled by the company?

The employee perspective is seen as another fundamental perspective. A DIE without users is nothing more than a hall with a wide variety of technologies and tools. It must therefore be ensured that the employees also actively support and carry the idea. For this reason, the relevant influencing factors that favor the fundamental use of DIEs by employees are also of the greatest relevance to the overall concept. These can be summarized in the following sub-research questions:

GQ2.1: How can employees be motivated to use DIEs?

GQ2.2: What conditions must be met for employee-friendly embedding?

In other contexts, it has been shown that development and innovation processes in DIEs are different from those in conventional research and development departments in companies [41]. Also on the process level, a synchronization of companies and DIEs has to be ensured for a successful embedding. Therefore, the following sub-research questions should also be addressed and considered:

GQ3.1: Under which general conditions do successful DIE development processes take place?

GQ3.2: Which process characteristics influence the integration of a DIE?

Finally, the technology and tools used in a DIE also represent a decisive dimension. It is only through the use of digital fabrication technologies that new concepts can be tested or new actors can be integrated into innovation processes [17]. Therefore, relevant influencing factors for the concept design should also be derived from this perspective through the following supporting research questions.

GQ4.1: What framework conditions must be in place for appropriate technology deployment?

GQ4.2: What factors influence technology use within DIEs?

The listed sub-research questions illustrate the complexity of the approach to integrate a DIE into existing business structures. Due to the limited available data, this study does not claim to develop a design down to the smallest detail, but rather intends to provide a basic structure with the most salient points. Also, the listed perspectives must not be seen as independent of each other, but rather an interrelation is to be expected. This is suggested by case studies from the DIE environment. To capture the influencing factors from different perspectives in the best possible way, this study makes use of different data sets and analyzes and interprets them with the help of complementary theoretical models. Expert interviews [42] with users of one of the few known permanently integrated DIEs in a company form the starting point [14]. These findings are supplemented with the results of a case study in which the product development processes in interdisciplinary DIE development teams were examined [41]. The whole is put into the context of already existing theoretical potential analyses on cooperations of DIEs and companies to identify overlaps but also contrasts [24, 38]. The chosen methodological multi-perspective approach thus makes use of different qualitative and quantitative research and analysis methods, so that it can be understood as a form of mixed-method approach [43]. The data sets used and the associated evaluation methods are presented below.

3.1 Expert Interviews

The expert interviews were conducted with employees of a medium-sized manufacturing company in Germany that maintains its own FabLab [14]. This FabLab meets the above definition. The employees came from different departments and all had experience in the FabLab. A total of seven employees from the areas of research & development, production, marketing, and administration were interviewed. Guidelines with previously identified dimensions were used for the interviews. These were deduced from established models and theories. Essentially, the dimensions were derived from Customer orientation [44], the Technology Acceptance Model (TAM3) [45], and the Innovation Diffusion Theory [46] and generalized in such a way that they could be applied to the DIE experience. For the guidelines, corresponding leading questions were formulated, which invited the interviewees to express their opinions freely [47]. At the same time, the interviewees were given sufficient space to express themselves freely to be able to capture influencing factors that are not covered by the existing models. After the comprehensibility of the questions could be confirmed in a pretest with two volunteers, the interviews were conducted in presence. The interviews were recorded and lasted between 40 and 65 min.

The interviews were then analyzed qualitatively, which is suitable for the exploratory research approach [47]. For this purpose, selective transcripts were made and only the passages relevant to the research questions were recorded [48]. Parallel to the recording, a categorization system was developed in accordance with the object-oriented theory formation (cf. Grounded theory [49]), which allows the structured classification of individual statements [50]. This inductive process of category formation is already part of the data evaluation and is particularly suitable for explorative study designs [51]. In subsequent steps, the individual statements were generalized with the help of qualitative content analysis in such a way that they can be applied to the research questions. The evaluation is thus divided into four analysis steps: paraphrasing, generalization to a defined abstraction level, first reduction, and second reduction [48].

3.2 Case Study

An interpretive case study [52] in which the development processes within a DIE are examined serves as an essential second data basis. This study is one of the few that covers both the socio-technological aspects and the resulting potentials and barriers [41]. Over a period of twelve months, 15 product development processes in the context of DIEs were monitored, and concluding interviews were conducted. All projects took place in the context of people with disabilities and pursued the goal of developing an individualized aid for a specific user. The development teams always consisted of the associated user, experienced makers from the DIE setting, and experts for the respective product to be developed and were characterized by a high degree of interdisciplinarity. The teams were able to freely design their processes and carry them out without external guidelines. They always had all the capabilities of one of the largest DIEs in Germany at their disposal. From the literature [22, 24, 38, 53–56], seven dimensions were derived in advance under which the processes were to be considered: participation, communication, organization, use of technology, resources, premises, and activities. During the case study, memos were continuously prepared to be able to reconstruct connections and relationships in the follow-up [57]. Both procedural and analytical memos were prepared to enable an accompanying evaluation [58]. In addition to the accompanying observation, guideline interviews were conducted with the actors involved after the development processes had been completed. The guiding questions were based on the same dimensions of the observation and were evaluated and interpreted according to a similar procedure as described above. In the evaluation of the 16 interviews, special emphasis was placed on the consideration of the hermeneutic circle and the individual statements were always embedded in the overall context [59]. In the final step of the analysis, the observations were checked for consistency with the statements of the interview partners and the findings were projected onto the underlying research questions.

3.3 Literature Review

In addition to the empirical data, a literature review was conducted to integrate findings from related contexts. Since DIEs have been used in academic and private contexts for some time and established concepts exist, corresponding studies can also serve as a source for relevant design aspects for the entrepreneurial context. For this purpose, thematically relevant study results were examined for their applicability and relevance to companies. In our search for suitable literature, we used the established Webster, Watson [60] methodology. In addition, we structured our search according to Cooper's taxonomy [61] and considered Vom Brocke et.al. Recommendations [62]. We operationalized the general review approach by using an iterative process of definition, clarification, and refinement within our research team to identify the most important keywords and search terms for our strategic search [63]. This identification process was based on scoping studies, initial literature findings, and discussions within our team [64]. The literature search is not limited to certain journals and conferences of Information Systems but considers interdisciplinary databases AIS Library, IEEE Explorer, Springer Link, ScienceDirect, and Elsevier Science. This interdisciplinary approach has already been identified as promising [65]. To expand our search, we also went forward and backward from our initial results [60]. To be considered for further exploitation, the resources had to fulfill the following criteria:

- The underlying environment meets the definition of a DIE;
- One of the five perspectives mentioned above is taken into account;
- Generalizability for the business context is possible;
- An empirical evidence base is given.

The references identified as relevant are used in the following to complete the design and are included in the respective perspectives at the appropriate point.

4 Multi-perspective Impact Factor Identification

In the following, the results of the two underlying data sets are presented in a structured manner supplemented by scientific sources from adjacent research settings. For this purpose, the relevant perspectives identified in advance are used as a structure. The guiding questions support the identification by setting the framework. Some aspects are relevant for several perspectives, but to avoid redundancies, they were assigned to the main perspective only.

4.1 Business-Perspective

Although empirical data on the effects of embedding a DIE in corporate structures are limited, a large number of influencing factors have already been identified [38, 54]. For example, DIEs represent an opportunity to establish new innovation approaches such as digital innovation [66] or open/user innovation [7, 67] in companies. In principle, DIEs can take on various functions in companies: Communication / Networking Platform, Digital Fabrication Environment, Digital Competency Incubator, and Market Research [38]. Thus, a DIE has both a direct and an indirect impact on a company. Direct impacts identified include the integration of digital innovation approaches [26], independent prototype development [28, 68], and the integration of additional players in the innovation process [24]. Indirect impacts are also to be expected, such as improved knowledge transfer, [69] increased innovation capability [28], or higher employee satisfaction [53].

In general, it can be observed that innovation processes have changed in the context of digital transformation and that digitalized activities are an integral part of them [70]. Some of these practices through the digitalization of innovation processes, such as the use of digital tools/software, the integration of digital platforms and networks, or the use of digital fabrication, are an integral part of innovation processes as they are known from the DIEs [70]. This also results from the observations and statements of the participants of the development processes within a DIE [41]. For example, during the ideation phase, open-source platforms were used to provide inspiration, and digital fabrication technologies were used to test initial approaches to solutions. DIEs thus intuitively support the new activities within corporate innovation processes. To actually enable these diverse changes to the existing structures, an appropriate mindset of the decision-makers within the company and a willingness for change are required. "Stakeholder Mindset" and "Willingness to Change" therefore seem to be a relevant facts for the implementation of a business-oriented DIE (GQ1.1).

In addition to the process level, the competency requirements within companies have also changed and digital competencies are increasingly required [71]. It is known from the academic context that these new competence requirements can be specifically addressed in DIEs [72]. The transferability to an entrepreneurial context was demonstrated in the case study, in which almost all participants stated that they had built up new digital competencies during the development process. Accordingly, DIEs can also support corporate needs at this level.

A DIE is therefore able to address a wide variety of needs in enterprises and thus make a contribution to sustainable competitiveness. The influencing factors can also be derived from these potentials because only if the embedding of a DIE can unfold the possible potentials, the company benefits from the initial expenses and the necessary structural adjustments. In a concept design, therefore, the deployment of potential should be presented as a prerequisite from the company's perspective and corresponding mechanisms that support this should be considered. "Grasping Potentials" thus represents another relevant factor (GQ1.2).

4.2 Employee-Perspective

Without users, a DIE is merely an area with a wide variety of tools and digital technologies. Only motivated and interdisciplinary users can unleash their potential. It must therefore be ensured that a company's employees are also motivated to use it and that appropriate framework conditions are created that make its use as uncomplicated as possible. For this perspective, we can draw on the comprehensive expert interviews, which focus on the factors influencing usage behavior [14]. In a previous study, seven relevant dimensions of influence were identified through structured analysis: User, Presentation, Offer, Perception, Structure, Contact Person, and Environment (Fig. 1).

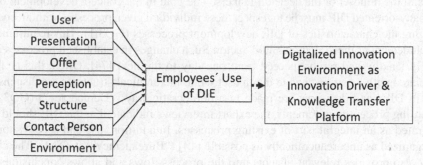

Fig. 1. Digitalized Innovation Environment Use Model [14].

It is noticeable that in the entrepreneurial context factors have an influence which has so far been largely disregarded in other contexts. For example, the image of the DIE within the company influences its use just like the relevance for day-to-day business [14]. Contrary to fears on the business side, employees even rate a high degree of work content relevance as a motivating factor. Also, the original intention of having as few hierarchical structures as possible does not seem to be appropriate for the corporate context [73]. On the contrary, the presence of a central, available, and competent contact person is named as a decisive factor. Private DIEs in particular are mostly self-organized without fixed structures and contact persons [53] (GQ2.2). Comparable results can be found in the case study on the development of aids. Here, as well, a competent contact person is considered positive by the non-experienced actors, especially in the case of technological issues [41]. However, great importance is still attached to exchange and open project design at eye level. Finally, it must also be concluded from the underlying data that not every individual can be motivated to use the system. A minimum of intrinsic motivation and openness must be brought along on the part of the employees (GQ2.1). The influencing factors listed can only make the entry as low-threshold as possible; forced use is not considered to be effective.

For the design of an integration concept, the identified factors are of the highest relevance and should be fulfilled as comprehensively as possible. Even if individual factors leave room for interpretation, no completely contradictory statements could be identified either within the studies or about the corporate perspective. For this reason, the identified factors of user behavior can also be adopted for the design of a business-oriented DIE. Only a small change is made by changing the factor "User" to "Intrinsic Motivation". This shifts the focus more towards the design approach. Individual sub-dimensions of this factor merge more appropriately into other perspectives.

4.3 Process-Aspects

Business workflows and processes are highly individual and therefore permit only limited general statements. In principle, however, it can be stated that innovation processes, for instance, are changing as a result of the ongoing digital transformation and are encompassing new activities and involving new players [70]. The extent to which this is already happening in companies depends on a variety of factors such as the branch, the size, the age, and the mindset of the decision-makers. The goal in the concept development of a company-oriented DIE must be to respect these individual given processes without counteracting the characteristics of DIE development processes (GQ3.1). This requirement is included under the "Integratability" factor. Such changes in established processes are usually lengthy and rarely succeed from one day to the next [74]. Often, this is also associated with a certain change in mindset when hierarchical structures are dispensed with in DIEs and decisions are made in a democratic way ("Democracy") (GQ3.2). Regarding process requirements, the expert interviews indicate that the DIE should be integrated as an integral part of existing processes. In addition, use and access should be organized as unbureaucratically as possible [14] ("Bureaucracy") (GQ3.1). The case study also provides relevant insights into the process flows and allows conclusions to be drawn about the requirements for successful embedding. Communication within the project teams was identified as a crucial factor [41]. Even if this could be maintained via digital channels, the personal meetings in the DIE were decisive for success. In general, it was found that the processes did not run in a linear sequence, but that several solution approaches were worked on in parallel in several iteration cycles [75]. This made the processes more difficult to plan and required flexible adjustments depending on capacities and intermediate results. A design of processes within a business-oriented DIE therefore should respect the "Agility" of this approach (GQ3.2). To exploit the dynamics of innovation processes within DIE and to be able to test different approaches to solutions, an appropriate "Error Culture" is necessary, which also tolerates the failure of approaches and sees these as part of progress (GQ3.1).

The processes thus show clear differences from the innovation processes of established companies, which are often planned over months or years. To exploit the potential of DIEs, a higher degree of flexibility must be made possible and linear top-down processes broken up.

4.4 Technology-Aspects

DIEs are characterized by extensive use of technology. Without these diverse technologies, some of the innovation approaches and methods would not be feasible and the overall characteristics would change [76]. It is, therefore, necessary to also take the perspective of the technology to identify relevant factors for a design. Even though various technologies create new possibilities, they often also pose requirements that have to be fulfilled for a value-adding application.

A fundamental prerequisite for any technology to unleash its potential is that it be used. The usage behavior of employees is often dependent on the acceptance of the technology [45]. For this reason, the expert interviews are suitable as a data basis for a more detailed investigation, since the leading questions used are partly based on established acceptance models (TAM3 [45]) and have captured this dimension. As a supplement, the observations from the case study are used, in which the use of technology was also observed and commented on in the subsequent interviews.

The user-friendliness of the technologies and tools used can be identified as a central aspect in both studies [14, 41] ("Usability") (GQ4.2). This applies to both the hardware and the software. Deficiencies in intuitive use can be mitigated to some extent by the presence of an expert, but since independent use by employees is desired at the same time, these deficiencies cannot be overcome in their entirety. A concept should therefore also provide sufficient leeway for the initial development of employee competence in the use of the technologies. In addition to ease of use, readiness for use and availability have also been mentioned as key factors (GQ4.2). Only if the tools and machines were available and functional at short notice could the potential of the DIE with its short iteration cycles be developed. In particular, new technologies such as 3D printers or laser cutters, while increasingly affordable, are also often still maintenance-intensive and error-prone. If innovation processes are delayed due to technical problems, this can even lead to the failure of the entire process [41]. "Functionality" and "Availability" are therefore central success factors.

In addition to pure availability and functionality, the relevance for the business purpose was also emphasized several times. Only if the technologies were seriously used in the further development of products or services that are also of commercial interest would they be positively received. Otherwise, there is a danger that the entire DIE will be misjudged as a playground and gain a negative reputation (GQ4.1). The technologies used must therefore fit plausibly with the business purpose ("Business Relevance").

4.5 Structured Mapping

After the individual dimensions have been examined in more detail based on different databases and supplementary literature, these findings need to be structured and appropriately processed to enable them to be used in practice. Furthermore, this structure is to be the basis for further discussion regarding the design of a DIE. To be able to transfer the evaluation to general business-oriented DIEs, a generalization is necessary. Due to the small amount of empirical data, this is done inductively and is based on Mayring's [48] process for increasing the level of abstraction. The specific characteristics of the identified factors, which can be traced back to the research setting, have to be abstracted to achieve better general validity for other contexts and companies.

The initial research question about the influencing factors remains at the center of the structuring process. Even though some assessment has already been made in the evaluation of the databases, the initial focus is on identifying these factors. To achieve maximum of clarity on this complex issue, an assessment of the individual factors and their effects on the presentation and visualization will be omitted from the beginning. The structure takes up the four dimensions of the research approach and divides the factors into the categories: Employee, Business, Technology, and Process. Some of the identified factors are cross-sectional topics, which could be assigned to several categories. In this case, an assignment was made based on the largest intersection. It should be noted that individual factors influence each other and should not be viewed in isolated instances.

The following visualization builds on the Digitalized Innovation Environment Use Model [14] and supplements it with the newly identified factors.

A total of 19 influencing factors were extracted from the existing database. These range from tangible factors such as the functionality of the available technologies to more social factors such as the mindset of the stakeholders or an appropriate error culture. The range of factors identified again underscores the complexity of the socio-technological construct of a DIE. Further studies would have to be conducted on each of the factors listed to capture them in their respective depths. Interaction between the individual factors can also be assumed. For example, technology factors are expected (Fig. 2).

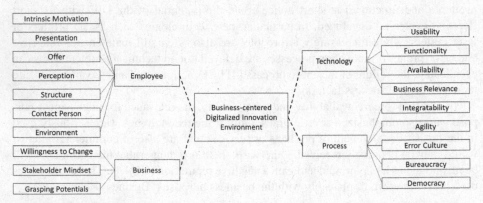

Fig. 2. Conceptual Model of Impact Factors of a business-oriented Digitalized Innovation

Environment to have a significant influence on process factors. Only if the available technologies are user-friendly and functional can appropriately agile processes be designed. This study initially intends to draw a general picture and lay the foundation for further investigations. Based on this, further recommendations for action for the realization of a business-oriented DIE will be derived in the next step.

5   DIE Design-Aspects

The 19 influencing factors identified are large of a subjective or individual nature. For example, "business relevance" depends on the business purpose of a company and can therefore not be supported by a general concept. The "Integratability" of the processes also depends on the existing processes and is therefore also influenced by a variety of other factors. A uniform concept that can be applied to all companies, therefore, appears to be unrealistic. Rather, the identified factors should serve as guidelines in the development of an individual concept.

Nevertheless, some basic aspects will be discussed below and evaluated about their consideration of the influencing factors. To turn the identified factors into a design theory, further evaluations are necessary. Quantification of the relationships using structural equation modeling would be a helpful addition [77]. The following design aspects can therefore be used as a basis for theory development. Thus, a further contribution to the transferability of the research results into practice should be made and a basis for subsequent empirical studies will be laid.

Basically, two different approaches to a business-oriented DIE can be distinguished: Internal and external (GQ1.2). While internal DIEs are a permanent part of the corporate structure and are also managed by it [78, 79], external DIEs are rather cooperations between companies and external providers [80]. Some universities now maintain their own DIEs, which they use for their students, but also increasingly offer special services to companies [41]. Due to the initial investment costs in setting up a DIE and the ongoing costs in maintaining it, internal solutions have so far only been known from large companies that are financially strong enough. However, these concepts must be examined to determine whether they still meet the criteria of a DIE and whether actors outside the company can also become involved in projects. Often, important potentials are not exploited here, since these internal facilities are accessible only to the research and development department of the respective company. Only partially and in defined event formats can external users get involved in predefined topics [24]. One of the best-known formats is the Makerthon, in which interdisciplinary small groups develop ideas on topics specified by the organizer [54]. A major advantage of internal DIEs is the possibility of optimally adapting the DIE to the company and its structures, both technologically and at the process level. However, it has been shown that with an internal administration and thus also internal contact persons, the company hierarchies cannot be overcome, and thus a democratic exchange of knowledge is made more difficult [14]. There is also a risk that projects will become bureaucratic due to the high commercial orientation and the associated documentation requirements. However, internal DIEs are also physically located directly at a company site, so that easy accessibility is possible without long distances. This also positively influences the visibility of activities within the DIE, which can have a positive effect on the perception factor.

On the other hand, there are external DIEs that are operated by universities, associations, or service providers and then support the companies through various forms of cooperation. The administration, organization, and also equipment are thus regulated externally by the company [41]. Thus, the company has much lower financial liabilities, which allows even smaller and medium-sized companies to access the potential. Thus, the entry barrier is generally lower, and also a lower willingness to change and a more reserved mindset of the decision-makers can lead to unlocking the potentials. However, the relevance for the individual business is not optimal due to the technological equipment, which is often as widespread as possible. In addition, structures and processes across company boundaries are often more complex and bureaucratic. Due to the less profit-oriented orientation of external DIEs, more pronounced error culture and more democratic decision-making can be assumed. Frequently, DIEs at universities are also accessible to a wide variety of user groups in parallel, which also results in changed potentials or these are more pronounced. Thus, external competencies can be accessed more flexibly and the DIE can also be used as a platform for knowledge transfer and networking. However, these broad user groups inevitably also lead to lower availability and functionality of individual technologies due to third-party or incorrect operations.

Only a few external DIEs have a permanent contact person, which can delay learning processes and maintenance measures.

The availability of a contact person has proven to be a very central aspect in previous studies. While inexperienced users of a DIE considered the support provided by a contact person who was available at all times to be helpful [41], other more experienced users in the corporate context tended to see this as restricting their flexibility and perceived it as an obstructive hierarchical structure [14]. In addition to the support function for dealing with a wide variety of technologies within a DIE, a contact person often also ensures the functionality and availability of all necessary technologies [81]. Thus, the design of the "contact person" factor also significantly influences other identified factors such as "functionality" or "availability". In addition to technical support, a contact person could have a supporting role in bureaucratic hurdles, which could reduce them. By taking over the administrative tasks surrounding the operation of a DIE, users could focus on the implementation of projects, leading to more targeted and business-relevant processes. DIEs without a defined contact person often lack adequate transparency and visibility. These tasks could also be taken over and thus the factors "Presentation" and "Perception" could be positively influenced. In summary, it can be stated that a contact person in a business-oriented DIE has a key role and involves very complex tasks. The recruitment of such a position should therefore be done with great care, as both technical competencies and an appropriate service mindset are required. The contact person has a decisive influence on the success of a business-oriented DIE and the utilization of its theoretical potential.

When considering the 19 identified influencing factors, in addition to the tangible factors, the mindset of the actors involved is also a very central factor [14]. This also has the potential to influence a large number of other factors and to make a decisive contribution to the success or failure of the integration of a business-centric DIE. The basic prerequisite for initiating a DIE is therefore the willingness of the decision-makers to change and appropriate support for the project. For the successful use of the theoretical potentials, the right attitudes of the employees, as well as a possible contact person, are also necessary. For example, an appropriate error culture can only be implemented with an error-tolerant attitude on the part of all involved. There must also be a willingness to dispense with hierarchical structures within the DIE to enable the transfer of knowledge and information on an equal footing. The mindset of the users is therefore also a very central factor, which influences many other factors. This mindset of the people involved is highly individual and can only be influenced to a limited extent. However, by addressing the factors of "Business Relevance" or "Integratability" in a targeted manner, reservations can at least be reduced.

Furthermore, the physical space of the DIE has been expressed by many users as a deciding factor. In addition to the technological equipment, an inviting and inspiring atmosphere also plays a central role [82]. A business-oriented DIE should therefore not be designed like a workshop or laboratory, but also as a meeting place and collaboration platform. In their comprehensive literature review, Rieken, Boehm, Heinzen, Meboldt [54] had already identified some elementary areas that address the different functions of a DIE. This ranges up to cafe areas in which an informal exchange is to be made possible. This is how the different functions of a DIE can be achieved. An appropriate environment in turn influences other identified factors such as "Usability" or the "Intrinsic Motivation" of employees. When initiating a business-oriented DIE, value should be placed not only on purely technological equipment but also on a motivating interior. However, the actual implementation is highly dependent on the available space and the required technical equipment.

Finally, the offer of different event formats could be identified as another central and exceptional influencing factor [14]. Especially in the respect that many DIEs, especially privately organized or based in the academic environment, do not offer fixed event formats. They are offered for free work without predetermined structures and agendas [21]. In a corporate context, this is considered desirable and may influence other factors. Targeted innovation formats or workshops on specific technologies can have a positive influence on both "Usability" and "Business Relevance". In addition, digital competencies of employees can be built up in this way, which represents a central motivation from a business perspective. Currently, there are no well-founded empirical studies on the influence of different event formats on the output of DIEs. The concept development of a suitable offer should therefore be carried out individually depending on the intended focus of a company.

Based on the influencing factors of a business-oriented DIE, more complex relationships between the influencing factors could be identified with the help of supplementary literature and their relevance explained during the concept design. The interdependencies of the influencing factors again show the complexity of a DIE and underline the fact that such an institution is more than a digitalized workshop. Rather, structures must be created that address all socio-technological aspects equally to be able to leverage the most diverse facets of the potentials. In this context, many of the identified influencing factors remain individual and depend on the framework conditions within the existing company. A uniform concept suitable for all companies is therefore not possible. However, important relationships between factors could be identified and their potential effects discussed. A plausibility check of the factors and correlations could be made through the supplementary theoretical literature. No contradictions were found, but the results should be validated in subsequent empirical studies. This thus provides a helpful basis for decision-making for future design processes for business-oriented DIEs and can make a valuable contribution to both practice and science.

6 Conclusion

The ongoing process of digital transformation confronts companies with new challenges. While on the one hand, a high level of innovative spirit is necessary for long-term competitiveness, on the other hand, motivated and digitally competent employees are required [83, 84]. Institutions are known from other contexts that address precisely these needs but have only been partially transferred to the corporate context [85]. These so-called DIEs allow novel open innovation processes through their high-tech equipment paired with an inspiring space. To be able to use these potentials in companies, it is first necessary to integrate such DIEs appropriately into the company structures. This paper aimed to identify relevant factors that need to be considered for successful integration. For this purpose, various dimensions were considered to obtain as complete a picture as possible. A DIE should be considered from the business perspective as well as from the employee perspective and at the same time aspects on the technology and process level should be reflected. Supplementary guiding questions defined the scope of the study and supported the identification of relevant factors.

Based on a study on DIE usage behavior of employees and a case study on development processes within DIEs, 19 influencing factors were identified through supplementary literature. Through further analysis of the data sets, it was also possible to qualitatively evaluate the individual factors and derive their influence on the potentials. The factors are of a very diverse nature and range from measurable variables such as the "Availability" and "Functionality" of the technologies to social factors of "Error Culture" or "Willingness to Change". The diversity of factors also reflects the complexity of a DIE as an ecosystem and underscores the need for more comprehensive investigation to better understand this phenomenon from both a practical and scientific perspective. Relevant factors could be identified for all guiding questions and thus the predefined scope of the study could be served. The initial research question about relevant factors in the design of a business-oriented DIE could be answered at various levels. Factors from the perspectives of business, employee, technology, and process were considered, and take into account the complexity of DIEs.

In a subsequent discussion, it was also possible to derive a large number of interrelationships between the individual factors and to make initial design recommendations for a business-oriented DIE. The basic approach of an internal or external DIE is of crucial importance. The availability of a contact person could be identified as a new and very central factor, which plays only a subordinate role in private or academic contexts. In the business context, this also requires concrete, targeted event formats and an appropriate mindset on the part of all the players involved. Finally, the physical design, including the atmosphere it creates, was also identified as a significant factor. All of these factors directly or indirectly influence a large number of the other factors and should therefore be given special consideration in their design. In general, it could be determined that the factors should not be considered in isolation from each other, but that they are much more correlated with each other. For this reason, no universal design of a business-oriented DIE is possible, but rather must be individually adapted to the framework conditions of a company.

The results of this study complement the existing body of knowledge by providing valuable insights into the targeted design of business-oriented DIEs. Previous studies on DIEs are often located in the private or academic context. The studies, which also consider the business perspective, are often limited to the potentials of DIEs or analyze the impact. The question of the design of a business-oriented DIE has so far been addressed only superficially. At this point, the findings of the study supplement the state of knowledge with central foundations for further research and close the gap to practice by deriving concrete recommendations for action. At the same time, a valuable basis is laid for further research, including quantitative research.

7 Outlook/Contribution

Since previous studies have already identified a large number of potentials for integrating DIEs into corporate contexts, this study aimed to lay a foundation for the concept design. Only with a suitable concept can the theoretical potentials be used in companies. Therefore, existing studies and databases were used to identify factors influencing the success of business-oriented DIEs. The complementary qualitative analysis of the factors and the identification of the first interdependencies of the factors allow a sound basis for future concept developments. The present work makes a significant contribution to practice and provides initial recommendations for action. The complementary assessment also allows an easy transfer into practice.

Furthermore, the phenomenon of DIEs is only superficially studied and only small amounts of empirical data are available. For further empirical investigations, the identified influencing factors can be used to prepare interventions in a targeted manner. In addition, the findings contribute to the fundamental understanding of DIEs and complement the existing results with the corporate perspective.

In the next step, further investigation of the identified factors would be useful to identify additional relationships and possibly quantify them. Also, a differentiation about the intended effects of a DIE would be a great added value, so that an even more targeted design would be possible. Furthermore, a validation of the factors in a practical study could consolidate and specify the findings and be established as a best practice concept. The potential uses and applications of these study results are thus as diverse as the identified factors themselves.

References

1. Vial, G.: Understanding digital transformation: A review and a research agenda. J. Strateg. Inf. Syst. **28**, 118–144 (2019). https://doi.org/10.1016/j.jsis.2019.01.003
2. Bharadwaj, A., El Sawy O.A., Pavlou, P.A., et al.: Digital business strategy: toward a next generation of insights. MIS Quart. **37**, 471–482 (2013). https://doi.org/10.25300/MISQ/2013/37:2.3
3. Piccinini, E., Gregory, R., Kolbe, L.: Changes in the producer-consumer relationship – towards digital transformation. Wirtschaftsinformatik Proceedings **2015**, 1634–1648 (2015)
4. Fitzgerald, M., Kruschwitz, N., Bonnet, D., et al.: Embracing Digital Technology: A New Strategic Imperative. MIT Sloan Management Review, 1–12 (2014)
5. Westerman, G., Calméjane, C., Bonnet, D., et al.: Digital Transformation: A Road-Map for Billion-Dollar Organizations. Report, Paris & Cambridge, MA (2011)
6. Magadley, W., Birdi, K.: Innovation labs: an examination into the use of physical spaces to enhance organizational creativity. Create. Innov. Manag. **18**, 315–325 (2009). https://doi.org/10.1111/j.1467-8691.2009.00540.x
7. Chesbrough, H.W.: Open innovation: The new imperative for creating and profiting from technology, [Repr.]. Harvard Business School Press, Boston, Mass (2003)
8. Iansiti, M., Lakhani, K.R.: Digital Ubiquity: How Connections, Sensors, and Data Are Revolutionizing Business. Harvard Business Review 92 (2014)
9. Nambisan, S., Lyytinen, K., Majchrzak, A., et al.: Digital Innovation Management: Reinventing Innovation Management Research in a Digital World. MISQ **41,** 223–238 (2017). https://doi.org/10.25300/MISQ/2017/41:1.03

10. Schumpeter, J.: Capitalism, Socialism and Democracy. Routledge, London (1943)
11. Hippel, E.v: The sources of innovation, 1. publ. in 1988, [repr.]. Oxford Univ. Pr, New York (2007)
12. Tidd, J., Bessant, J.: Managing innovation: Integrating technological, market and organizational change, Fifth edition, reprinted. Wiley, Chichester, West Sussex (2016)
13. Kantar Millward Brown (2020) BrandZ - Top 100 Most valuable global brands 2020. https://de.statista.com/statistik/daten/studie/162524/umfrage/markenwert-der-wertvollsten-unternehmen-weltweit/. Accessed 30 Oct 2020
14. Hellwig, L., Pawlowski, J., Schäfer, M.: Factors influencing the usage behavior of digitalized innovation environments in companies: a qualitative in-depth analysis. In: Proceedings of the 13th International Joint Conference on Knowledge Discovery, Knowledge Engineering and Knowledge Management. SCITEPRESS - Science and Technology Publications, pp. 90–101 (2021)
15. Jensen, M.B., Semb, C.C.S., Vindal, S., et al.: State of the art of makerspaces - success criteria when designing makerspaces for norwegian industrial companies. Procedia CIRP **54**, 65–70 (2016). https://doi.org/10.1016/j.procir.2016.05.069
16. Duh, E.S., Kos, A.: Fablabs as drivers for open innovation and co-creation to foster rural development. In: 2016 International Conference on Identification, Information and Knowledge in the Internet of Things - IIKI 2016: Beijing, China, 20–21 October 2016: proceedings. IEEE, Piscataway, NJ, pp. 214–216 (2017)
17. Cutcher-Gershenfeld, J., Gershenfeld, A., Gershenfeld, N.: Digital Fabrication and the Future of Work. Perspectives on Work, Labor and Employment Relations Association, pp. 8–13 (2018)
18. Capdevila, I.: Typologies of localized spaces of collaborative innovation. SSRN J. (2013). https://doi.org/10.2139/ssrn.2414402
19. Capdevila, I.: Joining a collaborative space: is it really a better place to work? J. Bus. Strateg. **86**, 84 (2018). https://doi.org/10.1108/JBS-09-2017-0140
20. Wolf, P., Troxler, P., Kocher, P.Y., et al.: Sharing is sparing: open knowledge sharing in fablabs. Journal of Peer Production. Issue 5 Shared Machine Stops: Beyond Local Prototyping and Manufacturing (2014)
21. Konopek, A., Hellwig, L., Schäfer, M.: A possible ubiquitous way of learning within a Fab Lab - The Combination of Blended Learning and Implementation-oriented Learning. In: Conference Proceeding: 10th International Conference on Computer Supported Education, pp. 265–271 (2018). https://doi.org/10.5220/0006780202650271
22. Dougherty, D.: The maker movement. innovations: technology. Governance, Globalization **7**, 11–14 (2012). https://doi.org/10.1162/INOV_a_00135
23. Hartmann, F., Lahr, M., Mietzner, D.: Maker movement as a path of digital transformation? current understanding and how it may change the social and economic environment. In: 2nd Annual International Conference on Foresight, pp. 29–30 (2016)
24. Zakoth, D., Mauroner, O.: Industry-specific Makerspaces: Opportunities for Collaboration and Open Innovation. Management International, pp. 88–99 (2020)
25. Lo, A.: Fab Lab en entreprise : proposition d'ancrage théorique. In: XXIIIe Conférence de l'AIMS, Rennes (2014)
26. Ruberto, F.: How the Fablabs Community Can Help the Italian Industry (2015)
27. Suire, R.: Place, platform, and knowledge co-production dynamics: Evidence from makers and FabLab (2016)
28. Bergner, A.: Make-Design-Innovate: Das Potential des Maker-Movement für Innovation, Kreativwirtschaft und Unternehmen, Coburg (2017)
29. Sein, M.K., Henfridsson, O., Purao, S., et al.: Action design research. MIS Q. **35**, 37 (2011). https://doi.org/10.2307/23043488

30. Boutillier, S., Capdevila, I., Dupont, L., et al.: Collaborative spaces promoting creativity and innovation. J. Innov. Econ. Manage.°**31**, 1 (2020). https://doi.org/10.3917/jie.031.0001

31. Capdevila, I.: How can living labs enhance the participantss motivation in different types of innovation activities? SSRN J. (2014). https://doi.org/10.2139/ssrn.2502795

32. Almirall, E., Lee, M., Wareham, J.: Mapping Living Labs in the Landscape of Innovation Methodologies. Technology Innovation Management Review 2 (2012)

33. Gershenfeld, N.: How to make almost anything: the digital fabrication revolution. Foreign Aff. **91**, 43–57 (2012)

34. Schmidt, S., Brinks, V.: Open creative labs: Spatial settings at the intersection of communities and organizations. Creat Innov Manag **26**, 291–299 (2017). https://doi.org/10.1111/caim.12220

35. The Fab Charter (2015). http://fab.cba.mit.edu/about/charter/. Accessed 02 Oct 2016

36. Aryan, V., Bertling, J., Liedtke, C.: Topology, typology, and dynamics of commons-based peer production: On platforms, actors, and innovation in the maker movement. Creat Innov Manag (2020). https://doi.org/10.1111/caim.12392

37. Capdevila, I.: A typology of localized spaces of collaborative innovation. In: van Ham, M., Reuschke, D., Kleinhans, R. et al. (eds.) Entrepreneurial Neighbourhoods. Edward Elgar Publishing, pp. 80–97 (2017)

38. Hellwig, L., Pawlowski, J., Schäfer, M.: How digitalised innovation environments impact companies' innovation capability - a review and research agenda. In: UK Academy for Information Systems Conference Proceedings 2021, vol. 8, pp 113–136 (2021)

39. Mortara, L., Parisot, N.: How do fab-spaces enable entrepreneurship? case studies of "makers" - entrepreneurs. IJMTM **32**, 16 (2018). https://doi.org/10.1504/IJMTM.2018.089465

40. Ruberto, F.: Fablabs to transform the Italian Industry: The Case of the Fablabs Community, University of Pavia (2015)

41. Hellwig, L., Preissner, L., Pawlowski, J., et al.: How digital fabrication technologies within digitalized innovation environments lead to participative aid development. Jet (2022). https://doi.org/10.1108/JET-01-2022-0013

42. Kaiser, R.: Qualitative Experteninterviews. Springer Fachmedien Wiesbaden, Wiesbaden (2014)

43. Venkatesh, V., Brown, S.A., Bala, H.: Bridging the qualitative-quantitative divide: guidelines for conducting mixed methods research in information systems. MISQ **37**, 21–54 (2013). https://doi.org/10.25300/MISQ/2013/37.1.02

44. Handlbauer, G., Renzl, B.: Kundenorientiertes Wissensmanagement. In: Hinterhuber, H.H. (ed.) Kundenorientierte Unternehmensführung, pp. 147–175. Springer Fachmedien, Wiesbaden (2009)

45. Venkatesh, V., Bala, H.: Technology acceptance model 3 and a research agenda on interventions. Decis. Sci. **39**, 273–315 (2008). https://doi.org/10.1111/j.1540-5915.2008.00192.x

46. Rogers, E.M.: Diffusion on innovations, 3rd edn. Free, New York (1983)

47. Döring, N., Bortz, J.: Forschungsmethoden und Evaluation in den Sozial- und Humanwissenschaften, 5. vollständig überarbeitete, aktualisierte und erweiterte Auflage. Springer-Lehrbuch. Springer, Heidelberg (2016)

48. Mayring, P.: Einführung in die qualitative Sozialforschung: Eine Anleitung zu qualitativem Denken, 5., überarb. und neu ausgestattete Aufl. Beltz Studium : Erziehung und Bildung. Beltz, Weinheim [u.a.] (2002)

49. Glaser, B.G.: Theoretical sensitivity. Advances in the methodology of grounded theory. Soc. Pr, Mill Valley, Calif (1978)

50. Urquhart, C. (ed.): Grounded theory for qualitative research: a practical guide. Sage, London (2013)

51. Mayring, P.: Gütekriterien qualitativer Evaluationsforschung (Quality Standards for Qualitative Evaluation Research). Zeitschrift für Evaluation **17**(11–24), 209 (2018)
52. Walsham, G.: Interpretive case studies in IS research: nature and method. Eur. J. Inf. Syst. **4**, 74–81 (1995). https://doi.org/10.1057/ejis.1995.9
53. van Holm, E.J.: What are Makerspaces, Hackerspaces, and Fab Labs? (2014)
54. Rieken, F., Boehm, T., Heinzen, M., et al.: Corporate makerspaces as innovation driver in companies: a literature review-based framework. JMTM **31**, 91–123 (2020). https://doi.org/10.1108/JMTM-03-2019-0098
55. Bosse, I.K., Pelka, B.: Peer production by persons with disabilities – opening 3D-printing aids to everybody in an inclusive MakerSpace. JET **14**, 41–53 (2020). https://doi.org/ https://doi.org/10.1108/JET-07-2019-0037
56. Schwartz, J.K., Fermin, A., Fine, K., et al.: Methodology and feasibility of a 3D printed assistive technology intervention. Disabil Rehabil. Assist. Technol. **15**, 141–147 (2020). https://doi.org/10.1080/17483107.2018.1539877
57. Glaser, B.G., Strauss, A.L.: The discovery of grounded theory: Strategies for qualitative research, 4. paperback printing. Aldine, New Brunswick (2009)
58. Esterberg, K.G.: Qualitative methods in social research, International ed. McGraw-Hill higher education. McGraw-Hill, Boston, Mass (2002)
59. Gadamer, H.-G.: The historicity of understanding. In: Critical Sociology, pp. 117–133. Selected readings. Penguin Books, Harmoondsworth (1976)
60. Webster, J., Watson, R.T.: Analyzing the Past to Prepare for the Future: Writing a Literature Review. MIS Quarterly 26:xiii–xxiii (2002)
61. Cooper, H.M.: Organizing knowledge syntheses: a taxonomy of literature reviews. Knowl. Soc. **1**, 104 (1988). https://doi.org/10.1007/BF03177550
62. Vom Brocke, J., Simons, A., Niehaves, B., et al.: Reconstructing the Giant: On the Importance of Rigour in Documenting the Literature Search Process (2009). http://www.alexandria.unisg.ch/Publikationen/67910
63. Higgins, J.P.T., Green, S(e).: Cochrane handbook for systematic reviews of interventions, Reprinted. Cochrane book series. Wiley-Blackwell, Chichester (2012)
64. Tranfield, D., Denyer, D., Smart, P.: Towards a methodology for developing evidence-informed management knowledge by means of systematic review. Br. J. Manage. **14**, 207–222 (2003). https://doi.org/10.1111/1467-8551.00375
65. Nambisan, S., Sawhney, M.S.: The global brain: Your roadmap for innovating faster and smarter in a networked world, 1. print. Wharton School Publ, Upper Saddle River, NJ (2008)
66. Kohli, R., Melville, N.P.: Digital innovation: A review and synthesis. Info Syst. J. **29**, 200–223 (2019). https://doi.org/10.1111/isj.12193
67. Hippel, E.v.: Democratizing innovation. Creative Commons, Merzig (2010)
68. Allen, D.: Hackerspaces as Entrepreneurial Anarchy, vol. 2016 (2016)
69. Capdevila, I.: Co-Working spaces and the localised dynamics of Innovation in Barcelona. Int. J. Innov. Mgt. **19**, 1540004 (2015). https://doi.org/10.1142/S1363919615400046
70. Hellwig, L., Pawlowski, J., Schäfer, M.: An innovation activity framework for digital innovation. In: Laumer, S., Quesenberry, J., Joseph, D., et al. (eds.) SIGMIS-CPR'20: Proceedings of the 2020 ACM SIGMIS Conference on Computers and People Research: June 19–21, 2020, Nuremberg, Germany. Association for Computing Machinery, New York, pp. 10–19
71. Hellwig, L., Pawlowski, J., Schäfer, M.: A business competency framework within digital transformation - an empirical study. In: Association for Information Systems (ed) ECIS 2021 Proceedings, vol. 39 (2021)
72. de Filippi, P., Troxler, P.: From material scarcity to artificial abundance: the case of FabLabs and 3D printing technologies. In: van den Berg, B., van der Hof, S., Kosta, E. (eds.) 3D Printing: Legal, Philosophical and Economic Dimensions, 1st edn. 2017, vol. 26. T.M.C. Asser Press, The Hague, s.l., pp 65–83 (2016)

73. Garcia-Ruiz, M.E., Lena-Acebo, F.J.: FabLab global survey: characterization of FabLab phenomenon. In: 13th Iberian Conference on Information Systems and Technologies (CISTI), pp. 1–6 (2018). https://doi.org/10.23919/CISTI.2018.8399154

74. Markus, M.L., Robey, D.: Information technology and organizational change: causal structure in theory and research. Manage. Sci. **5**, 583–598 (1988)

75. Vinodh, S., Sundararaj, G., Devadasan, S.R., et al.: Agility through rapid prototyping technology in a manufacturing environment using a 3D printer. JMTM **20**, 1023–1041 (2009). https://doi.org/10.1108/17410380910984267

76. Böhmer, A.I., Beckmann, A., Lindemann, U.: Open Innovation Ecosystem - Makerspaces within an Agile Innovation Process. ISPIM Innovation Summit, Brisbane, Australia (2015)

77. Urbach, N., Ahlemann, F.: Structural equation modeling in information systems research using partial least squares. J. Inf. Technol. Theory Appl. **11**(2) (2010)

78. Lô, A., Fatien Diochon, P.: Unsilencing power dynamics within third spaces. The case of Renault's Fab Lab. Scandinavian J. Manage. (2018) . doi:https://doi.org/10.1016/j.scaman. 2018.11.003

79. Hartmann, R.K., Svenson, P.: Policies to Promote User Innovation: Evidence from Swedish Hospitals on the Effects of Access to Makerspaces on Innovation by Clinicians (2015)

80. Capdevila, I.: Different inter-organizational collaboration approaches in coworking spaces in Barcelona (2014)

81. Wilczynski, V.: Academic maker spaces and engineering design. In: ASEE Annual Conference and Exposition, Conference Proceedings 122 (2015)

82. Farritor, S.: University-Based Makerspaces: A Source of Innovation. Technol. Innov **19**, 389–395 (2017). https://doi.org/10.21300/19.1.2017.389

83. Theyel, G., Hofmann, K.H.: Environmental practices and innovation performance of US small and medium-sized manufacturers. JMTM **26**, 333–348 (2015). https://doi.org/10.1108/JMTM-07-2012-0070

84. Laforet, S., Tann, J.: Innovative characteristics of small manufacturing firms. J. Small Bus. Enterp. Dev. **13**, 363–380 (2006). https://doi.org/10.1108/14626000610680253

85. Lewis, M., Moultrie, J.: The organizational innovation laboratory. Create. Innov. Manag. **14**, 73–83 (2005). https://doi.org/10.1111/j.1467-8691.2005.00327.x

Author Index

© The Editor(s) (if applicable) and The Author(s), under exclusive license
to Springer Nature Switzerland AG 2023
A. Fred et al. (Eds.): IC3K 2021, CCIS 1718, p. 173, 2023.
https://doi.org/10.1007/978-3-031-35924-8

Printed in the United States
by Baker & Taylor Publisher Services